TEENSET, TEEN FAN MAGAZINES, and ROCK JOURNALISM

TEENSET,
Teen Fan Magazines, and Rock Journalism

Don't Let the Name Fool You

Allison Bumsted

UNIVERSITY PRESS OF MISSISSIPPI / JACKSON

The University Press of Mississippi is the scholarly publishing agency of
the Mississippi Institutions of Higher Learning: Alcorn State University,
Delta State University, Jackson State University, Mississippi State University,
Mississippi University for Women, Mississippi Valley State University,
University of Mississippi, and University of Southern Mississippi.

www.upress.state.ms.us

Publication of this book was supported in part by the UPM First Author's initiative.

All materials from *TeenSet* magazine are used by permission of Scholastic Inc.

The University Press of Mississippi is a member
of the Association of University Presses.

Copyright © 2024 by University Press of Mississippi
All rights reserved
Manufactured in the United States of America

∞

Library of Congress Cataloging-in-Publication Data

Names: Bumsted, Allison, author.
Title: TeenSet, teen fan magazines, and rock journalism : don't let the name fool you / Allison Bumsted.
Description: Jackson : University Press of Mississippi, 2024. | Includes bibliographical references and index.
Identifiers: LCCN 2024028933 (print) | LCCN 2024028934 (ebook) | ISBN 9781496853264 (hardback) | ISBN 9781496853271 (trade paperback) | ISBN 9781496853288 (epub) | ISBN 9781496853295 (epub) | ISBN 9781496853301 (pdf) | ISBN 9781496853318 (pdf)
Subjects: LCSH: TeenSet. | Journalism—United States—History—20th century. | Music and youth—Social aspects. | Rock music—Periodicals—History. | Popular music—Social aspects. | Popular culture—United States—History—20th century. | Mass media and teenagers.
Classification: LCC PN4900.T42 B86 2024 (print) | LCC PN4900.T42 (ebook) | DDC 070.4/4978166—dc23/eng/20240729
LC record available at https://lccn.loc.gov/2024028933
LC ebook record available at https://lccn.loc.gov/2024028934

British Library Cataloging-in-Publication Data available

THIS BOOK IS DEDICATED TO JUDY SIMS, NANCY CHESTER, CAROL GOLD,
AND ALL THE CONTRIBUTORS TO AND READERS OF TEENSET MAGAZINE.

AND TO ALL OF US WHO READ AND CHERISHED
TEEN FAN MAGAZINES THROUGHOUT THE DECADES.

Judith Sims during a Beatles press conference held at DC Stadium before their evening concert,
August 15, 1966. Photographer unlisted. Provided by Jeff Hoganson.

CONTENTS

ix   ACKNOWLEDGMENTS

3   INTRODUCTION: AGE, GENRE, AND JOURNALISM IN POPULAR MUSIC

22   **CHAPTER ONE. A *CAPITOL* IDEA!**
The Origins of Teen Fan Magazines and *TeenSet*

61   **CHAPTER TWO. IT'S ONLY ROCK 'N' ROLL JOURNALISM**
The Absence of *TeenSet* Within a History Shaped by Critics

91   **CHAPTER THREE. SHOW ME *TEENSET*!**
TeenSet as a Valuable Source in Popular Music

128   **CHAPTER FOUR. TAKING POPULAR MUSIC SERIOUSLY**
Judith Sims and the Women on the Scene

167   **CHAPTER FIVE. "A NIFTY MUSIC MAGAZINE WITH A MISLEADING NAME"**
TeenSet's Duality, Representation of and Interaction with an Evolving Musical and Cultural Landscape

207   **CONCLUSION. "ETC. ETC."**
Reconsidering the Popular Music Journalism Historical Discourse

217   APPENDICES

221   NOTES

243   BIBLIOGRAPHY

257   INDEX

ACKNOWLEDGMENTS

My whole life, I have been a fan, and I want to thank my parents for enabling my fandom from the beginning by accepting my love of popular music and culture and enduring my obsessive playing of my "oldies" tapes and the few CDs I had. I thank my mother for the expensive teen fan magazines with Hanson or JTT on the covers, the book fair money, and embracing my ten-year-old Spice Girls–inspired "Girl Power" obsession. Thank you both for the gift of a turntable and receiver and the ability to pick through your albums, which are still in my possession, where I became intimate with the Doors, Whitney Houston, Prince, and Janis Joplin—all of which helped lead me to the Beatles and to this research.

As a teenager, my music fandom was enhanced and encouraged by my dear high school friend Daniel Barto—the one who, for my birthday, gifted me my first (nonhits) Beatles record, *Sgt. Pepper's Lonely Hearts Club Band* (1967). The moment it was in my hands, he laid down with his elbows behind his head and said, "Let's listen." Over the next few years, we spent hours not only listening to the Who, the Beatles, and whatever was playing on the (now-defunct) Houston radio station 93.7 The Arrow but also discussing music and bands at all hours. Dan always included me in movie nights and outings where I was introduced to *Spinal Tap* (1984), The Who's *The Kids are Alright* (1978), and so much more. When we were still teens, he once defended me when I was called a "hair twirler" during a game of music trivia (I won that game), and he just could not understand why others doubted my knowledge. I will always love him for that. At the 2003 Doors concert (with Ian Ashbury as Jim Morrison), I'll never forget, as I was slightly embarrassed, that Dan yelled (while they were filming the crowds), "We don't need instructions to know how to rock." Yet now, I reflect on that moment and that statement and think how this book carries on that spirit, Dan's spirit. No one can tell us what type of fans we need to be, how we need to act at a concert, or what we should listen to or read to be authentic.

When I began my research, I was focused on the male canon of rock criticism. Yet I noticed a problem in the historical discourse surrounding the rock narrative and traveled off the beaten path (even when encouraged to stay the course), where I found *TeenSet*—or rather, it found me. From that moment on, my glass was shattered, and how I viewed teen fan magazines and rock history would never be the same. I cannot claim to be alone on said path because no good idea is formed or executed without the influence and help of others, and I am very thankful to all those who have believed in me.

I would like to begin by thanking Dr. Jacqui Miller and Dr. Noel Brown—two individuals who believed in me, my vision, and the value of *TeenSet*. I am forever grateful. Thank you to Craig Gill, Katie Turner, and the staff of the University Press of Mississippi for not only believing in me and my work but also recognizing the importance of Judith Sims, *TeenSet*, and female fandom by proudly publishing this book. Thank you to Dr. Renold, Dr. Deidre Lannon, Rick Henderson, and Lee Moore for showing me that my passions were of value early in my studies.

Researching can often be a lonely task, but I was never alone in the wonderful city of Liverpool with my dear friend, fellow student, and Beatle lover Dr. Beth Easton at my side. Beth, thank you for listening, understanding, encouraging, and *growing* with me—I am forever grateful for our friendship. Rebekka Jolley, thank you for also being an amazing support throughout the pandemic and our PhD studies. Thank you to Liverpool's own Joe Mckechnie for welcoming me and showing me a Liverpool I could have never known.

I further owe a debt of gratitude to those who actively encouraged me and graciously devoted time and effort to contribute their words, thoughts, sources, or images to this book: Debbie Gendler, Ann Moses, Richie Furay, Ken Mansfield, Amelia Davis and the Jim Marshall Archives, Nancy Furlong, Jeff Hoganson, Joel Selvin, Ben Fong-Torres, Steve Kern, Van Dyke Parks, Dr. Matt Brennan, John Mendelsohn, Scholastic Inc., The University of Nevada Las Vegas Special Collection Archives, Malcolm Lubliner, Larry Marion, Alison Livaditis, Robert Rodriguez, Dr. Howard Owens, Allison Boron, Dr. Ken Womack, Dr. Christine Feldman-Barrett, Rococo Cafe, and to all my friends who have been supportive of me over the years.

Most importantly, I would like to thank Michael for encouraging me to pursue my dreams and celebrating my many interests. Thank you for the countless hours you have spent reading *TeenSet*, teen fan magazines, and helping me develop my thoughts. Your unwavering support and encouragement are invaluable—you helped fuel my passion. A special thank you to our puppy, Rufus, for keeping me company during many edits.

Finally, I am grateful to all my supporters and readers. I hope *TeenSet* and all teen fan magazines will be celebrated and explored further.

TEENSET, TEEN FAN MAGAZINES, and ROCK JOURNALISM

INTRODUCTION

Age, Gender, Genre, and Journalism in Popular Music

TeenSet Mag. was the precursor and template for *Rolling Stone*, *Mojo*, and other music journals.
—Van Dyke Parks[1]

I never expected to encounter *TeenSet* Magazine. That is, I never thought something like *TeenSet* existed, because rarely have published historical accounts of popular music history discussed the magazine, unless to further dismiss teen fan magazines. When I first obtained issues, I was surprised by the content—Frank Zappa, Jefferson Airplane, Tim Buckley, Janis Joplin, considerations of racism, the blues, Cream, the Who, Jimi Hendrix, music scenes, music and meaning, the Monterey Pop Festival, and many famous iconic Jim Marshall photographs. By every account, *TeenSet* surely should be discussed in many rock journalism or popular music history texts, but, at the time of writing, little consideration was to be found. It led me to wonder: why is *TeenSet* not discussed more broadly, and most importantly *why* was I surprised by its existence? A question this book aims to better understand by exploring the current historical popular music journalism discourse.

The 1960s American teen fan magazine *TeenSet* was an early example of a peer-edited popular music magazine that has been forgotten and remains mostly unacknowledged in prior scholarship. This book establishes *TeenSet* as a contributor to popular music and shows how, under the leadership of editor Judith Sims, *TeenSet* engaged with fundamental discourses of late 1960s US counterculture across broad issues of music, politics, race, and gender. The 1960s was a time of social and political change within American culture, and as it evolved, so did *TeenSet*; it not only reflected the culture of the period but actively contributed to it, considering popular music and culture through a critical lens.

In America, teen fan magazines were the first magazines in the mid-1950s to embrace rock 'n' roll in an accessible print form, were often led by strong female editors and writers, and read by a diverse cross section of music fans. As this book shows, all teen fan magazines have been viewed wrongly as indistinguishable from one another, and their impact on rock journalism, popular music, and culture has been underestimated—as they are often proclaimed by rock critics to be unimportant or lacking "seriousness" in their coverage of popular music. This book aims to show that *TeenSet* holds a unique place in 1960s American popular culture; however, its gravity has been significantly underappreciated, and its role has been widely misconstrued due to the tendency in both scholarly and journalistic accounts to marginalize all 1960s teen fan magazines.

Although the current discourse would lead one to believe the majority of popular music editing and writing was executed by men and men alone, this is grossly inaccurate. This book attempts to redress the balance, and alongside a thorough analysis of *TeenSet* and its wider cultural influence, it will explore the leadership and authorship of editor Judith Sims as well as female *TeenSet* staff writers such as Carol Gold and the voices of first-generation *TeenSet* readers. More broadly, it presents a necessary counternarrative to the dominant historical male-oriented discourse in popular music journalism. Additionally, the sub-title of this book, *Don't Let the Name Fool You*, is a direct response to the dismissal, marginalization, and overlooking of *TeenSet* within the current rock journalism discourse and gestures to one of my key intentions, namely, investigating how the historiography of how rock and popular music journalism history has been established by men. While it is central to my argument that *TeenSet* belongs within this discourse, I also want to convey how different aspects of popular music journalism history, especially teen fan magazines and women's voices that are featured within them, can be considered through the case study of *TeenSet*. Thus, this book serves as a critical response to the current male-dominated narrative encompassing popular music (specifically American rock journalism) history and the long-standing dismissal of American teen fan magazines. It advances historical popular music journalism discourse and challenges a deep-rooted history through a consideration not only of the American magazine *TeenSet* but also the broader questions of genre, gender, and rock aesthetics that *TeenSet* navigates.

While scholarly studies considering teen lifestyle magazines[2] such as *Seventeen*[3] and considerations of Hollywood fan magazines such as *Photoplay*[4] exist, these works have not addressed teen fan magazines. However, interest in historical popular music print media has steadily grown since the 1990s with publications such as Motti Regev's "Producing Artistic Value: The Case of Rock Music" (1994), Steve Jones's collection *Pop Music and the Press* (2001), Devon Powers's *Writing the Record* (2013), and Matt Brennan's *When Genres Collide* (2017). However, as argued, within academic or general texts, there has been little consideration of teen fan magazines of the 1960s (or of any era). A few exceptions consist of Diana L. Belscamper's unpublished PhD dissertation, "'Your Ticket to Dreamsville': The Functions of *16 Magazine* in American Girl Culture of the 1960s" (2014); journalist Margaret Moser's *Austin Chronicle* articles "Dreamsville: Gloria Stavers, *16 Magazine*, and the Roots of Rock Journalism" (2007) and "The Singer Not the Song" (1999); and Brian Ward's "'The "C" is for Christ': Arthur Unger, *Datebook* Magazine and the Beatles (2012). Indeed, as I will show, teen fan magazines have been underrepresented in the historical discourse of the rock press and, more generally, in the popular music press. By redressing the balance through a close examination of *TeenSet*, this book will fill a significant gap in prior scholarship. Although *TeenSet* and teen fan magazines, in general, have not yet received their due consideration in popular music history (except in cases where they have been summarily dismissed), there is a growing body of scholarship that reconsiders the roles of women (preteen to adult) in popular music that is considered below; this book will contribute to this field of research. More generally, it will also serve to question a number of prevailing generalizations and stereotypes regarding popular music and prompt a deeper look at teen fan magazines and women's roles in 1960s popular music journalism.

Age and Gender in Popular Music

As this book is about a magazine mostly written by women with an evidenced large female reading base, it is important to place it within this scholarship about women with the intention of reestablishing its rightful place within the history of popular music journalism. Historically, popular music divisions between genders have been drawn by the press, musicians, and academics. For example, Simon Frith and Angela McRobbie's 1978 article *Rock and Sexuality* further constructs a division between boy music and experience as "cock rock" and girl music and experience as "teenybop."[5] They present boys as musicians and active in popular music and girls as teenyboppers—young, inactive female fans confined to their bedrooms.[6] Within this discussion, girls are discussed as passive, and in this generalization, the authors fail to consider the ways in which many women were active. The word "passive" implies that young women were not interested or that they did not respond to popular music. In positioning girls as passive (as fans, consumers, performers, writers) and as preparing for their domestic life, Frith and McRobbie place boys as the ones "who are intellectually interested in rock, who become rock critics."[7]

Frith and McRobbie's argument has been challenged by multiple texts that have considered gender and popular music, such as Marion Leonard's book, *Gender in the Music Industry: Rock, Discourse and Girl Power* (2007), and Christopher R. Martin's 1995 article, "The Naturalized Gender Order of Rock and Roll." In response to Frith and McRobbie, Leonard finds that dividing genders by "cock rock" (male) and "teenybop" (female) is problematic, suggesting that "by assuming that the rock performer is male, they erase the history of female practitioners while also failing to acknowledge the popularity of 'cock rock' among girls and women."[8] However, it is evident that *TeenSet* readers were interested in "rock," as were the mid-1960s readers of *16 Magazine* and *Tiger Beat*. Christopher Martin presents a challenge to their argument, noting that:

> The gender lines have not always been so clear, especially at times when young women shaped early rock and roll as its undeniably active and passionate fans. The traditional gender order of rock and roll is not natural but naturalized. The acceptance of rock and roll as a naturally masculine medium is possible only by ignoring the historical marginalization of the female audience of rock and roll.[9]

Christine Feldman-Barrett argues that these divisions between boys and girls "separate the experience of rock music into production and critical appreciation (male) on one hand and consumption and emotional response (female) on the other."[10]

Considering Beatlemania sparked an explosion of teen fan magazines that would later heavily focus on the Monkees, these publications have often been labeled as magazines for "teenyboppers"—despite the fact that males, some of whom became rock journalists, were reading them, too. Yet they have been labeled as being for "girls," and over the last twenty years, multiple scholars, including Norma Coates, Sheila Whiteley, Jacquline Warwick, and Helen Davies, have evidenced that "girl," like "groupie," is a pejorative term in rock and in general. In regard to music journalism, Coates contends that in "popular music scholarship and journalistic criticism, 'teenybopper' is a very dirty word."[11]

Fan scholar Daniel Cavicchi found that many felt "fans represent negative effects of modern media and are often stereotyped as unhealthy and dangerous,"[12] but this is particularly evident in the portrayal of young female fans throughout popular music history and especially in the time of Beatlemania and the rise of teen fan magazines. The screaming of young female Beatles fans has been regularly criticized, and at various Beatles events, I have heard passing comments by older male fans and self-proclaimed "authorities" that screaming girls ruined others' chances of seeing the Beatles live. Feldman-Barrett's *A Women's History of the Beatles* (2021) addressed the negative connotations associated with Beatlemania and the screaming girls, "the same girls who were sometimes disparaged in mainstream press accounts as immature 'screamers' were taking on challenges and responsibilities that demonstrated maturity, resilience, and grit. Their fandom may have given them a clear 'mission' (meeting the Beatles), but it also helped them realize their own capabilities."[13]

In an interview with Beatles fans Debbie Gendler and Carol Tyler at the Fab4ConJam's Beatles online conference, I asked what the screaming meant for them. Gendler instantly responded: "It was love. It was the way we could show our love."[14] Tyler and Gendler both substantiated Feldman-Barrett's argument by claiming that the Beatles opened the world to them as young women. Tyler claimed that it was the Beatles who made her realize "I could get out of Fox Lake [Illinois],"[15] and Gendler agreed: "I could get out of Oakland, New Jersey."[16] This dismissal of the teen fan is not limited to Beatlemania, as "girls are consistently cast as hysterical, uncritical, and driven by primal and primitive sexual desire, the very opposite of the thinking subject normatively associated with intellectual criticism."[17]

Understanding how female fandom in popular music is stereotyped provides a sense of why *TeenSet* and teen fan magazines, in general, have been overlooked or dismissed as lacking "seriousness" in popular music. Fandom studies are continuing to grow and challenge the negative connotations surrounding all-female popular music fans, but as Coates observes, females are still often classified as teenyboppers or groupies.[18] Whiteley's *Too Much Too Young* (2005) provides evidence that women in the male musical domain are presented as highly sexualized figures or little girls.[19] Helen Davies's consideration of the overall portrayal of women in the British press advances this point, arguing that "the music press views all teenage girls, and indeed often all women, as teenyboppers, an assumption that is repeated in most academic writing about popular music."[20] Even women who are active professionals in popular music are marked as teenyboppers. For example, Elizabeth Weinstein's consideration of popular music journalist Jane Scott, the so-called "grandmother of rock journalism," found that after a lifelong career writing about music, she continued to be referred to as the world's oldest "teenybopper,"[21]—no male counterpart has been labeled the same. Matt Brennan also observes that while female performers had been often sexualized in rock criticism (see Coates and Leonard), "worse off were female fans, who were represented as either tasteless teenyboppers (the opposite of the authentic rock fan) or disposable sex objects, also known as 'groupies.'"[22] The early rock text, *Groupies and Other Girls*, authored by rock critics John Burks and Jerry Hopkins, considers women (fans and professionals)[23] in popular music and, as the title implies, positions females as either groupies or "other girls." Although they initially acknowledge groupies as girls and boys "who have given themselves to rock and roll,"[24] the authors do not include any consideration of male groupies, and they refer to grown women as groupies and to the likes of *16 Magazine*'s Gloria Stavers as one of the "other" girls—at forty-three years old. They proceed to define groupies as "the all-purpose girls who pursue rock and roll stars from dressing room to dressing room and motel to motel."[25] However, as Cheryl Cline argues in her study of fandom, "the idea that women rock fans want to be groupies of the most craven sort is a strictly masculine daydream—Them as the rock stars surrounded by Us, the groupies."[26]

Many scholars agree that *Rolling Stone* helped establish the current rock discourse by "keeping them [women] firmly on rock's margins,"[27] maintaining this dual identification as either groupies or teenyboppers. The term "teenybopper," as Coates observes, "acquired its current, less savory and thoroughly value-laden meaning in the mid-1960s, or more accurately, as a result of later analyses of mid-1960s music and trends."[28] This is evident in Burks and Hopkins's text, as no "in-between" label was offered to females (as with Frith and McRobbie's academic text, published seven years later). These works contributed, in this period, to a larger positioning of female fans, performers, and professionals (such as journalists) of all ages as continuing to exist in a perpetual state of "groupiedom" or "teenybopperdom." Chapter 2 will revisit this consideration by highlighting the past and current dismissal of teen fan magazines by rock critics and academics alike.

This belittling of female fans, especially young ones, ignores their active roles and purchasing power. Scholars and writers such as Ann Powers and Sheryl Garret have shown that females were buying "records in millions and made a massive contribution to the early success of Elvis, the Beatles, the Stones, Marc Bolan, and Michael Jackson."[29] Thus, the purchasing power of young female fans seems to have been underestimated in many accounts of popular music history. Although this book does not focus on fandom per se, *TeenSet* was a teen fan magazine, and the consideration of the historic dismissal of teen girl fans as "teenyboppers" cannot be ignored; it was the same female fans who bought these records and have historically been positioned as passive who read *TeenSet* and other teen fan magazines. In cases where female popular music fans are labeled as teenyboppers, a "dirty word,"[30] it is not surprising that what they are reading (and who is writing it) is viewed through a similarly pejorative lens. Yet this consideration of *TeenSet* (as well as teen fan magazines) will further counter the idea that young females are passive in popular music by instead evidencing their activeness, and it will also show that female fandom is not easily defined through two categories.

POPULAR MUSIC JOURNALISM AND GENDER

There has been a strong but scattered response to the idea that, in general, women were (or are currently) not writing about popular music. Multiple texts have attempted to reposition women as active participants in popular music journalism. One foundational example of this scholarly tendency is Evelyn McDonnell and Ann Powers's edited collection of works by women popular music journalists, *Rock She Wrote: Women Write About Rock, Pop, and Rap* (1995). The editors argue that "the need for this book was reinforced when a number of rock histories and collections were published, and women authors were notably MIA [missing in action]."³¹ Their text includes a collection of sixty-two popular music articles, but McDonnell and Powers make it clear that "we wound up finding too much, and selection became a painful process."³² They seem surprised by how much they found, perhaps because these women, both rock journalists themselves, were the first to compile such a collection in which they list over ninety other women they "wish" they could have included, such as Gloria Stavers. No women involved in the production of *TeenSet* are listed, a fact that suggests that the list of over ninety significantly underestimates the true extent of the phenomenon; as Powers argues, "After what we've found, we know there could be a whole library full of these vibrant, sassy, nasty, brilliant women's voices."³³

In consideration of *Rock She Wrote*, Daphne A. Brooks argues that "because of this volume alone, we can trace a visible 'history of the women who've been sustaining a tradition of writing about rock since the '60s that has been 'largely hidden' in American culture."³⁴ *Rock She Wrote* is now over twenty-five years old, and since then, many more women have contributed to popular music journalism (see Crawford and Friedlander). Weinstein's 2006 article "Married to Rock and Roll: Jane Scott, Grandmother of Rock Journalism," for example, examines one of the first American women to write about the Beatles and who continued to have a lifelong career in popular music journalism, Devon Powers's *Writing on the Record* (2013) considers Ellen Willis's role at the *Village Voice*, and *Tiger Beat* editor Ann Moses's autobiography, *Meow* (2017), examines Moses's career with the magazine. In addition, Robert Millican's biography, *Lillian Roxon: Mother of Rock* (2005), examined Roxon's life. More recently, Roxon's role as a rock journalist was considered in the documentary *Lillian Roxon: Mother of Rock* (2010). Musicians such as Alice Cooper and Iggy Pop appeared in the film and testified to Roxon's important role in popular music journalism.

Brooks's 2008 article, "The Write to Rock: Racial Mythologies, Feminist Theories, and the Pleasures of Rock Music Criticism," also questions the way rock is mythologized by and about men through the consideration of the portrayal of rock as male in *Tenacious D and the Pick of Destiny* (2006) and *High Fidelity* (2000). Building on Brooks's argument, this book will consider the portrayal of Lester Bangs in *Almost Famous* (2000). Liz Evans's 1997 book, *Girls Will Be Boys: Women Report on Rock*, is another collection of work by female critics and contributes to the canon of female popular music journalists. The title of the book, which may be perceived as a statement about the lack of women considered in popular music journalism, seems to participate, perhaps unwittingly, in the perceived assumptions that women do not have a significant role in rock writing and are merely participating in something that is for men. However, what this book does serve to illustrate is that women were writing about popular music before the rise of what is generally regarded as the beginning of rock journalism.

It is not surprising that, as musicologist André Doehring observes, "We tend to view the history of popular music journalism as a history of 'single great men,'"[35] and as this book will evidence, this view is incorrect. Rock journalism history is often said to have begun with Paul Williams and *Crawdaddy!* and then bolstered by the creator of *Rolling Stone*, Jann Wenner, and the men writing for it. Yet this narrative leaves a void in popular music journalism history that does not take account of the period of the early to mid-1960s or the women who were writing about popular music. This is largely a consequence of how rock critics have positioned themselves as the first to "seriously" consider popular music, claims that Brennan and Weinstein (and this book) directly challenge.

A more recent consideration of early and mid-1960s popular music women journalists, Kate Mossman's BBC4 radio special "The Women Who Wrote Rock" (2016), illuminates early popular music journalism in the UK written by women. Mossman explores five journalists: Dawn James of *Rave*, June Harris of *DISC* and *Rave*, Nancy Lewis of *FABulous* and the *NME*, Maureen O'Grady of *Boyfriend* and *Rave*, and (perhaps most famously in the Beatles canon) Maureen Cleave of the *London Evening Standard*. Mossman explores their pioneering work writing about popular music and argues that these women were "fearless pioneers who bore little resemblance to the music writers of later years."[36] It is evident here that women were the ones writing about popular music, with the rise of the Beatles in the UK in 1963 and Beatlemania in 1964 before the rise of "rock" journalism. Mossman alludes to the "established" male-dominated rock journalism discourse but focuses on the women who were writing about popular music first. She claims that "these are vivid alternate realities of men who became fixed in the public imagination as the formula for writing about them established itself. This was uncharted territory, with a sense of trust between journalists."[37] Most importantly, and as this book will argue in relation to *TeenSet*, she argues that not only were these women "on the front line,"[38] but "serious social history was being made through journalistic observation and levels of access that writers today can only dream of."[39] That level of access could not have been dreamed of even in 1970, and as this book addresses, a serious social history of women writing about popular music is still being written.

In general, teen fan magazines were often edited and written by women, a fact that may reflect the limited roles available to female journalists in the 1950s and 1960s. Although many works have considered the role of women in journalism, including Deborah Chambers, Linda Steiner, and Carole Fleming's *Women and Journalism* (2004), Nan Robertson's *The Girls in the Balcony: Women, Men, and the New York Times* (1992), and Suzanne Franks's *Women and Journalism* (2013), scholars are in general agreement that women's roles in the field of journalism were (and still are) limited. Povich's *The Good Girls Revolt: How the Women of Newsweek Sued Their Bosses and Changed the Workplace* (2012) conveys how women filed a discrimination case against *Newsweek* for not allowing them to become staff reporters. More recently, Amazon dramatized Povich's account in a miniseries titled *Good Girls Revolt* (2015). As Franks argues, in the early 1970s (and beforehand), in addition to *Newsweek*'s exclusion of staff women reporters, "discrimination against women in journalism could be found across the profession, in print and broadcasting."[40]

This became evident in popular music journalism, too, with the rise of rock journalism. Although Ellen Willis and Lillian Roxon are gaining more recognition and many women before them covered the Beatles and continued to write about popular music, popular music magazines excluded women writers. The practice of not allowing women to write for publications that eventually became established authorities surely contributed to their positioning as passive. The early days of *Crawdaddy!* did not include women writers, and *Rolling Stone* only employed female secretaries until the hiring of writer Robin Green in 1971, who earned a Masthead. (Judith Sims also began writing for the magazine in 1971, and her appointment as LA Bureau Chief would not be far after.) *Rolling Stone* played a large part in the exclusion of women as it is historically placed as the pinnacle in establishing the legitimacy of popular music or rock journalism. In conversation with rock critic John Mendelsohn, he referred to the lack of women writing for early *Rolling Stone* as well as the dismissal of female rock stars, as "sickeningly misogynistic."[41] If *Rolling Stone* had hired women staff writers before the early 1970s, the established historical discourse would be different because if more women were *allowed* to write for *Rolling Stone*, they would have. This is different in the case of teen fan magazines (in the US and UK), as evidenced in Mossman's "The Women

Who Wrote Rock (2016)." Many of the writers from the late 1950s onward, as well as the editors of teen fan magazines, were women, including the high school stringers/campus reporters who featured in *TeenSet* and other teen fan publications. Although Gloria Stavers is often discussed as "the only female editor of a teen magazine,"[42] this book shows that this is untrue. Not only was Judith Sims the editor of *TeenSet*, but Ann Moses edited *Tiger Beat*, Janey Milstead edited *TeenScreen*, and Bess Coleman edited *Teen Life* (while Dana Ohlmeyer was its managing editor); there were others. The work of these women needs to be explored in much greater depth; in relation to *TeenSet*, this will be the primary focus of chapter 4.

GENRE AND THE DISTINCTION BETWEEN ROCK AND POP

When considering the categorization of teen fan magazines and specifically *TeenSet*, it is evident that genre is extremely complex and not defined solely by sound or production but also by cultural aesthetics, as there are cultural connotations attached to genres. As Frith, Negus, Holt, and Brennan suggest, genre can be discussed as *genre cultures*, which are not limited to how music sounds or how it is produced. For example, Franco Fabbri argues that genre is "a set of musical events (real or possible) whose course is governed by a definite set of socially accepted rules."[43] Holt advances Fabbri's argument by suggesting that genre is "in the minds and bodies of particular groups of people who share certain conventions,"[44] such as smaller groups of people like rock critics. Yet all genres (music, film, literature, etc.) "create boundaries ... and draw attention away from more important matters."[45] With regard to television, Jane Feuer argues that "genre limits the field of play of the interpretive community."[46] By comparing genre theory with taxonomy, she poses the idea that considering genre is a question of ideology and "cultural value"[47] and builds on Rick Altman's argument that "genres are thus not neutral categories."[48] This book will further evidence that genre is more than just sound per se and that genres are also defined by cultural aesthetics.

Within the growing interest in magazine studies, magazines are often discussed as categories or types. However, they are typically categorized with little or no recourse to analysis. As Marcia Prior-Miller argues, many "communication scholars generally agree that the universe of magazines, journals and other non-newspaper periodicals can be clustered by titles with shared characteristics."⁴⁹ But as Prior-Miller points out, these communication scholars "differ on category criteria, on definitions for commonly used labels and on relationships between characteristics."⁵⁰ Her study shows that categorical descriptions can signify more than one meaning and can be extremely misleading and restricting. This study of *TeenSet* supports Prior-Miller and Holt's contentions, showing that *TeenSet* cannot easily be categorized by its title. While this book does differentiate between "teen lifestyle," "teen-type," and "teen fan" magazines, these classifications are based on a consideration of prevalent content only. Although I acknowledge that boundaries between these categories can occasionally blur (especially by the late 1960s), differences remain. Nonetheless, these publications are often lumped together because of their presumed audience demographics as "teenbooks." Yet teen fan magazines rose to prominence alongside rock 'n' roll and considered popular musicians and music more than, say, *Seventeen*. Thus, even though throughout this book, I argue genre and categorization can be limiting, I find it important to *emphasize* that not all magazines marketed to teens are the same, and it is very restricting to argue they are.

As *TeenSet* is argued to feature musicians and cultural issues that are historically categorized as or associated with rock, it is necessary to consider the distinction between the genres of rock and pop. As noted above, teenage girls have been contrasted as "teenyboppers"—passive, inauthentic "pop" fans—and boys as active, authentic "rock" fans. The genre of rock is conventionally understood as an authentically male genre, and this contrast has been ingrained in our understanding of popular music history. As mentioned previously, genre is not easily defined, and the relationship between rock and pop is highly contested. Keir Keightley's 2001 essay "Reconsidering Rock" argues that "the idea of rock involves a rejection of those aspects of mass-distributed music which are believed to be soft, safe, or trivial, those things which may be dismissed as worthless 'pop'—the very opposite of rock."⁵¹ Miles Parks Grier advances this claim, arguing that "rockers would like to think their genre thrives on the naked power of its raw sound while vacuous pop survives only because its empty sounds are paired with expensive visual supplements."⁵² Jody Rosen has found that, in contrast to rock, "pop hits reside on a lower aesthetic plane, a source of fleeting, and often shameful, enjoyment."⁵³ For example, by the late 1960s, while the word "pop" was still used to describe rock in music periodicals such as *Rolling Stone*, it was used less frequently. So much so, in fact, it makes one question whether the

Monterey Pop Festival would have been called the Monterey Rock Festival if it had taken place in 1969. In considering Paul McCartney and Wings, I found the word "pop" began to be used to question and describe music accused of lacking rock aesthetics[54] (and is still today in some circles), "as every review [of Wings] used the word or genre of 'pop' to question and criticize."[55]

It is evident that rock and pop are not defined purely by sound or production, and rock aesthetics are embedded within the genre, contributing to the definitions of rock and pop. For Keightley, "it is more useful to approach it [rock] as a larger musical culture."[56] Although there is not a definitive definition of rock or pop, it is evident that within the rock and rock journalism discourse, rock has been long established as a culturally authentic form of music, and in comparison, pop as vapid and meaningless. If all female fans are labeled as teenybopper (pop) fans, then by default, and throughout history, what they are reading about popular music would also be designated as meaningless.

There is a consensus among scholars that the genre of rock is positioned as "serious," thereby placing pop and teenyboppers as lacking "seriousness"—but in whose eyes? And did *TeenSet* not offer "serious" considerations of music simply because it was a teen fan magazine? I did not encounter one teen fan magazine reader (from the 1960s to the 1990s) who thought what they were reading was unimportant to them or lacking in "seriousness." However, this book illustrates that *TeenSet*, as with all teen fan magazines, has routinely been charged with not upholding "serious" journalism. Serious journalism is not readily defined, and the majority of journalism textbooks do not define what is or is not serious but rather subjectively define what *good* journalism entails.[57] Here, I adopt Keightley's definition of serious "as something 'more' than mere entertainment or distraction."[58] It is not that teen fan magazines like *16 Magazine* were not "serious," but rather they lacked loosely set criteria expected (and imposed) by rock journalists. When I asked *Tiger Beat* editor Ann Moses how she felt about the marginalization of teen fan magazines throughout history, she was surprised, because in her experience, *Tiger Beat* mattered to her fans and, as evidenced on her social media, it still does. Chapters 3, 4, and 5 will revisit this discussion and position *TeenSet* as serious journalism, not only arguably by rock critics' standards but by editor Judith Sims.

At the time of writing, these histories are yet to be fully examined. While scholarship on women's roles in popular music journalism is steadily growing, it is surprising how little has been published to date about *TeenSet* or Judith Sims and disheartening to see how teen fan publications have been portrayed in popular music journalism history, specifically within rock criticism texts. Yet as noted by many of the scholars above, rock music is often perceived and perpetuated as a masculine form for boys. While many of the texts discussed thus far attempt to position women as important contributors to popular music and correctly so, they still seem to exist outside the prominent historical discourse. However, this book will begin to fill a clear gap by reassessing *TeenSet*'s role and perception within history and popular music history and challenging the current limitations of the historical popular music journalism discourse and dismissal of *TeenSet*. Ultimately, it argues that *TeenSet* (and its staff) not only reflected popular music and culture of the mid-1960s in multiple ways but actively contributed to our understanding of it.

Lacking Access

Acquiring copies of *TeenSet* and teen fan magazines, in general, has proven to be a monumental task. During the time of researching, *TeenSet* has been listed at anywhere from five dollars to $250 for a single issue on eBay, Etsy, and other sites. The large wall posters have also sold from fifty dollars to hundreds of dollars. I was able to acquire all five posters *TeenSet* offered—all removed from the magazine. In addition, many copies of *16 Magazine*, *Tiger Beat*, and *Teen Life* (among others) have also been collected in order to place *TeenSet* into a deeper context (these will be archived in the near future). To my knowledge, there is not an extensive public digital or microform archive of any teen fan magazine from the 1950s to the present.[59] Bowling Green State's Ray and Pat Browne Library for Popular Culture Studies does house some physical copies of teen fan magazines; however, the collection is incomplete. It is not easy to access many popular music magazines such as *Rolling Stone*—which had been digitally archived through CDs using the now outdated Bondi Reader software (which can only be used on older operating systems from 2007 to 2014) and at one point on their website, but their current site does not have digital copies of their older magazines to browse through.[60] *Creem* and *Rolling Stone* can both be found in their entirety in some libraries as microform or selected articles through an annual subscription to *Rock's Backpages*.[61] *Creem*'s digital archives can now be accessed through a yearly subscription of seventy-nine dollars. Due to these fees, both archives are unobtainable for many. Yet there has been no evidence of an accessible and complete archive of *16 Magazine* or *Tiger Beat*, with the exception of a few issues scanned on music fan sites such as the *Sunshine Factory*[62] or on sites of collectors of 1960s memorabilia.

As this book will suggest, one of the lasting consequences of the lack of teen fan magazine archives (physical or digital) has been the ongoing scholarly neglect of the format. During his research, Anthony Slide found a similar problem finding archives of Hollywood fan magazines: "Because of their ephemeral quality, not to mention the low regard in which they were held, fan magazines have not withstood the test of time well. Public libraries seldom, if ever, subscribed, and many of those that did discarded an old issue once the new one arrived."[63]

One of the problems is the long-term tendency for popular culture, and especially popular music, to be marginalized. This has occurred not only in the field of musicology,[64] but, as Frank Hoffman, B. Lee Cooper, and Wayne Haney argue, can be adduced in what was and is valued by other institutions controlling our access to reading materials. Considering popular music, Cooper and Haney suggest that, in general, libraries do not necessarily value popular culture texts, and, as I found, especially ones admired by young girls. They argue that "if librarians are to succeed in providing present and potential patrons with comprehensive information services, they must collect and circulate popular culture materials. It is regrettable that so few libraries can currently be cited as models for offering such services or resources."[65] While this argument is now over twenty-five years old, it is still relevant today, as the majority of the popular music sources needed for this book were difficult to retrieve and had to be purchased, especially out-of-print texts dating from the 1960s, 1970s, and 1980s, which were either not kept by libraries or were never acquired. As teen fan magazines have (at the time of writing) almost disappeared with changing technology, it is important to rescue the surviving copies and create an open-access archive. This is one of my future priorities for research in the field.

Along with archiving physical resources, obtaining firsthand accounts has proven invaluable to this book. I was presented with the opportunity to interview several individuals who were key players in 1960s music culture, beginning with Ken Mansfield, a 1960s Capitol Records executive, well-known Beatles fan Debbie Gendler, and 1960s and early 1970s *Tiger Beat* editor Ann Moses. After these first interviews, I began to reach out to readers, writers, and musicians featured in *TeenSet*, such as Buffalo Springfield's Richie Furay, *Rolling Stone*'s Ben Fong-Torres, Van Dyke Parks, Jim Marshall's estate holder Amelia Davis, author Joel Selvin, and Apple Scruff[86] Nancy Furlong. Additionally, I attempted to contact individuals who wrote letters to *TeenSet* that were published in the magazine, but as many of the names are common or were changed due to marriage, I had very little success tracking down specific individuals. Yet eventually, I had readers reach out to me, and first-generation reader Steve Kern and collector Jeff Hoganson's voices are included. Every participant had the option of withdrawing their responses or remaining anonymous. *TeenSet* (and the 1960s in general) is moving beyond living memory, and including voices with firsthand experience of the publication adds valuable historical insight to research of this kind.

The book is divided into five chapters. Chapter 1, "A Capitol Idea! *TeenSet* and Teen Fan Magazines," explores the development of 1950s/'60s teen fan magazines such as *16 Magazine*, *Tiger Beat*, and, specifically, *TeenSet*. This chapter (among others) includes voices of 1960s teen fan magazine readers such as Debbie Gendler and *Tiger Beat* editor Ann Moses, considering the hitherto unexplored value of teen fan magazines, such as a sense of community and knowledge of popular music. This chapter goes on to consider Capitol Records' promotional creation of "the teen set" and its release of dominant control of the publication in 1965 to the Kimtex Corporation, upon which Judith Sims is given editorial control over the renamed (*The*) *TeenSet* magazine. The format, coverage, and brief evolution of *TeenSet* are considered to provide a foundational historical understanding. It ends with an exploration of how *TeenSet* and Sims have been discussed historically and reveals a gap in scholarship research that this book will attempt to fill. Ultimately, this chapter contextualizes teen fan magazines and *TeenSet* within the mid to late 1960s, presents *TeenSet* as a phenomenon in the popular music press, and introduces *TeenSet*'s liminal role between teen fan magazines and the rock press, setting a foundation for the entire book.

Chapter 2, "It's Only Rock 'n' Roll Journalism: The Absence of *TeenSet* within a History Shaped by Critics," primarily argues that the historical popular music journalism discourse has been monopolized by a dominant rock criticism/journalism narrative, overlooking teen fan magazines and *TeenSet*. In general, the scant consideration teen fan magazines have received within popular music journalism has overwhelmingly been dismissive. This chapter shows that throughout the years, without many early challengers, male rock critics have written their own history within popular music journalism, and rock criticism's seemingly elite status has allowed for the dismissal of other narratives in rock journalism and popular music, such as *TeenSet*'s. Readers have been presented with a dominant narrative of a few men, at times referred to as the "founding fathers,"[67] elevating rock music to a high status in comparison to pop music. This chapter also analyzes Cameron Crowe's presentation of rock journalists in *Almost Famous* (2000), specifically its portrayal of Lester Bangs as a wise literary sage, which arguably blurs reality and fiction and, in turn, contributes to hagiography within the field of rock criticism. Importantly, this chapter conveys the extent to which the dominant narrative has allowed for a problematic and uneven historical discourse of hagiographical proportions that has allowed a contributing historical narrative like *TeenSet*'s to be marginalized.

Chapter 3, "Show Me *TeenSet*! Combating the Historical Discourse: *TeenSet* as an Authentic Source," examines the use of *TeenSet* in popular music histories and biographies. In many ways, this chapter is in response to the dominant narrative that popular music was only taken seriously by the established rock press and male rock critics. By exploring biographies and academic texts and their authors' use of *TeenSet*'s content, we gain an understanding of how *TeenSet* has shaped our perceptions of various artists or musicians over time, such as Laura Nyro, Neil Young, and Jimi Hendrix, and that these texts have regarded *TeenSet* as a legitimate source. Furthermore, many of the photographs have become highly recognizable in the popular music canon, several of them being iconic portraits of individuals and historic events that inform and advance our understanding of the subject. This chapter also examines celebrated rock photographer Jim Marshall's involvement in *TeenSet*, presenting a semiotic analysis of selected Marshall photographs and photography from a Beatles and Rolling Stones tour manager, Bob Bonis. The chapter ends by analyzing the visual use of *TeenSet* to illuminate Jim Morrison's 1960s fame in Oliver Stone's film *The Doors* (1991). Ultimately, this chapter shows, through an examination of sources that utilized *TeenSet*, that it has made an impact on popular music and culture despite its absence from the archives.

Chapter 4, "Taking Popular Music Seriously: Judith Sims and the Women on the Scene," explores *TeenSet*'s role in taking popular music seriously. By considering Judith Sims's leadership of *TeenSet* and her role as editor, it becomes clear that *TeenSet* addressed popular music from multiple angles—separating *TeenSet* from other teen fan magazines of the time. This chapter also presents Judith Sims as a peer editor and as present and active in the popular music scenes of the period. Sims and her freelancers participated in the Hollywood, San Francisco, and London scenes, and (unlike rival teen publications) they presented their readers with many up-and-coming musicians in these scenes. Through the leadership of Judith Sims and the magazine's articles and regular columns, *TeenSet* challenged the expected gender norms of not only teen fan magazines but also women fans by reporting on the blues, issues surrounding race, and musicianship. The chapter concludes by emphasizing Carol Gold's and Judith Sims's scene coverage and love of popular music, which defies many generalizations of women's roles in popular music and leads into chapter 5's consideration of how Sims transformed *TeenSet* by 1969.

Finally, chapter 5, "'A Nifty Music Magazine with a Misleading Name': *TeenSet*'s Duality, Representation of and Interaction with an Evolving Musical and Cultural Landscape," advances the central claim that *TeenSet* not only presented serious considerations of popular music but also constructed, reflected, and navigated an evolving musical and cultural landscape. This chapter contends that *TeenSet*, again via the editorial leadership of Judith Sims, conveyed the then-growing countercultural and revolutionary rhetoric in the rock genre in multiple ways, including its record reviews, cover formatting, content focus, and design. Here, revolutionary rhetoric refers to political commentary and actions that may propel, persuade, or encourage rapid change; these include *TeenSet*'s inclusion and discussion of Grace Slick's performance in blackface, *TeenSet*'s (and Hendrix's) consideration of Black Power and the Black Panthers, and its open support of protests and peaceful social movements in which music or musicians are involved—all persuasive attempts to consider and possibly encourage rapid change.[68] Here, *TeenSet* is presented as a historical source that provides insight into the cultural evolution of the late 1960s and addresses the evolving concept of the teenager, which is finally emphasized by the changing of the name *TeenSet* to *AUM (America's Underthirty Magazine)*. In no other popular music magazine of this period can such a transformation be detected. This final chapter will advance *TeenSet*'s historical value within popular music journalism and emphasize that *TeenSet* is a unique phenomenon of 1960s US culture.

Collectively, these chapters establish *TeenSet*'s position within the history of popular music and rock journalism and show *TeenSet*'s engagement with and contribution to the US's cultural discourses of the 1960s. *TeenSet* fits within the discourse of rock journalism and should not only be recognized in this context (a discourse that has contributed to its omission from standard narratives of popular music history) but also celebrated and considered in its own right. This book builds on a number of recent publications that maintain that female voices of any age deserve to be taken seriously in popular music—that one narrative is not more "serious" than another. Ultimately, this book challenges and contributes to a corrective history that upholds *TeenSet* as not only meaningful to the rock journalism canon but valuable as a historical artifact when considering the late 1960s and popular music and culture.

Finally, throughout this book, rock journalism and rock criticism refers to all serious considerations of rock music, specifically in the mid-1960s to the mid-1970s and at times are used interchangeably. As Brennan found in *When Genres Collide: Downbeat, Rolling Stone, and the Struggle Between Jazz and Rock*, it is difficult to separate these terms as many rock journalists often blurred the lines between criticism and journalism by offering their thoughts and opinions on musicians, music, and culture. Addtionally, I refer to rock journalism as a branch of popular music journalism. Although popular music journalism will be used when discussing popular music coverage as a whole (which refers to any media coverage and consideration of popular music including rock journalism), I will use rock journalism or criticism when discussing music journalism concerned with the rock genre, criticism, and rock aesthetics.

CHAPTER ONE

A CAPITOL IDEA!

THE ORIGINS OF TEEN FAN MAGAZINES AND *TeenSet*

TeenSet raised the bar. They catered to diverse musical tastes, in-depth interviews, and detailed record reviews.
—APPLE SCRUFF NANCY FURLONG (ALLEN)[1]

THE BEGINNINGS OF THE TEEN LIFESTYLE, TYPE, AND FAN MAGAZINES

By the 1950s, with the development of rock 'n' roll and a growing understanding of and attempt to gain the expanding teenager dollar, the teen-type magazine (and shortly after, the teen fan magazine) thrived. Not only did teenagers want to listen, watch, and dance to rock 'n' roll, but they wanted to read about it, too. Thomas Doherty argues that "the first 'teen-type'[2] magazines, *DIG* and *Teen*, appeared by 1955, and a dozen more were on the market by 1960. Circulation averaged a few hundred thousand each, but actual readership might well have tripled that . . . the teen magazines that flourished in the mid-1950s were no instructional manuals designed under the approving eyes of parents and teachers."[3] Teen-type magazines were not the same as teen lifestyle magazines such as *Seventeen* or *Teen*, which mostly focused on one's transitioning to adulthood before the 1960s. Rather, they focused on being a teen and "making the 'teen time' more enjoyable."[4] In general, these magazines were teen general interest magazines that included rock 'n' roll or at least considered stars such as Elvis but were not founded by peers, teenagers, or individuals fairly close in age (nor would teen fan magazines). The first of these, and the most notable, was *DIG*, which was first published in November 1955. *DIG* and the early teen-type magazines advertised to both

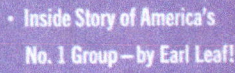
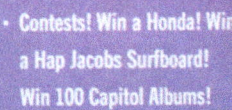

Figure 1.1. *The TeenSet* cover, Volume 1, Fall 1964. Used by permission of Scholastic Inc.

sexes. Within *DIG*'s first issue, not only did it feature Black musicians, rock, and jazz, but it also included a free R&B record[5] and an article titled "Learn How to Rock and Roll." However, the extreme rarity of this particular issue, as well as the majority of 1950s *DIG*s, hinders closer analysis. While the new mid-1950s teen-type magazine format may have been different from the 1940s teen lifestyle magazine, these magazines were ultimately an amalgamation of Hollywood fan and teen lifestyle magazines but with an attempt to market to teens directly with a devotion to the growing teen culture.

The focus of teen fan magazines, unlike any other category of teen *publication*, was popular music rather than an attempt to center more broadly around teenage life. The focus on musicians and groups was the differentiating factor. Hollywood fan magazine writer Dixie Dean Harris[6] noted in *Esquire* in 1965:

> Teen books concentrate on recording stars, and particularly on the groups. The last count netted about thirty vocal groups, with names like The Kinks, The Animals, Manfred Mann, The Searchers, Gerry and The Pacemakers, The Rolling Stones, and the Ronettes. The magazines do run stories on teenage movie stars, like Hayley Mills, Patty Duke, and Paul Petersen, but their real interest is the record people. In the movie books, the proportions are almost exactly reversed.[7]

Moreover, throughout the 1960s, teen-type and even teen lifestyle magazines such as *Seventeen* featured popular musicians, groups, and teen idols; thus, the lines can often be blurred. It would be incorrect to say teen fan magazines did not consider teenage life at all as *16 Magazine* and the majority of teen fan magazines absolutely did, but by the 1960s, they were not as broadly focused on all things teen as teen-type magazines were. In most cases, the early teen fan magazine followed many Hollywood fan magazine practices such as sensationalism, reprinting articles, and "stretching" facts. After all, before the existence of the teen fan magazine, Hollywood fan magazines would be the only place to find a plethora of information on stars, some of whom, such as Frank Sinatra, were also popular music idols. Thus, the teen fan magazine's origins lie within Hollywood fan magazines rather than in music periodicals.

Hollywood fan magazines[8] historically were and are often portrayed and criticized as a lower form of journalism that embellished stories or blackmailed stars. As Mary Desjardins found, "fan-magazine [Hollywood] writers and editors relied heavily on studio publicity departments (and often on independent press agents employed by some stars) for information about or access to the stars, which kept the practitioners of this genre open to criticism from other journalists."[9] The same concept crosses over into the teen-type magazines or in the early years of teen fan magazines as the personae of stars were heavily controlled by their press agents or their film studios. This argument may be applied to teen fan magazines with musical acts and pop stars. Consider that, as Erin Weber argues, the portrayal of the Beatles was heavily controlled by Brian Epstein, among others, and "elements that contradicted the more sanitized official version [of the Beatles] were suppressed for years."[10] Similarly, no discussion of the Monkees' marijuana use was ever to grace *16 Magazine* or *Tiger Beat*. While I do not believe that teen fan magazines of the 1960s were "mouthpieces" for record companies or Hollywood studios, the reputation of the Hollywood fan magazines carried over to teen-type and teen fan magazines due to their sensationalistic nature. Teen fan magazines have clear origins within Hollywood fan magazines, but they are also precursors to rock journalism, and unlike other teen fan magazines, *TeenSet* developed alongside the rock press.

In contrast to the Hollywood fan magazines, music periodicals often considered classical music, featured sheet music, and advertised to musicians. While throughout the nineteenth and early twentieth century, magazines such as *Etude* were directed toward professionally educated musicians and music teachers, the early 1920s ushered in a growing popularity of popular music genres such as jazz, blues, and country. However, popular music articles[11] were rare in music magazines in contrast to classical sheet music into the mid-twentieth century. Early cultural magazines, such as *Vanity Fair*, were where one may have read about popular music and culture in the 1920s, such as Carl Van Vechten's 1925 and 1926 pieces on the blues and Bessie Smith (see Van Vechten). In the 1930s and 1940s, one may find sheet music for popular Shirley Temple songs or Tin Pan Alley songs in musical periodicals such as *Song Hits* (a lyric periodical) or *Hit Parader* but would not find in-depth discussions of popular music and culture. By 1934, the jazz magazine *DownBeat* successfully began to seriously consider jazz.[12] *DownBeat* also featured small articles on country, folk, and, by the 1950s, even the blues. Yet with the exception of contributors such as Ralph J. Gleason, Nat Hentoff, Ruth Cage, and Barbara Gardner, *DownBeat* openly dismissed rock 'n' roll and popular music or completely ignored it in the 1950s. As Brennan argues,

DownBeat did not attempt to consider rock music until the mid-1960s with ad pressure in attempts to gain readers, but even then, this was very inconsistent. Folk periodicals like *People's Songs* and, later, Pete Seeger's cofounded *Sing Out!*, contained folk sheet music and discussions pertaining to social issues but were sharply focused. Trade papers such as *Billboard* and *Cashbox* considered popular music and musicians but from an industry standpoint. It was not until the rise of the teen fan magazine that popular musicians (rock, pop, soul, etc.) were considered throughout the pages of a magazine.

The Rise of the Special-Interest Teen Fan Magazine: *16 Magazine*, *Tiger Beat*, and Teen Fan Magazines

David Abrahamson has suggested that by the 1960s, "the 'special-interest' publication began to flourish."[13] These magazines were different in multiple ways from general interest magazines such as *Life* or *Look* or even teen-type magazines as they were tailored to special interests such as a specific hobby, sport, or craft, or in this case, teen fan magazines that were tailored to popular music fans. As Abrahamson points out, "As many of the mass-circulation publications suffered, magazines addressing the specific interest of specific readers prospered. Between 1955 and 1965, the circulation of a wide variety of more targeted publications enjoyed significant growth."[14] During this time, multiple teen fan magazines began and many were successful, even with heavy competition as "large print runs were no longer necessary, and small circulation magazines suddenly became more profitable."[15] Teen fan magazines were created for profit, and some profit came from advertising; in most cases, merchandise or fan clubs for the Monkees, Beatles or Cowsills were advertised. However, many teen fan magazines, such as *16 Magazine* and *Tiger Beat*, advertised items that were created by the magazines themselves, such as posters and detailed fan books. While fan magazines were not new, teen fan magazines with a focus on popular music were, and they began to develop by the end of the 1950s with the New York-based *16 Magazine*, and more importantly, with Gloria Stavers's placement as *16 Magazine*'s editor in late 1958.

Teen fan magazines of the 1960s "not only informed their readers of the favorite snack foods of John, Paul, George, and Ringo, but offered predictions and previews of what act would be the next major transatlantic import into the domestic teen culture."[16] Largely, by the 1960s, these publications served as special interest magazines concerned with the popular music realm directed at the lucrative teenage market—specifically marketed to girls. Unlike the early issues of *DIG*, the mid-1960s teen fan magazine audience is generally argued to be "composed almost exclusively of girls, ranging in age from eleven to seventeen."[17] As *Time* highlighted in a 1967 article titled "The Press: Aiming at the Hip": "Brothers and boyfriends mostly stick to *Mad*, car magazines, and *Playboy*. So teen publishers tune their message to girls between ten and 18,"[18] but that is not to say boys did not also read teen fan magazines, and as this book shows, they did. In the same article, *Flip*'s editor Stephan Khan told *Time*, "'The kids are straight,' he contends. . . . 'These books are sexless, innocent, good books. When the girls get older and begin to think about sex, they can go on to other magazines. We're through with them.'"[19] *16 Magazine* editor Gloria Stavers confirms that the reading age is young and suggests the title of her magazine is the age that girls typically stop reading the magazine: "The average reader's age is about 14. . . . We have a lot of readers who are 11, but it seems to drop off considerably at about 16. When a girl reaches that age, she gets more interested in the boy next door and moves out of the *16* world."[20]

16 Magazine is arguably the first popular music teen fan magazine, and many followed suit or adapted elements of Stavers's methods, such as *Tiger Beat* or *Teen Life*. *16 Magazine* was originally founded in the origins of the Hollywood fan style but for a younger audience. The magazine was created by men—Jacques Chambrun, Desmond Hall, and George Waller—in 1957, with a focus on Elvis, and for the first two years, "there were no interviews with the actual subjects, but rather press releases, photos, and even drawings of the subject if the proper photo couldn't be obtained at his price."[21] The magazine was targeted at teenage girls with the slogan "The magazine for SMART Girls."[22] Early *16 Magazine* had "no competition. Fans were quick to realize that *16 Magazine* was the only place they could go to find information (such as it was) and photos. It was a fan book for them, a *Photoplay* or *Life* magazine, filled with young stars they cared about."[23]

It is evident, by the few sources that consider *16 Magazine* (Belscamper, Moser, Eldrige, and Fields), that *16 Magazine* was shaped more by the leadership of Gloria Stavers than by its original creators. At the time of writing, *16 Magazine*'s Wikipedia page discusses Stavers and her role as editor but does not mention the founders of *16 Magazine*, which advances the argument that *16 Magazine* became important under Stavers's control. This is of interest because the majority of consideration given to teenage girl fandom from the 1960s or that examines *16 Magazine* is solely focused on Stavers. In *Who's Your Fave Rave: Teen Idols as You Knew Them . . . And as They Really Were!* Fields and Reisfeld argue that "everything *16* ever was, it was because of her."[24] She "sought a slightly younger audience than *Seventeen*, and featured popular music and television stars, rather than fashions."[25] *16 Magazine* presented elements of popular music and teen culture through sensationalism on many levels, but on others, provided thoughtful insight into popular music stars. However, as Belscamper argues, *16 Magazine* was not interested in representing the changing political, cultural, or musical landscape associated with the counterculture but rather, to stay hip, adopted "lingo generally associated with a counterculture lifestyle"[26] as it became more popular. This is also evident in the lack of consideration of certain musicians and groups directly connected to the counterculture, such as Janis Joplin or Jefferson Airplane, and the declining Beatles coverage by 1967. Rather, it mostly included stars and musicians who were in the Top 40 and had a young readership. The "magazine maintained continuity, including the specific columns that featured Stavers herself and the advice features that generally fell in line with the gender and generation social norms and expectations of the era."[27] Stavers "used *16* every issue . . . to express her absolute loyalty to a specific version of teen culture."[28] This is not to say it did not contribute to popular music journalism or that it did not thoughtfully consider popular music, but rather that it was not concerned with any type of changing rock rhetoric, counterculture, or growing up with its readers, as I will argue *TeenSet* did. The magazine followed a specific formula, and Stavers's version of teen culture was safe and supportive in that it included fantasy with the concept of Dreamsville, but it was not ready for sex or war. On multiple occasions, *16 Magazine* and Stavers have received acknowledgment for being the first to consider popular music in print media but quickly dismissed for lacking seriousness, and this, in regard to all teen fan magazines, will be fully considered.

As Nicolette Rohr points out, "The Beatles came to the United States in February 1964 and sparked the American iteration of 'Beatlemania,'"[29] and teen fan magazines contributed to this "mania." With this arrival, *16 Magazine* gained in popularity but began to see a large rise in competition from new teen fan magazines, teen Hollywood fan magazines, and teen-type magazines as they began to focus on popular music more. It was easy for magazines such as *TeenScreen* or *Movie Teen* to consider popular music artists as many of them were in movies or on television, such as Elvis, Doris Day, the Beatles, or the Monkees. The surf craze of the 1960s (a period of time when surfing was popularized in TV and movies) also allowed for a crossover to consider the Beach Boys and others such as Jan and Dean.

By the mid-1960s, especially after the arrival of the Beatles, the teen fan magazine was in full swing. In addition to the teen-type *DIG* and the original teen fan magazine *16 Magazine*, multiple monthly teen fan magazines appeared: *Teen Life, Teen DateBook (Datebook), Flip, Fifteen, Tiger Beat, Teen Beat, TeenScreen, Movie Teen, For Teens Only, Teen Talk, Teen World, Today's Teens, FABulous Teen, Hollywood Go Go Teen Album, FaVE, Top Teen, Keen Teen, Teen Pin-Ups, SPEC* (by *16 Magazine*), *Teen Scoop, Teen Circle, Teen Stars, Outasite,* and *TeenSet* (originally *the Teen Set*). Also, the Beatles (and later the Monkees) would inspire many one-offs or limited-issue teen publications such as *BeatleDom, Welcome Back Beatles,* and *Beatles Movie,* often released by various publishers. In 1965, Harris noted, "It is estimated that twenty-one shots on the Beatles were put out. They sold an average of a million copies apiece, at prices ranging from thirty-five cents to a dollar."[30] She further suggests that in the early to mid-1960s, there were between seventy and eighty magazines published and aimed at teenagers at once, but by 1965, only approximately twenty survived; nonetheless, many were selling half a million copies.[31] If her calculations are accurate, many of the magazines are unaccounted for and no formal archive exists; due to the lack of archives, titles may be missing from the previous list. *Tiger Beat, TeenSet,* and multiple others began to compete with Stavers and *16 Magazine*. Yet when *Tiger Beat* (1965) arrived, the competition became a reality for Stavers, as *Tiger Beat* was highly circulated. Unlike the New York-based *16 Magazine,* both *TeenSet* and *Tiger Beat* were located in LA, home to many popular bands and record companies. *Tiger Beat* editor Ann Moses, a then-peer of her readers at age nineteen, describes in her book *Meow! My Groovy Life with Tiger Beat's Teen Idols* (2017), "*Tiger Beat's* Los Angeles proximity to stars, coupled with the fact that Gloria's was no longer the only teen fan magazine on the stand, had to have troubled her."[32]

Like *16 Magazine,* these new teen fan magazine arrivals resembled one another.[33] They often featured crowded, bright covers, which promised several features attempting to entice multiple fans, but this meant the features were often short and lacked in-depth detail. For example, figure 1.3 illuminates how much information is considered in one issue of *16 Magazine.* Within

Figure 1.2. Multiple 1960s teen fan magazines. Used by permission of Scholastic Inc.

the sixty-seven pages (including the front and back cover) of the particular issue of *16*, there are twenty-nine features, but this was not uncommon.

In general, many of the formats were similar, as well as the content and subject matter, but departments varied from magazine to magazine, such as the Letters to the Editors, Pen Pals, Self-Help, and Astrology. Many teen fan

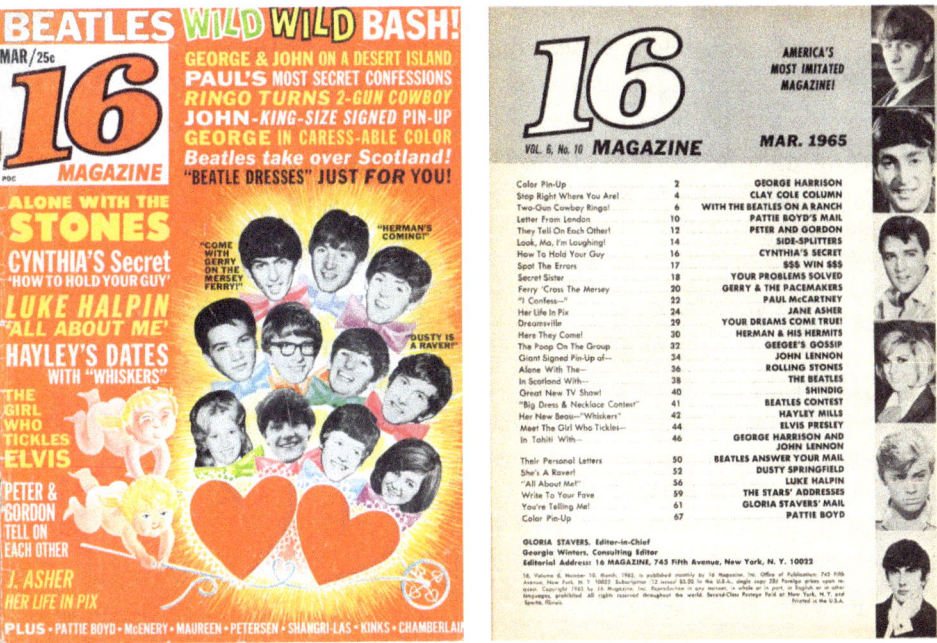

Figures 1.3A and 1.3B. *16 Magazine* cover and table of contents, March 1965. Author's collection.

magazines did not have a consistent letter from the editor as part of their format as other special interest magazines would (except for *TeenSet*). While *Tiger Beat* initially provided an introductory piece from its sponsor TV host (Lloyd Thaxton),[34] the magazine did not provide an introductory editorial from an involved peer-fan editor and eventually dropped the introductory name and association with Thaxton. While, at times, there was an introductory letter from a popular musician, and Ann Moses did have a consistent feature titled "Meow," it was more informative and contained information about the featured artists and stars rather than an openly analytical opinion considering culture, controversy, or musicianship as *TeenSet* did. *16 Magazine* did not provide a consistent editorial from Stavers. *TeenScreen*, although at times providing a letter from the editor (mainly during Janey Milstead's short time as editor), lacked a consistent editor and did not provide the voice and the involvement that Sims contributed to *TeenSet*.

Like the Hollywood fan magazine, teen fan magazines (at times) created catchy or zany headlines and stories, even if they were loosely based on factual information. *16 Magazine* was evidently guilty, as was *Tiger Beat* and *Datebook* in their early years. *16 Magazine* included headlines such as "Monkees-Saj Fight! Whole Terrible True Story."[35] However, the issue contains one article about various struggles of Micky's and Mike's childhoods and a separate article on Saj's struggles. There was no actual fight between the five men, as the headline suggested. In our correspondence, Ann Moses recalled a headline and story from the 1970s that followed the sensational style:

> Did we do some stories that were taken from one sentence from an interview? Yes. Like when David Cassidy had a scary accident (running out of air when he was diving in Hawaii—our photographer was with him at the time), and we ran the headline "The Day David Almost Died" on the cover, and it was a four-page article with pics and described how he ran out of air while diving. This was typical fan mag writing, presentation, but it was not wholly fiction.[36]

These headlines were common throughout the existence of print teen fan magazines until the 2000s.

In general, 1960s teen fan magazines had little coverage of Black musicians in comparison to white musicians. While Ann Moses did cover James Brown in 1965 for *Tiger Beat* as well as other Black artists and acts throughout the 1960s, they were not considered equally within teen fan magazines or necessarily featured on the covers (with the exception of Jimi Hendrix on *TeenSet* in 1969 and Motown acts on *Teen Life* in 1968). With the 1970s popularity of the Jackson Five, Michael Jackson was featured multiple times on the cover of *Tiger Beat* and *16 Magazine*, but the coverage of Black artists was still insufficient. Later on, in 1971, *Tiger Beat* developed a Black-focused teen magazine titled *Right On!* and, in 1973, Good Publishing Co. produced the little-considered Black teen fan magazine *Soul Teen*.[37]

Teen fan magazines offered removable pinups (or pullouts) and posters (often in color) of specific stars or musicians to their readers. Pinups and articles could be hung in lockers and on walls and shared with friends who were also interested, and these magazines provided information that could not easily be found elsewhere. The 1960s did not have the social media platforms and constant bombardment of information about musicians and stars, and therefore, the teen fan magazines opened an avenue to announce concerts and provide coverage of popular music events with information on multiple musicians and stars in a way that television did not.

While the general teen fan magazine was not often concerned with the actual musical process or discussing music per se, it provided a platform for music fans to learn more personal information about their favorite musicians or stars. Ann Moses says her role as editor of *Tiger Beat* was to present the stars from a very specific perspective:

> Ralph [Benner, cocreator of *Tiger Beat* along with Chuck Laufer] explained right away that *Tiger Beat* readers didn't want to know about their idol's sex-capades, and they didn't get a hoot if they wrote their own songs. I was told to focus on things teenaged and preteen girls could relate to: Mick's favorite color or what Paul liked to eat for lunch. We turned our attention to a pop star's thoughts on girls with short hair or why they always wore a particular strand of love beads. You wouldn't find us writing about Davy's new girlfriend; everyone was presented as single and free and looking for just the right girl, one who liked sunshine and home-baked cookies and thought the color green was just groovy![38]

The 1960s teen fan magazine featured materials that fans wanted and could relate to, such as commonalities between the fan and the star or musician. As Moses highlights, individual celebrities were presented as single, and these omissions deepened the distrust of teen fan magazines that printed the actual relationship status of their features.

Devon Powers argues the teen fan magazine lens was from a "celebrity-oriented perspective."[39] There is no doubt that the majority of teen fan magazines did focus on "teen idols"; as Moses says, "Our magazine [*Tiger Beat*] was in the business of teen idols,"[40] but it did not make their contributions unable to influence popular music journalism. In our correspondence, Moses made a point to highlight that *Tiger Beat* included non-"teen idol" groups too, and it was not only idolization printed within the pages of *Tiger Beat*:

> *Tiger Beat* was one of the early ones to publish a huge, four-page article (written by me from my interview in 1965) on James Brown. I paid my dues by working for a local music newspaper in Fullerton, CA, which was distributed to music stores all over So. [Southern] California called Rhythm 'n News. Because the editor's slant was blues music, she would assign me to interview the Negro acts that played at mostly Black clubs in South LA. I was so surprised at their excitement at my interviewing them for what I knew was a

small, local circulation music newspaper. They were literally flabbergasted to get "press coverage." The amazing shows I saw—Ike and Tina Turner, Smokey Robinson and the Miracles, Little Stevie Wonder, James Brown—were a bonus for me. *Tiger Beat* was not intending to go in that direction, but when I presented the James Brown story, for example, they ran it and got lots of reader mail in response. That's one contribution.[41]

Teen fan magazines of the mid-1960s covered pop, rhythm and blues, and rock, as well as the burgeoning counterculture, before the late 1960s when the majority of them moved to cover younger pop stars such as Sajid Khan. The typical stars chosen for the magazine were young or representative of youth. While the teen fan publications in the late 1960s and early 1970s and thereafter considered extremely young stars and musicians such as David Cassidy, the Osmonds, and Michael Jackson, there was a period where the musicians that became associated with authenticity and meaning within the rock press were considered in teen fan magazines. The musicians and stars (such as the Monkees, Moby Grape, or the Beatles) were not necessarily teens. In addition, in the 1960s, readers could find themselves reading about the Yardbirds, the Rolling Stones, the Kinks, and other groups that became connected to the counterculture before the existence of *Crawdaddy!* or *Rolling Stone*.

Teen fan magazines covered the Top 40, as many British (as well as American) rock groups charted. The mid-1960s was an interesting time: the Beatles had broken the US market, which encouraged the growth of many teen fan magazines. This was a period in which political rhetoric entered the genre of rock via folk, and teen fan magazines considered what was popular. Many of the musicians and music they featured eventually became attached to the counterculture or revolutionary rhetoric. These magazines were the first to feature the Rolling Stones, the Beatles, the Byrds, Donovan, Frank Zappa, and multiple others, but as will be conveyed, *TeenSet* (as well as *Datebook*) continued to feature groups such as the Rolling Stones throughout the late 1960s, whereas *16 Magazine* did not. As Belscamper argues, "As the Stones followed a similar path as the Beatles with drug arrests, more progressive music, and maturity and facial hair, they gradually disappeared from the pages of *16 Magazine*."[42]

Teen fan magazines arguably progressed the careers of artists as well. As noted, for some time, they were the main purveyors of popular music information. When I asked if teen fan magazines advanced the careers of musicians and idols, Moses replied:

Without a doubt. As far as I know, in the early sixties, *16 Magazine* was the only one that featured teen idols, other than occasional feature in movie magazines of the day (but movie and TV stars were their bread and butter, and the fan-base for the movie magazines was older). *16* was first published in 1957 and was the #1 seller for many years (because of their early start).

Of course. All of a sudden, garage bands like the Standells, groups like the Byrds, the Mamas and the Papas, Jefferson Airplane, and all the British groups that were part of the British Invasion . . . were more popular and sold more records because they were covered extensively in *Tiger Beat*. Remember, groups like Crosby, Stills, Nash and Young were not teen idols, but they were loved around the world. While our bread and butter were teen idols, boys were definitely buying our mag to read about music groups, and *Tiger Beat* had quite a bit more than mags like *16* because I was going to The Trip, The Whiskey-A-Go-Go, The Fillmore Auditorium in San Francisco—all the clubs where acts like Elton John, James Taylor, the Byrds, Jefferson Airplane, and so many more were getting their early appearances—long, long before they were playing stadiums.[43]

Buffalo Springfield's Richie Furay contributed to this discussion when I asked him if *TeenSet* advanced Buffalo Springfield's career: "I know the magazine gave awareness to Buffalo Springfield—anytime you're getting print (and that was the model for the day), it had to help."[44]

By the early 1970s, the teen fan magazine had fully transitioned to a younger audience, and this is evident by the included content and the musicians whom the magazines focused on. However, even though the targeted audience was younger, the magazines still included interesting or impactful features such as *Tiger Beat*'s two-page spread[45] on Glam Rock, focusing on David Bowie and Marc Bolan, which is nothing to dismiss. Throughout the 1970s, 1980s, and 1990s, teen fan magazines continued to thrive; some, like the 1980s *TEENSET*, completely unrelated to the 1960s *TeenSet*, did reach beyond preteen audiences but were concerned with popular culture in general and were not as focused on popular music. I personally read many magazines in the 1990s, and it is undeniable that they were crush-focused—there was never a shortage of posters of Jonathan Taylor Thomas, Leonardo DiCaprio, Hanson, or the Spice Girls. However, like in the early 1950s and on, until the development and affordable accessibility of the internet, it was the only place to find a plethora of information on my *then* favorite musicians—as *Rolling Stone* and others were not concerned with preteen interests.

Teen fan magazines would continue to adhere to a similar format until their demise in the early 2000s. While *Tiger Beat* had a website, the format was not in the style of a magazine. The teen fan magazine flourished in print for over sixty years, but considering the easily accessible information at our fingertips, in general, these magazines have ceased publication. *16 Magazine*'s last issue was printed in 2001, *Tiger Beat*'s in the winter of 2019, and others have come and gone. In 2018, I went to the American book chain Barnes & Noble to explore their current teen fan magazine selection, but in the vast array of magazines, not one teen fan magazine was to be found. The current *Rolling Stone* magazine, while still considering politics and music production, features spreads of popular musicians' photographs (and captions) as the teen fan magazines had before.

Fundamentally, considering these early origins and contributions of 1960s teen fan magazines, these magazines created a platform to discuss popular music that music periodicals failed to do, and they further conveyed that readers were interested in popular music. As shown above, the origins and contributions of 1960s teen fan magazines are of value not only in popular music journalism but also because, in contrast, it provides a foundation for understanding why *TeenSet* is an exception to the typical format of the teen fan magazine and shows that *TeenSet* cannot be categorized solely as a teen magazine.

A Valued Community

A very important aspect of teen fan magazines that is often overlooked is the role they played in encouraging a communal space. In correspondence with Beatles fan and author of *I Saw Them Standing There: Adventures of an Original Fan during Beatlemania and Beyond* (2024), Debbie Gendler[46] openly proclaims teen fan magazines vital from her perspective as a 1960s teen fan. Specifically, Gendler remembers that 1960s teen fan magazines offered a sense of community through pen pals and letters to the editors:

> Teen magazines became a vital part of my life because they kept me in touch with what was going on in the music community. Communication and information flow wasn't like we have today. The magazines that I purchased at the newsstand kept me up to date with upcoming tours, single and album releases, and most importantly, insider info on my favorite performers. The

magazines brought together people—we could write in to the editor with hopes of being published and find pen pals across the globe who shared the same interest. They gave many of us food for thought and inspired our lives beyond the small confines of home and our little universes as we were growing up. We learned that there were people in Japan who loved the same groups as we did in New Jersey. The magazines defined a community for me.

Many publications also had beautiful photos of my favorites that I would clip out and hang on my bedroom walls or corkboard. I would share my magazines with only select friends who would take care of them and return them when they were finished. Several of my friends had to sneak peeks because their parents wouldn't tolerate their obsessions. My parents received criticism from their friends and other family members for permitting me to buy and read teen magazines. My parents felt otherwise. They believed that as long as I was reading, I was learning. How wise they were.[47]

Carolyn Kitch argues that "a magazine's readership may itself be a peer group, even if its members are not physically together."[48] She further presents magazines as a community, which, to fans of teen fan magazines, not only provided them with information about musicians, groups, and stars but also a sense of community with shared popular music interests. This is evident in many teen fan magazines, as letters to the editor were often responses to others' letters to disagree or debate information between peers. *Tiger Beat* editor Ann Moses recalls her readers as active:

> 100% active, they wrote letters to the editor, they wrote letters to their faves c/o *Tiger Beat* (one way we knew who was most popular/in demand, they sent presents to their faves c/o *TB*). They spent their money on love beads and neck chokers and our one-shot special "books" on the latest faves, plus addresses of the stars books and fashion/makeup books from the female celebs.[49]

Consider these 1964 Clinton Wright images of four young African American girls (figures 1.4A and B) who are not only shopping for teen fan magazines but also reading them together. Local man and *Las Vegas Voice*[50] photographer Clinton Wright attempted to document Black life in a segregated Las Vegas, and Wright felt these ladies' actions were worth photographing. These particular photos not only offer a window into the shopping experience of the young women but also convey young African

Figures 1.4A and B. Four young women in 1964 Las Vegas shopping for teen fan magazines. Photograph by Clinton Wright. Courtesy of UNLV Libraries Special Collections.

American women's interests not only in the Beatles (a narrative often overlooked) but in teen fan magazines. As Gendler highlighted, she shared issues with her friends, thus one can infer that different magazines would have been purchased and then shared between not only these ladies but others for maximum experience.

The Teen Set

While the value of *TeenSet* is not necessarily in its origin, its beginnings are unusual when compared to other teen fan magazines. The specialty magazine was on the rise in the early 1960s, and by 1964, many teen fan magazines were finding success by covering the Beatles and others. In the 1950s and early 1960s, Capitol Records featured artists such as Judy Garland, Jackie Gleason, and zitherist Ruth Welcome. Capitol did have success with rock 'n' roll musician Gene Vincent and rockabilly musician Wanda Jackson, but the label was in no way rock-centric. As previously noted, teenage consumers were on the rise and this has been well documented in historical accounts (see scholar Thomas Hine or Doherty), but it is of note here as Capitol began to sign more artists who marketed well with 1960s rock 'n' roll fans such as the Beatles and the Beach Boys.

What is unusual about the origin of *TeenSet* (originally *The Teen Set*, then *The TeenSet*, before becoming known simply as *TeenSet*) is it was created as a promotional tool to sell records and gain access to multiple mailing addresses, not to become a monthly teen magazine. Publishing a magazine was not an entirely surprising venture for Capitol Records, as "it published a money-making music magazine (*Capitol News*[51]) which attained a worldwide circulation of 800,000 copies monthly"[52] in the 1940s. *Capitol News*, later renamed *Music News* (arguably a trade paper), is an example of early popular music journalism and marketing[53] that has not received its due attention in popular music journalism history. Additionally, *Music News* included multiple artists from other record companies, such as Decca (Louis Armstrong) and RCA Victor, as *TeenSet* did after it was released from Capitol control.

As stated, *The Teen Set* was not created to become a Capitol Records' monthly teen magazine or a magazine to be targeted at teen girls; it was, as Capitol executive and former US manager for Apple Records Ken Mansfield explained, "a promotional tool."[54] Mansfield's comment is verified by the Capitol Records Distribution Channel's (CRDC) advertisement to record dealers featuring *The Teen Set* and announcing its "biggest promotion of the year"[55] in the October 24, 1964, issue of *Cashbox*.[56] The advertisement encouraged businesses to carry the various Beach Boy albums and free copies of *The Teen Set* magazine. It claimed, "*TeenSet* is a quality magazine. The first issue featuring 36 pages of Beach Boys info and pics. It's a natural!"[57]

The original *Teen Set* was listed as edited by Capitol's chief executive, Brown Meggs, Hollywood photographer and guest editor Earl Leaf, and featured other high-level Capitol staffers such as Fred Rice, all older men who were not peers of their readers and some of whom did not necessarily like popular music. Meggs himself was a promoter and "always said he had little interest in popular music, yet his instincts in that field proved crucial to Capitol's financial success in the 1960s."[58] Unlike *16 Magazine* or *Flip*, *The TeenSet*'s first issue focused solely on the Beach Boys, and the second featured multiple Capitol artists. From the beginning, *The Teen Set* was concerned with popular music.

Historically, the Beach Boys would seem a prime choice during a cultural wave of surfing popularity among teenagers in the early to mid-1960s, as "surfing was identified as a hot new sport with a youthful focus epitomizing the ideal Californian lifestyle."[59] During the peak of the teen surf films,

Figure 1.5. *The Teen Set* cover, Volume 2, Summer 1965. Used by permission of Scholastic Inc.

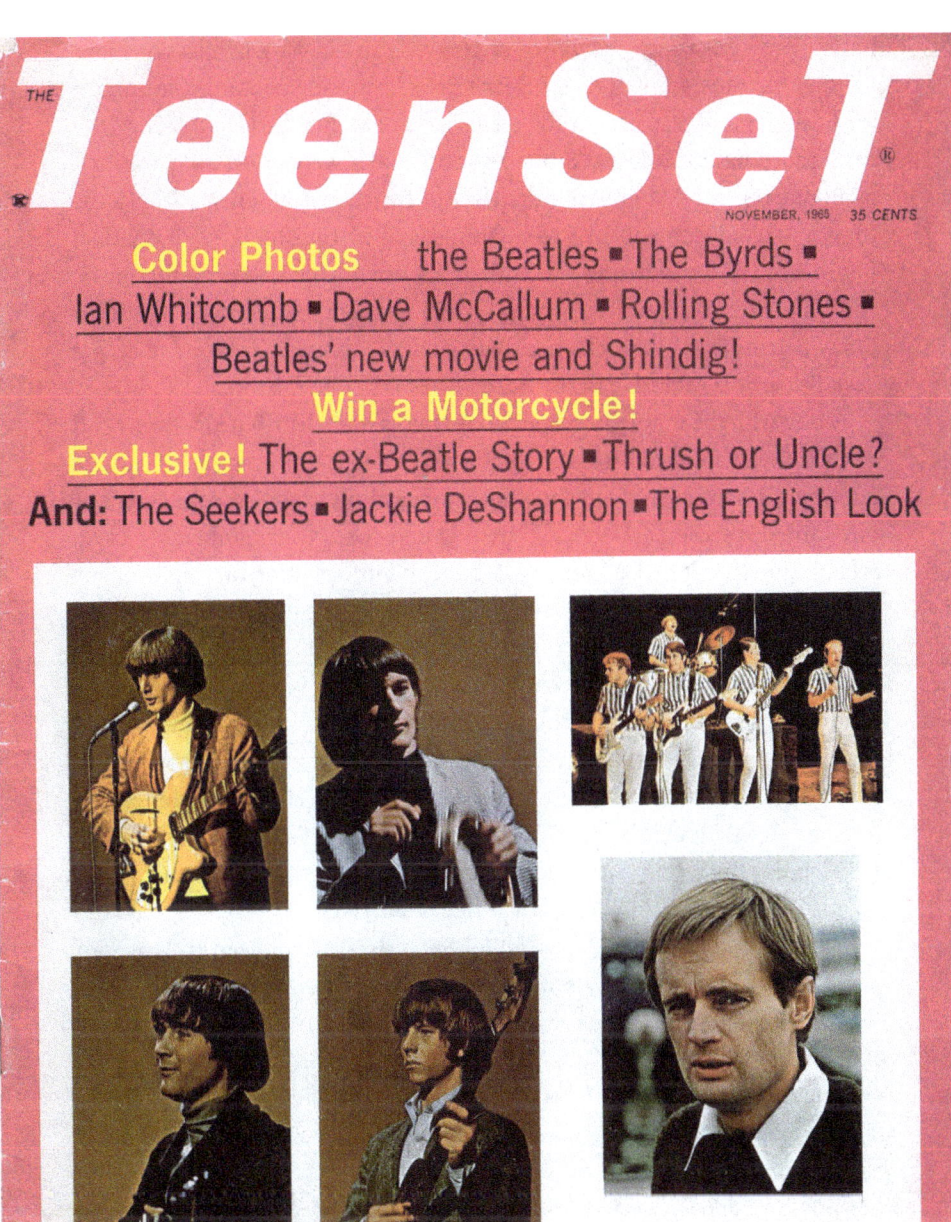

Figure 1.6. *The TeenSet*'s first nonpromotional issue. *TeenSet* cover, November 1965. Used by permission of Scholastic Inc.

Capitol provided record-buying teenagers with an exclusive publication highlighting the musical lives of the Beach Boys, who sang about the hot hobby (or lifestyle) that was part of the teen scene, or rather for Capitol, *The Teen Set*. According to *Cashbox*, "Some 750,000 copies were given away through retail outlets and tied in with purchases of Beach Boy albums."[60] This issue (figure 1.1) had elements of a teen fan magazine by profiling the individual Beach Boys and discussing fun and girls, but it also considered the music and Wilson's creative writing process and time spent in the recording studio. Many Beach Boys biographies and fan sites cite this particular issue of *The Teen Set*, as it is exclusive to the Beach Boys.

Along with the magazine, paper book covers were distributed to teens and contained "an application blank to be used by teenagers in joining Capitol's Hollywood-based 'Teen Set' fan club."[61] According to the advertisement, if one joined for the cost of "$1,"[62] they would receive a membership card, records, photographs, Capitol newsletters, and information on Capitol stars. This promotional tool was clever in design and similar to the popular record clubs; however, Capitol took it a step further. Instead of paying to receive multiple records, one would receive direct in-home advertisements and possible one-off records. In October 1964, Brown Meggs told *Cashbox* magazine that: "This is clearly the time of the teens. Our present teenage population now spends a billion and a half dollars a year on entertainment alone. This population will double by 1970. Accordingly, our *Teen Set* magazine attempts to reach this burgeoning market by speaking to young people directly in the language—and with the ideas—that they understand."[63]

Considering the Beatles on Capitol Records, Bruce Spizer gives a brief context to the early successes and sales of *TeenSet*. Spizer provides circulation data after the release of volume one (1964), noting that "within a few months, nearly 20,000 'teeners' had joined the *Teen Set* Fan Club,"[64] and by volume two (1965), "CRDC shipped 350,000 copies of *TeenSet* to its accounts. The remaining 150,000 copies were distributed to newsstands to be sold for 35 cents a copy. Over 60% of the magazines were purchased."[65] On August 28, 1965, *Billboard Magazine* announced that *TeenSet* was to become a full-fledged teen fan magazine:

> In a diversification move, Capitol Records is going into the publishing business with a teen fan magazine. The label has contracted with the Kimtex Corp. to produce and expand its *Teen Set* publications for newsstands. The first issue

of the expanded *Teen Set* publication will sell for 35 cents on newsstands.... The new issue, dated November, has stories about record and movie acts by Capitol people but is not an exclusive Capitol vehicle.... Capitol's delight with newsstand sales of the second prompted the company to get into the teen fan magazine business.[66]

By late 1965, Capitol outsourced *The Teen Set*, now *TeenSet* (although "The" is still in the title, it is very small and almost unnoticeable on the cover), to become a bimonthly magazine (it never became a bimonthly magazine) to the Kimtex Corporation and to be edited by *Drag Racing* and *Modern Racing* editor and creator of Kimtex, Lou Kimzey. While Capitol may have relinquished control, their original marketing of the magazine, content, and very colorful glossy covers gave it a promising start and alluded to a future discussion of popular music beyond solely that of a celebrity nature. The choice of Kimzey is not as out of place as it may seem, as Kimzey produced the 1950s teen-type magazine *DIG*[67] and had experience with the teen magazine market, unlike Capitol. However, unlike Kimzey's early *DIG*, the new monthly *TeenSet* would originally be marketed mostly to teen girls, attempting to follow the established formulaic teen fan magazine. Kimzey is only listed as editorial director through September 1966 (Kimtex went bankrupt, and by October, Regensteiner Publishing Enterprises took control); but from the first issue in October 1965, the name of Judith Canon[68] is listed as editor. From February onward, she was listed first as Canon-Sims but then transitioned quickly to her maiden name, Sims. She went on to be the only editor of the magazine until its demise.

The appointment of Judith Sims was unusual.[69] In college, she was extremely active in theater, involved in the Radio Club, and consistently made the dean's list, but she had no background in journalism, with the exception of small unaccredited reports for her Iowa Coe College newspaper (although she was an Illinois native), and there is no evidence she was attempting to become a popular music writer. Judith was hired from within the Kimtex Corporation as a supposed representative of contemporary American youth. An acting secretary who loved popular music, Sims was the first peer editor of a popular music magazine, and "*TeenSet* thus is extremely interesting as the first recorded example of peer group writing."[70] Capitol Records released control to the Kimtex Corporation, and there is no evidence that Capitol played a role in selecting Sims or controlled any nonadvertising content.

Through my correspondence with Ken Mansfield, he did not recall anything to do with *TeenSet* after the first two issues. Brown Meggs and other Capitol elite were not active within *TeenSet* beyond internal advertising and possibly providing Sims and her freelance staff exclusive connections to Capitol artists and musical events. Unlike the Capitol's *Music News* trade approach or the first two volumes (as they were originally referred to) of *The Teen Set*, Sims considered popular music more broadly as a female peer who actively participated in music scenes, a first for any teen fan magazine (Stavers was active, but not a peer of her audience. Moses was a peer editor but did not have content control like Sims). While the connection to Capitol was of value for possible promotions and exclusives, *TeenSet*, from this moment on, was shaped by Judith Sims. Subsequent references to *TeenSet* in this book do not refer to Capitol Records' first two promotional issues of *The Teen Set*. After the Capitol issues, the magazine's coverage still considered musicians and, at first, some movie stars (specifically Britain's David McCallum, who also released records) but moved on to solely consider popular music, with elements of culture, politics, and race.

TeenSet Magazine: An Introduction

The surf craze peaked in 1964, and *TeenSet* was entering a time of many transitions and changes culturally and musically. The genre of rock 'n' roll meant something different than it did in the 1950s or early sixties as, by the mid-sixties, rock and revolutionary rhetoric were becoming intertwined with the evolving genre of rock. *TeenSet* came and went during the mid to late sixties and ended before the Beatles broke up and before Jim Morrison, Janis Joplin, or Jimi Hendrix died.

TeenSet under Judith Sims was not the same magazine that Capitol had created and did not move in the direction Capitol thought or intended it to when it was outsourced. As *Billboard Magazine* announced, Capitol was entering the teen fan market,[71] which would suggest that *TeenSet* was to be like *16 Magazine* or the newly created *Tiger Beat*. *TeenSet* was a contributor to a changing musical and cultural landscape, and it broke the successful format of other teen fan magazines and attempted to grow with its readers. The magazine under Judith Sims's leadership was not a typical fan magazine, and as will be considered, she recognized this. However, the label was used by

Sims herself until the name changed to *AUM*, and for this reason, *TeenSet* is referred to here as a teen fan magazine. There are aspects of *TeenSet* that did resemble the then-current teen fan magazines that came and went throughout its existence, but, slowly, starting in 1966 until the transition of *TeenSet* to *AUM*, many articles within the magazine were different from the formulaic teen fan magazines. When asked about *TeenSet* and Sims, Moses did not recall either (even though they were in the same city), suggesting that they were not in competition and *TeenSet* was reaching a different market. *TeenSet* rarely reprinted articles, and it moved away from the typically zany or sensational headlines that characterized other teen fan magazines. Many of the features and articles were contributed by women, such as Carol Gold, Janey Milstead,[72] Sue Cameron, Kassy Gerrick, Marilyn Doerfler (the Association's publicist), Ginni Ganahl, Jeannie Simons, Lee O'Dill, Jacoba Atlas, and Nancy Chester (art director), among many others. Other important popular music journalists such as Tom Nolan, Jerry Hopkins, Ben Fong-Torres, and Pete Johnson, like some of the women above, also wrote for various newspapers, other teen fan magazines, or music magazines simultaneously when contributing to *TeenSet* or *AUM*. Photographers such as Chuck Boyd, Bruce McBroom, Gene Trindl, Bob Bonis, and, more significantly, Jim Marshall also contributed multiple photographs to *TeenSet* and then *AUM*. Many of these individuals' works will be considered later on.

TeenSet was originally sold on stands for thirty-five cents until November 1967; by December, it was fifty cents. *16 Magazine* continued to sell it for twenty-five cents (without any outside advertising) and *Tiger Beat* for thirty-five cents. *TeenSet* did print in color more than its competitors, and by December 1967, it began including large 2×3-foot centerfolds into mid-1968, which offers up a possible reason for the price changes. *TeenSet* also did not offer in-house publications beyond a one-time offer to purchase a large photograph of Janis Joplin (the same image photographed by Jim Marshall on the September 1968 cover—excluding the cover lines). Additionally, there were promotional issues, specifically the Sears Special Summer "Back to Cool" issue that was "in conjunction with the Sears Roebuck store chain."[73] Finally, some radio stations agreed on promotional deals to "present" *TeenSet* with Regensteiner to obtain and give away copies of *TeenSet* with the radio station's logos printed on the cover, such as Los Angeles's KRLA (a well-known station for having their own popular music newspaper titled *KRLA Beat*, which notably featured many female writers). Unlike most teen fan magazines,

Figure 1.7. *TeenSet* cover, February 1966. Used by permission of Scholastic Inc.

Figure 1.8. *TeenSet* cover, April 1966. Used by permission of Scholastic Inc.

TeenSet only included an average of twenty-three features (including the "Mail Scene") in its approximate sixty-page magazine.

TeenSet never presented the musicians' favorite foods or colors as a feature. That is not to say that there weren't elements of teen fan magazines that lingered; they most certainly did. For example, *TeenSet* housed another magazine (no author was listed) within the magazine pages titled *A Go Go*: "The teenager's 'insider's' magazine." The introduction of the first *A Go Go* appears in the November issue of 1965: "In case you don't think that we have what every other teenage magazine has."[74] The magazine only consisted of a few pages and used old Hollywood images with funny captions and stories, as well as quizzes and jokes. It was not relevant to the overall content of the magazine but clearly was an attempt to retain an element of established teen fan magazines. Notably, it was not intended to be considered part of *TeenSet* but separate. *TeenSet* ended *A Go Go* magazine by 1968 as, by that point, *TeenSet* was focusing more on music, culture, and rhetoric associated with rock music and the counterculture such as protests, race, drugs, and youth culture. Moreover, the statement above suggests that, in 1965, Sims already considered *TeenSet* as distinct from other teen fan magazines.

TeenSet changed hands three times over the course of its existence. First, as mentioned above, it was produced by Capitol Records, then by Lou Kimzey's Kimtex Corporation, and finally, by 1966, it was acquired by the now defunct Regensteiner Publishing Enterprises based in Chicago after "Kimtex filed for bankruptcy."[75] Sims did not necessarily get along with the publishers overseeing *TeenSet*, and she openly refers to them in her editorial column as "the Powers That Be."[76]

TeenSet included some fictional stories, self-help articles, and poems dedicated to the Beatles and other stars, but not enough to expect these types of articles in each issue, as the format was constantly being negotiated. *TeenSet* did have a "Letter to the Editor" department titled "Mail Scene" but did not have a self-help question section or a pen pal section as other teen fan magazines did. Mail Scene always considered popular music, artists, and *TeenSet* itself. Articles and stories within the magazine ranged in genre from pop to blues and rock and considered multiple elements within popular music. *TeenSet* was the only teen fan magazine to include a record review section in every issue, and *TeenSet* always considered the actual music itself as well as the personal information of pop and rock stars. Articles such as "Color It Blues" (1966) considered the origins of the blues; "What Ever

Happened to Rock 'n' Roll" (1966) was a discussion of the evolving rock genre; "Boston Scene: Happening or Hype" (1968) explored whether or not Boston was a growing music scene; "The Beatles and Their Music" searched for meaning within lyrics; and there were constant features and coverage of the Hollywood, London, and San Francisco music scenes.

TeenSet covered a wide range of artists, from the Monkees to Frank Zappa.[77] The coverage of the Beatles is especially of note as Sims toured with the Beatles in 1966 and spent time in EMI during the recording of *Sgt. Pepper's Lonely Hearts Club Band* (1967), and articles from Mal Evans, Neil Aspinall, and Derek Taylor appear in early issues of *TeenSet* While many of the featured musicians were white, *TeenSet* also included many Black artists such as the Supremes, Little Stevie Wonder, the Four Tops, Percy Sledge, Billy Stewart, Bobby Hebb, James and Bobby Purify, Brenton Wood, the Chambers Brothers, Billy Preston, the Ramsey Lewis Trio, Muddy Waters, Lou Rawls, Otis Redding, Brenda Holloway, Dionne Warwick, Verdelle Smith, Fontella Bass, and Jimi Hendrix. Many of these artists were considered individually, and some were featured in articles about the blues, Motown, and soul. Although the coverage of Black musicians was not equal to white musicians, this amount of coverage was not common in other teen fan magazines of the 1960s. By 1969, *TeenSet* had begun to consider race and culture more in depth, starting with articles such as "Jimi Hendrix, Black Power, and Money" or the March article "Black and White" about a young Black man and his interest in the Black Panther Party.

By mid to late 1968 and into 1969, *TeenSet* had only a few similarities to other teen fan magazines. The musical acts considered by *TeenSet* mostly differed (although the Monkees were still discussed but much less than before). The Raiders and the Monkees were no longer featured on the cover, but rather musicians such as Grace Slick, Jim Morrison, Cream, Janis Joplin, Mick Jagger, Jimi Hendrix, and the Beatles (individually and together). The covers and imagery began to reflect and contribute to the growing psychedelic San Francisco trends, and by 1968, *TeenSet* was covering politics, race, social activism, fashion,[78] and music. *16 Magazine* and *Tiger Beat* were covering the Monkees, Saj, Dino Jr, the Raiders, Brendan Boone, Sally Field, Barry, and advertising "huggable color pinups."[79] *TeenSet* still offered pull-outs of various sizes and was openly always proud of its color photographs, but these were of Frank Zappa, Cream, the Monkees, the Beatles, Jimi Hendrix, Neil Young, and Janis Joplin (among multiple others). *TeenSet*'s Judith Sims was no longer concerned with the Top 40 or worried about what would easily sell the magazine. Most interestingly, she began to engage with the evolving idea of what it meant to be a "teenager," or rather, what it meant to be young. This was unique to *TeenSet*, as the publishers were not invested in the magazine itself. Sims attempted to grow *TeenSet* with her readers and engage with evolving teenagers rather than seeking out the then-current pop idol of the time like Stavers did.

The magazine's name changed to *AUM* (*America's Underthiry Magazine*) in May 1969. *AUM* did not claim to be a teenage fan magazine but found its short-lived niche as a cultural and music magazine. Sims stressed the importance of a cultural youth fan magazine: "Cheetah[80] died a long time ago, and now Eye[81] is gone. Suddenly, *AUM* is the only youth-oriented, general interest magazine in this country, and that's scary."[82] It is evident by its articles that *AUM* leaned more toward a cultural magazine than *TeenSet* did, but music was still included. For example, the June 1969 issue of *AUM* contained articles about vegetarianism, the then-current voting age, the Delano grape strike and Cesar Chavez, astrology, and the Vietnam War, in addition to music.

The first *AUM* cover featured the GTOs (Girls Together Outrageously) surrounded by various issues of *TeenSet*. The cover was a reference to *TeenSet* for those who were unaware of the name change due to the fact that *TeenSet* did not announce it in its last issue. Choosing the GTOs for the cover signified another change: for the first time, *TeenSet* featured an obscure, non-commercially successful rock group on the cover. While *AUM*'s articles were aimed at the college-age youth culture and presented compelling coverage of Cesar Chavez, and even with well-known contributors such as Jacoba Atlas, Henry Diltz, John Mendelsohn, *Los Angeles Free Press* poet Liza Williams, *TeenScreen* editor Janey Milstead, Ben Fong-Torres, and Jim Marshall, *AUM* folded after three issues.

It is important to stress that when Capitol outsourced *TeenSet*, the intention was to compete in the teenage fan magazine market. *TeenSet* was to be seen and categorized as a teen fan magazine, but what was presented in *TeenSet* broke away from the growing teen fan magazine content and format. All magazines evolve somewhat to stay current, but *TeenSet*, under Sims's leadership, evolved into another publication that focused on music and culture rather than attempting to strictly appeal to young fans. To argue that *TeenSet* wasn't a teen fan magazine would not be correct, but to argue it was like other teen fan magazines would also be untrue. Rather, this book argues that *TeenSet* was not only a guide or template for the early rock press but should be considered more than a precursor to the rock press, perhaps as a contributor to popular music and cultural commentary.

Shortly after *TeenSet*'s beginnings, the rock press began to develop. Paul Williams's *Crawdaddy!* was first issued in a self-published, low-circulation format in February 1966. Jann Wenner's first issue of *Rolling Stone* arrived on November 9, 1967. The way popular music was being written about in the rock press was more derived from music periodicals such as *DownBeat* and jazz criticism than from teen fan magazines. This is not to say the teen fan magazine did not impact the new rock press, underground press, or fanzines. The underground press began to discuss popular music through tropes of meaning and authenticity and did not focus on the celebrity of the groups or individual artists (unless they were questioning it). While this style of rock criticism was then still developing (Lester Bangs was first published in *Rolling Stone* in early 1969), *TeenSet* was already seriously considering aspects of music. However, at first, it was not necessarily focused on culture and politics, which popular music often was (and historically has been) attached to in the late 1960s. As *TeenSet* developed, so did the rock press. Here, the rock press is considered to be magazines like *Crawdaddy!* and *Rolling Stone* that were not originally mainstream newspapers or teen fan magazines but (mostly) peer-run periodicals that focused on popular music and industry through a critical social and political lens. *TeenSet* hired individuals such as Tom Nolan, Jerry Hopkins, Jacoba Atlas, Ben Fong-Torres, Chuck Boyd, Jim Marshall, and others—who were either already working with or went on to work or freelance for *Rolling Stone* or other popular music publications after *TeenSet* folded, including Sims herself. From this history, it is clear that the rock press developed in parallel to the evolution of *TeenSet* and will be fully considered in the next chapter.

WHERE IS *TEENSET* IN HISTORY?

With few exceptions, *TeenSet*'s position in discourses on popular culture is lacking. Typically, if one is to consider teen fan magazines, *16 Magazine* and *Tiger Beat* are the two publications most often listed, but this is perhaps due to the longevity of the magazines. Only one teen fan magazine editor, Ann Moses, has written an autobiography about her career. Although other texts

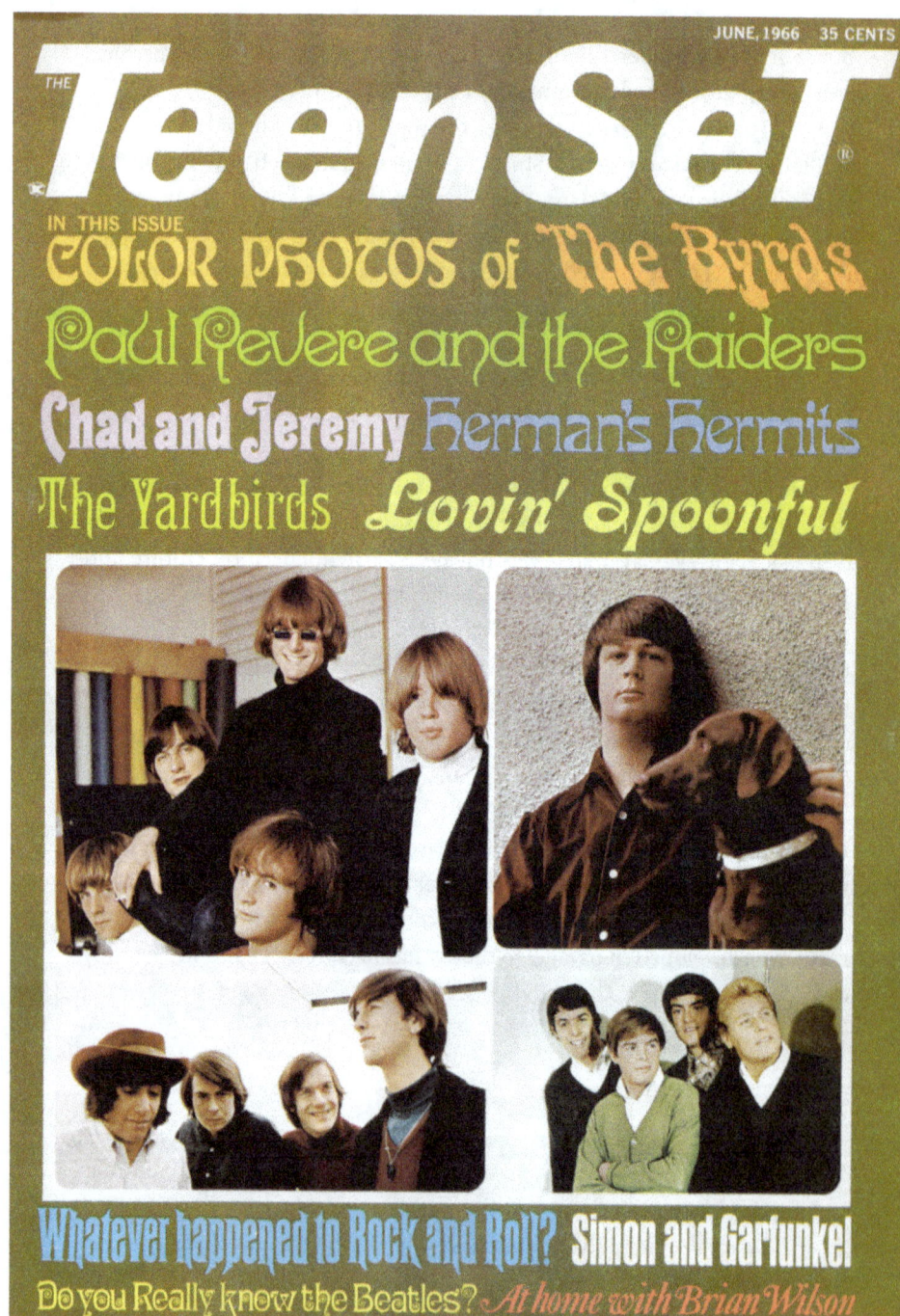

Figure 1.9. *TeenSet* cover, June 1966. Used by permission of Scholastic Inc.

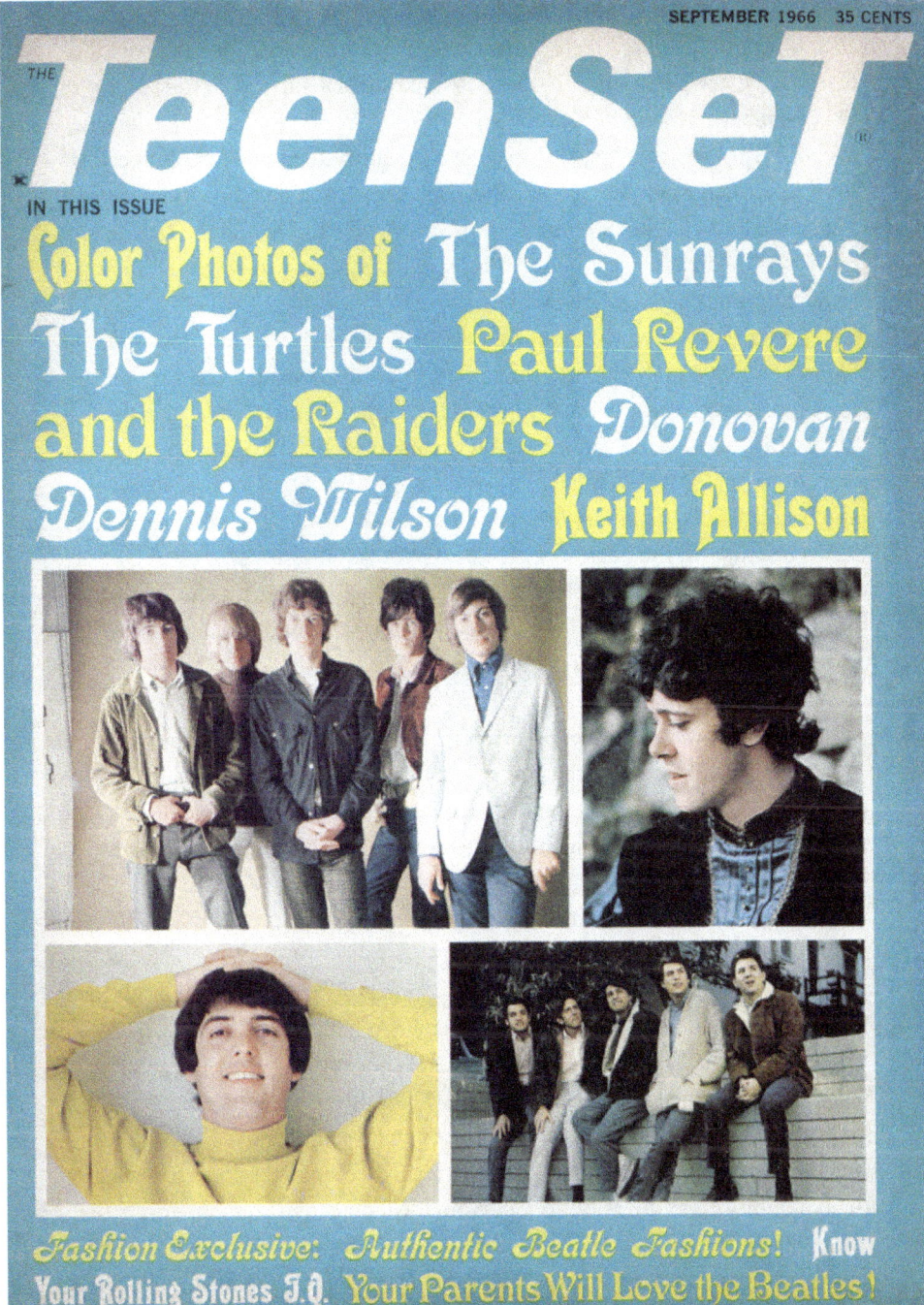

Figure 1.10. *TeenSet* cover, September 1966. Used by permission of Scholastic Inc.

have used *TeenSet* as a primary source, here I will consider the only attempted accounting of *TeenSet*'s history. These four brief considerations consist of Chester ("Chet") Flippo's MA thesis, "Rock Journalism and *Rolling Stone*"; Bruce Spizer's *The Beatles' Story on Capitol Records: Part 2: The Albums*; Richard Morton Jack's article, "*TeenSet*: The story behind This Pioneering 1960 American Rock Magazine"; and Don Armstrong's blog posts, "*TeenSet* Magazine Part 1," "*TeenSet* Part 2," and "*TeenSet* Part 3." While the four texts discussed below are useful for this research, they come from very different understandings of what *TeenSet* was.

Chester Flippo's[83] 1974 unpublished thesis, "Rock Journalism and *Rolling Stone*,"[84] was the first recorded document to briefly consider *TeenSet* within rock journalism and the most significant. Flippo opens his 189-page thesis discussing teen fan magazines as precursors to rock journalism with a specific focus on *TeenSet*. While Flippo does discuss the cleanliness, sexlessness, and beauty-focused nature of the teen lifestyle and some teen fan magazines, he argues that "in the beginning, rock was not taken seriously except by the teen magazines."[85] Flippo claims that *TeenSet*, with thanks to Judith Sims, marks the beginning of the first peer-edited magazine and collection of rock journalism, regardless of its connections to Capitol Records:

> Generally, however, the notion of writing about rock music as something other than a distasteful, although potentially profitable, phenomenon found no acceptance in the Sixties until a secretary [*TeenSet*'s Judith Sims] in Los Angeles and a young [Richard Goldstein] Columbia University journalism graduate—both simply trying to discover what they would like to do—inadvertently helped to found rock journalism.[86]

Flippo does not consider or analyze any context of *TeenSet* but rather places Sims as important to popular music journalism history. In doing so, he further applies Jon Landau's adaptation of the concept of "cultist to careerist," and he presents Sims (as well as others, such as Lester Bangs) as a cultist: "The young music fan who became a writer through love of music."[87] Flippo argues that Sims presented music as a "cultist," a term defined in dictionaries as "one who exhibits great devotion to a person, idea, object, movement, etc."[88] "in an unconventional manner."[89] As Flippo asserts, for Sims, this "idea, object, movement" was popular music: "Sims's experience is the story of most rock editors: they started out because they loved the music, period. Loving the music wasn't enough; they had to write about it too; their enthusiasm could not be contained. To borrow Jon Landau's term, they were cultists. Their early writings were acts of love."[90]

Flippo argues that many young rock writers who began to write about music began as cultists, those who love all things music, and eventually move to writing as a career, becoming "careerists," where the love or passion within the writing may be overshadowed by the waning interest in the subject or the assignment, paychecks, free records, or ego of the writer.[91] The concept of "cultist to careerist" was popularized in film critic Andrew Sarris's 1970 text, *Confessions of a Cultist: On the Cinema 1955/1969*, where Sarris refers to himself as a cultist of all things film, somebody "who loved movies beyond reason."[92] Other film critics, such as Roger Ebert, openly acknowledged that Sarris was the "jolliest"[93] critic "who loved movies,"[94] reflecting a perception among his peers that Sarris was genuinely passionate about movies. It is evident that the term had been used in a similar fashion to describe dedicated film and music lovers in *Fortune Magazine*[95] in 1933 and *Billboard*[96] in 1949. However, Sarris presents the concept of "cultist to careerist." The idea was adapted to rock critics by well-known critic Jon Landau in *It's Too Late to Stop Now: A Rock and Roll Journal* (1972). Landau argued that, in general, many rock critics began as or were/are cultists: "Critics are usually people who began as cultists.... Some initial love of an art form ... drives them to express themselves through writing about it,"[97] but if their interest begins to wane (for multiple reasons) they can become careerists—claiming, then, that the writing lacks passion. By 1974, Flippo further applied Landau's adaptation of the term "cultist" to Judith Sims during her tenure as editor of *TeenSet*. Although Flippo is building on rock critic Landau's consideration of the cultist figure, it does not take away from the application of the concept to Sims. Landau is referring to why he and many others began writing about music: because they loved every aspect of it.

Flippo ultimately argues that *TeenSet*'s entire run was influenced by Sims's undying love of popular music. However, this does not mean her writing was devoid of criticism or analysis, as the term was embraced by a film critic; rather, it presents her as coming from a place of absolute devotion. Sarris admits to not liking the term at first but eventually espousing it, as—even with the apparent religious connotation—he felt it was a correct description of himself.[98] While Flippo is the first to refer to Sims as a popular music cultist in her tenure with *TeenSet*, he argues that she became a careerist (due to her lack of interest in the then-current music and the regulations) when working for *Rolling Stone*. Sims, for the most part, had more freedom to feature whomever and report on whatever she wanted to than other editors/journalists did—as she did when steering the direction of *TeenSet*. With regard to Sims's tenure at *TeenSet*, I do not disagree with Flippo's contention that it was filled with passion and devotion to all things popular music. While here, the term "cultist" is defined as a matter of passion and a religious-like devotion, its meaning has evolved in more recent years, particularly in studies of fandom. Brian Longhurst, for instance, places it on a continuum, suggesting that goth cultists are "more engaged and may dress in a Goth way."[99] This book is not concerned with positioning Judith Sims's editorial practices in relation to her identity as a music fan, but it remains of historical interest that the "cultist" label was applied to her because it shows how she was perceived by peers—as someone who had a strong personal stake in the music and cultural scenes of the period and not merely as a disinterested professional.

Sims's brief testimony included with Flippo's text is invaluable and utilized to further her role with *TeenSet* and in popular music. This is the first academic writing considering rock journalism that gave credit to Sims and *TeenSet* and was also written relatively close to the existence of *TeenSet*. However, while Flippo argues that "*TeenSet* is important as prototype"[100] for the rock magazine, he does not further consider that *TeenSet* was more than just a beginning of rock journalism or a precursor. Flippo offers a brief but important account of teen fan magazines, that of a female peer editor, and specifically places Sims within rock journalism. As *16 Magazine*'s formula and success are historically attributed to Stavers's role, Flippo correctly attributes *TeenSet* to Sims—not to Capitol Records, Kimtex, or Regensteiner Publishing Enterprises. Flippo's interviews and access to multiple *Rolling Stone* staffers of the early 1970s, such as former *TeenSet* Judith Sims and founder/editor Jann Wenner, have contributed to a body of knowledge,[101] and after completing his master's degree, Flippo went on to become an editor of *Rolling Stone*. His thesis was out of reach for many until the more recent digital archiving of thousands of past theses, or as in my case, access to the physical University of Texas libraries. Regardless, at the time of writing, it is still not well known.

At the moment of writing, one text provides a Capitol Records-related history, Spizer's 2000 *The Beatles' Story on Capitol Records: Part 2: The Albums*. Spizer presents a brief consideration of the creation of *TeenSet* concerning the Beatles and Capitol Records. Spizer's book is highly valuable as it is out of print. More recently, his text has been offered as an e-book[102] valued at fifty dollars, suggesting the brief discussion of *TeenSet* was and is fairly inaccessible to researchers and the general public—I had difficulty retrieving this book myself. While he provides extremely insightful information, such as how *TeenSet* was presented within record shops and that Capitol provided paper book covers to students inviting them to join *TeenSet*, the book does not consider *TeenSet* beyond the Beatles. However, Spizer does argue that "although *TeenSet* was aimed at the teen and preteen market, its articles were often informative and insightful, going beyond the hero worship and love life rumors typically found in teen magazines."[103] Although it is understandable that Spizer's discussion of *TeenSet* was to consider Capitol's role for promoting the Beatles, it failed to mention how little Capitol had to do with the magazine after 1965 beyond possibly passing press or advertising information until Capitol's distant association was no longer listed in November 1968.

In addition to Spizer, Richard Morton Jack's article in 2014 in *Flashback* magazine titled "*TeenSet*: The story behind this pioneering 1960s American rock magazine" considered *TeenSet* for the first time as a pioneering "serious rock publication . . . predominantly written by women."[104] The article spends little time discussing the origins of *TeenSet*, and rightfully so, as *TeenSet*'s legacy began with the editorial control of Judith Sims. The four-and-a-half-page article makes many solid points considering various elements of *TeenSet* and Sims, such as her time with the Beatles, and most importantly, it contains a brief interview with London correspondent Carol Gold and contributor Janey Milstead. Jack is the first to notice that *TeenSet* was changing as the music scene did, but Jack also claims, "By 1967, the music scene was changing beyond recognition, and *TeenSet* gleefully reflected the colorful new attitudes of its readership without descending into hippie cliché."[105] While I agree the music scene was evolving, *TeenSet* was not merely a reflection of this, but it contributed to the changing musical landscape of the 1960s. Jack tunes into the magazine's changing subtitle in mid-1968 but does not further address why it was changing. Rather, Jack attributes the changes to the influence of *Crawdaddy!* and *Rolling Stone*. While this could be a contributing factor, *TeenSet* began evolving from the time Judith Sims was hired to edit the magazine. Like Spizer's text, it is not easily accessible, but it supports my argument by recognizing that *TeenSet* was a pioneer as one of the first to "seriously" consider popular music, though it does not fully crystallize this point.

Don Armstrong's 2019 blog posts "*TeenSet* Magazine Part 1," "*TeenSet* Part 2," and "TeenSet Part 3" consider *TeenSet* of value in popular music journalism history. Armstrong began his brief three-part blog post by simply stating, "*TeenSet* was an anomaly,"[106] to which I agree, as no other teen fan or music magazine was like *TeenSet*. He further argues that "*TeenSet* exemplifies the complicated interface between aesthetic and commercial intentions in music journalism. Founded as an advertising giveaway by Capitol Records, it evolved into a credible source of information and opinion about rock music during the 1960s."[107] His understanding and presentation of *TeenSet* is not focused on Capitol Records per se; rather, he quickly argues *TeenSet* to be a contributor to popular music. While Armstrong does not necessarily argue that Capitol Records let go of full control of *TeenSet* or that women were not often considered as important in rock journalism, he does consider Judith Sims and her abilities: "By 1966, *TeenSet* had shown a capacity for solid reporting and excellent photography. This was largely due to the presence of editor Judith Sims, writers like Sue Cameron, and photographers like Jim Marshall."[108] Armstrong does mention Capitol's connections to many stars but ultimately gives credit to the staff of *TeenSet*. His argument is brief, but it openly acknowledges Judith Sims and *TeenSet* as contributors to popular music journalism. Armstrong continues his interest in *TeenSet* and popular music journalism beyond his website into a private Facebook group he founded titled "Music Journalism History." On occasions, Armstrong posts *TeenSet* covers or articles to encourage discussion. Flippo's, Armstrong's and Jack's consideration of *TeenSet* all assert its historical significance.

The internet has arguably created a platform for marginalized sources such as *TeenSet*. I have seen *TeenSet* become more present on various social media websites such as Pinterest, Instagram, Tumblr, and Facebook. Whether individuals are posting images, covers, or articles, the presence of *TeenSet* is growing. Grace Slick herself has posted the May 1968 cover[109] in which she was featured, suggesting she finds value in having been on *TeenSet*'s cover. If the internet had then existed as it does now, she most likely would have shared it in 1968. Other individuals have blogged about aspects of *TeenSet*, such as https://www.afka.net/Mags/TeenSet.htm, where articles and images from *TeenSet* are posted and, at times, discussed, such as the September 1967 issue on the diverse website theavacdo.org.[110] Many 1960s teen fan magazine discussions, such as *16 Magazine* and *Tiger Beat*, exist mostly on an online platform, particularly in blogs or on Wikipedia. In the case of *16 Magazine*,

The TeenSeT

OCTOBER, 1966 — 35 CENTS

In this issue

Color Photos of The Beach Boys

The Mamas and Papas

Herman's Hermits

Chad and Jeremy

Mark Lindsay

The Animals

Simon and Garfunkel

Mike Love

The Standells

Figure 1.11. *TeenSet* cover, October 1966. Used by permission of Scholastic Inc.

the majority of online publications and discussions have originated about individuals who have found value in the magazine or in Stavers's personality and contribution to literature. Margret Moser of the *Austin Chronicle* published two articles considering *16 Magazine* and Stavers (which will be explored later). During this research, in 2019, musician Van Dyke Parks posted my personal Twitter message to him on Instagram regarding the value of *TeenSet*, asking his followers if he should accept an interview or not: "Do I dare?"[111] His followers' comments encouraged his participation, and musician Benmont Tench, a founding member of Tom Petty and the Heartbreakers, commented that he read *TeenSet*. "Dare! I loved *TeenSet*! They covered so many great bands & musicians."[112] Although Tench did not respond to my request to answer a questionnaire, *TeenSet*'s value was openly acknowledged by a male rock musician.

As of September 12, 2020, a Wikipedia page was created for Judith Sims and *TeenSet*. The page sources various *TeenSet* magazines, Don Armstrong's website, *Cashbox*, *Flashback Magazine*, and a few other websites previously listed in this book. On December 20, 2020, Peter Jackson announced that his film *The Beatles: Get Back* (2021) was delayed due to COVID-19. As part of his announcement, Jackson released an approximately six-minute sneak peek "of the spirit of the film."[113] Within this clip, John Lennon and Yoko Ono are shown reading the February 1969 issue[114] of *TeenSet* featuring John Lennon on the cover, and this same clip is featured in the second part of the three-part documentary. Given these developments, it is only a matter of time before *TeenSet* and teen fan magazines, in general, spark other people's interests, as it has mine.

CHAPTER TWO

IT'S ONLY ROCK 'N' ROLL JOURNALISM

The Absence of *Teenset* within a History Shaped by Critics

> Personally, my patience is exhausted. If one more person asks what I do for a living only to reply, "Oh, that junk" when I tell them, I shall quite certainly flatten that person. The people I write about are not junk. Nor do I write junk about them.
> —Janey Milstead, teen fan magazine editor[1]

Currently, an examination of 1960s teen fan magazines is lacking not only in popular music studies but also in other academic studies. Very few sources discuss 1960s teen fan magazines as historically valuable, if at all.[2] In 2007, *Austin Chronicle* contributor Magaret Moser's article, "Dreamsville: Gloria Stavers, *16 Magazine*, and the Roots of Rock Journalism," openly noted that for *16 Magazine*'s fiftieth anniversary there was no celebration of Stavers or *16 Magazine*'s success or contribution to rock journalism: "With absolutely no fanfare, fawning memoir, *VH1* special, or even *People* magazine blurb, the most important milestone in rock journalism turned fifty this year. Not *Rolling Stone*, which turned forty, but *16 Magazine*. 'The magazine for smart girls' boasted the spine of its May 1957 debut. Elvis Presley waved from the cover."[3] Moser's comment highlights that the reader would have instinctively thought that *Rolling Stone*, rather than *16 Magazine*, would be the subject of her article.

Figure 2.1. Dylan and Lennon *TeenSet* cover, November 1966. Used by permission of Scholastic Inc.

On more than one occasion, authors have called for future attention to such studies of teen fan magazines but often to be studied as separate from the popular music journalism discourse. If one is to search for such consideration within the rock canon, it is more common to read negative comments regarding teen fan magazines in rock journalism than to find historical accounts of teen fan magazines. For example, in *Let It Blurt* (2000) (in reference to the development of rock writing and Lester Bangs), Jim DeRogatis claims:

> Rock 'n' roll had thrived for more than a decade without anyone to criticize it when mainstream media wrote about fifties rockers such as Chuck Berry, Little Richard, and Jerry Lee Lewis, it was often in terms of an encroaching cultural plague, which only made fans love it more. Magazines such as *Song Hits, Hit Parader, Beat,* and *16* lauded teens' heroes by printing lyrics, photos, and occasional interviews about the stars' favorite foods and colours, but there was very little "real" journalism and absolutely no criticism.[4]

Like DeRogatis, Devon Powers refers to 1960s teen magazines as lacking real criticism or journalism, going as far as to state, "I would like to qualify any blanket dismissal of the teen books [regarding criticism]. Read *charitably* [emphasis added], these magazines engaged their primarily young female readerships with the burgeoning rock and roll culture, establishing celebrity gossip as its own form of critique."[5] Her textual evidence to uphold her statements consists of *Datebook*'s reprinting of Maureen Cleave's article, "How Does a Beatles Live? John Lennon Lives Like This"[6] (an article quoting John Lennon that caused outrage and protests among Christians against the Beatles in the American South). However, this is an insufficient example to support Powers's case against teen fan magazines, as editor Art Unger and managing editor Danny Fields's[7] intentions were very different than, say, Gloria Stavers of *16 Magazine*. Brian Ward argues in "'The "C" is for Christ': Arthur Unger, *Datebook* Magazine and the Beatles" (2012) that "virtually nobody has paused to ask who Arthur Unger was"[8] or "why he chose to feature Lennon's five-month-old interview in his magazine,"[9] because he found *Datebook* was often dismissed as a lesser form of journalism—a teen fan magazine.[10] Thus, there has been a historical tendency to uphold the idea that Cleave's article was sensationalized by a teen fan magazine—*Datebook* and Unger's intent was (and is still) assumed. Yet Ward found that "*Datebook* was

...rather a politically progressive publication that gay publisher-editor Unger used to expose various kinds of intolerance and bigotry to American teens."[11] Unger clearly had hoped for a strong reaction to Paul McCartney's dismay at the open racism in America by featuring a racist word and McCartney's image on the cover. While the McCartney coverline may have been slightly rewritten for effect, the articles were "not reproduced out of context or edited for sensational effect."[12] Although author Robert Rodriquez argues that Art Unger "recognized media dynamite when he saw it,"[13] it did not mean the intent was *only* to sell magazines and stir trouble but rather to continue to position *Datebook* as a progressive magazine concerned with pressing cultural issues—some of which were personal to Unger. Moreover, a well-established British female journalist wrote this article for the reputable *London Evening Standard*, yet it is of interest that it is seen as nonserious when placed in the context of a teen magazine. It cannot be denied that many teen fan magazines do focus on the celebrity of a musician or artist, but one cannot blanket all teen fan magazines. Powers does qualify that a study of teen fan magazines is needed, but she makes it clear that this study would not focus on a contribution to "serious" rock journalism, further perpetuating the dismissal of all teen fan magazines within rock journalism.

Considering the development of rock journalism, scholar and former rock critic Simon Frith claims that "in the 1950s and early 1960s, the USA had no music papers between the trade press on the one hand (*Cash Box* and *Billboard*) and the teeny-bop magazines on the other."[14] While this comment suggests that these do cover music in some fashion, he specifically singles out teen fan magazines as "teenybop" (as discussed in the introduction, young and often female). Furthering this sentiment, Frith remarks that "teenage magazines have used pop star images, male and female, to illustrate their romantic fantasies and practical hints since their origin in the fifties."[15] Again, while this may be accurate to some extent, Frith, like Powers and DeRogatis, blankets all teen fan magazines and all teen fan magazine content. Brennan's *When Genres Collide* questions this notion:

> Teen magazines have been routinely neglected or dismissed in accounts of popular music criticism on the grounds they did not take music seriously... but this ignores the fact that the teen press industry was substantial in both size and content, developing a discourse that valued pop music (especially in the case of *16*) and appealed to a large market of young female music fans.[16]

Unlike most popular music texts, Brennan suggests a possible contribution of teen fan magazines and that these magazines are of value to the development of a "serious" popular music journalism discourse. However, as this book will argue, *TeenSet* was *more* than just a contributor to the developing acceptance of valuing popular music.

As previously mentioned, there was a period in the mid-1960s when teen fan magazines covered the burgeoning rock culture before the growth of *Crawdaddy!* or the existence of *Rolling Stone*. Critics themselves grew up reading teen fan magazines. DeRogatis briefly mentions in *Let It Blurt* that Lester Bangs read teen fan magazines before he became a rock critic, but historically, that narrative is not explored; rather, what is espoused is the consistent tale that rock was only taken seriously with the creation of *Crawdaddy!* For example, longtime *Rolling Stone* critic David Fricke states, "Before the music had any serious outlet . . . Paul Williams, a seventeen-year-old college freshman, published 500 copies of the first issue of a new adventure he called *Crawdaddy!*"[17] Again, one has an instance of the dismissal of teen fan magazines as Fricke declares *Crawdaddy!* the first "serious outlet."[18] Fricke (among many others) seems to treat Williams as the first peer to edit a music-centered magazine and the first to take popular music "seriously." Yet the word "serious" is not defined here or in most texts. Whatever is considered to be a "serious" outlet, the current discourse does not recognize teen fan magazines as contributors. However, *16 Magazine* did receive admiration from critics such as Dave Marsh and late-1960s *Datebook* editor Danny Fields in 1997. They argue that the main interest of *16 Magazine* is Stavers herself, specifically for her "vision" and poise, but she is not credited with "serious" journalism. Margaret Moser credits Stavers and *16 Magazine* with providing "roots" to rock journalism, and as discussed previously, a close examination of Stavers and *16 Magazine*'s contributions to popular music is still lacking.

The majority of texts that feature rock history narratives in a general or biographical sense often quote teen fan magazines, especially *TeenSet*, because, for a period of time, *TeenSet* and other teen fan magazines were the only places that featured such material. However, one text stands out by directly referring to *TeenSet*: Richie Furay[19] and John Einarson's Buffalo Springfield biography, *For What It's Worth*.[20] The authors discuss Buffalo Springfield's inclusion within *TeenSet*, *Tiger Beat*, and *Teen Screen* and include the voice of Judith Sims (*TeenSet* was the first magazine to cover Buffalo Springfield). Although Einarson and Furay credit *TeenSet* with enhancing

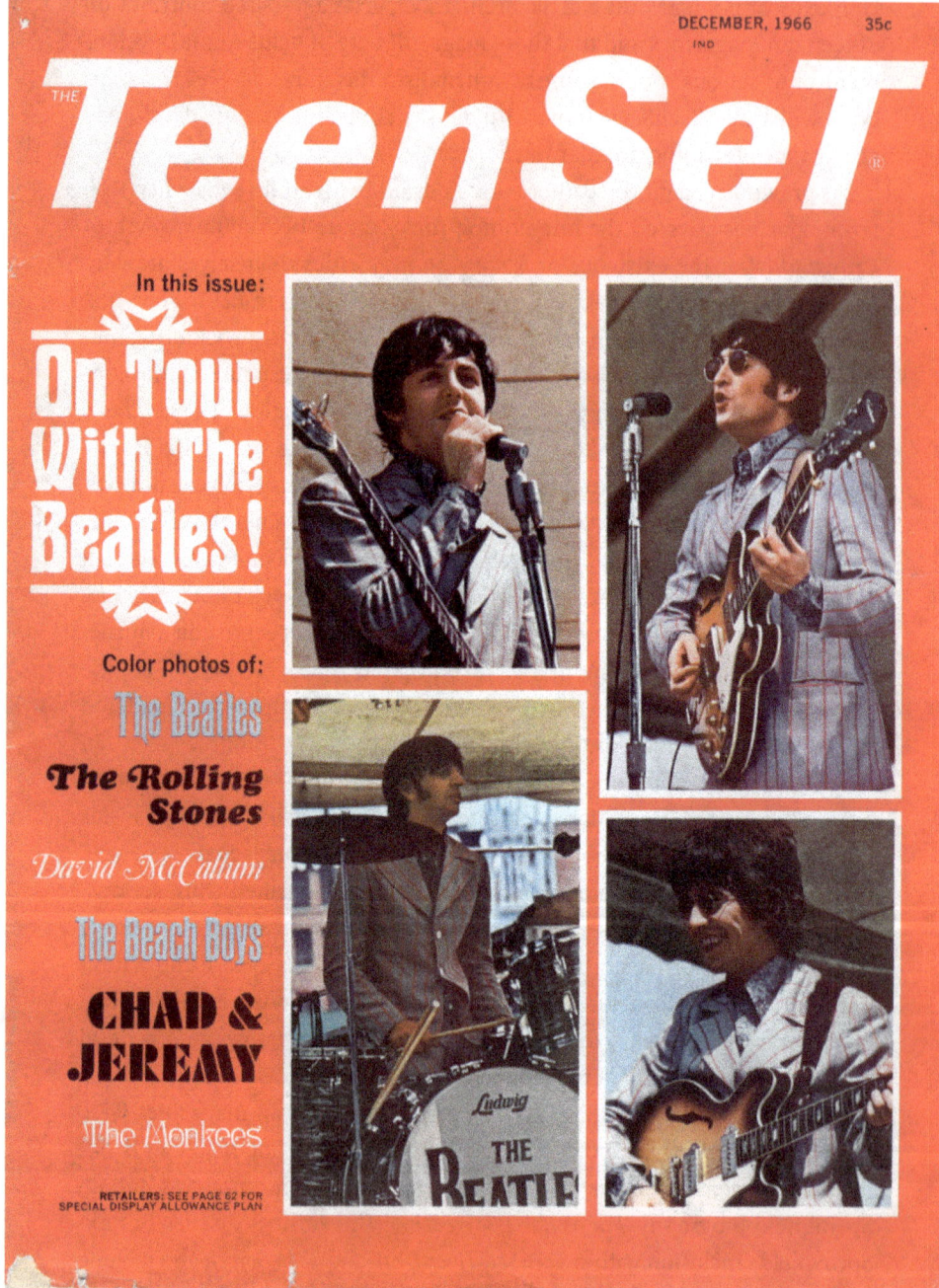

Figure 2.2. Bob Bonis's Beatles Tour *TeenSet* cover, December 1966. Used by permission of Scholastic Inc.

Figure 2.3. Bob Bonis's Paul McCartney *TeenSet* cover, January 1967. Used by permission of Scholastic Inc.

the group's profile, they ultimately claim teen magazines hurt or "plagued"[21] the image of the group by interviewing them as individuals. They state, "The dilemma is that the Springfield's music transcended the teenybopper, pop idol idiom and their individuality proved unsuited for such simplistic presentation. Being marketed as the teenybopper flavor of the month ultimately became a hindrance to their progress in being accepted as artists."[22] This statement is not supported by any evidence within the biography. However, it does suggest a "rockist"[23] attitude toward teen fan magazines as simplistic and unworthy of featuring "transcending" artists.

Furay and Einarson's statement would suggest that *TeenSet* (and other teen magazines) negatively affected the profile of the group. However, any serious evaluation of this claim would need to consider whether *TeenSet* hurt the profile of the Beatles, Janis Joplin, Frank Zappa, the Rolling Stones, or multiple other groups that were featured. As previously evidenced, a teenybopper is defined as "a teenage girl,"[24] thus, this statement suggests that young females are not worthy of the music and could not accept the group as artists (or possibly as "auteurs"). Again, teen fan magazines are marginalized; the authors seem to underestimate not only the magazine but the readers.

THE HISTORY OF ROCK DEVELOPS THROUGH ROCK CRITICS

The historiography of rock journalism of the early 1960s to mid-1970s (as well as the history of rock) has been written mostly by all-white male rock critics who have presented themselves as the first to "seriously" discuss rock music for magazines such as *Rolling Stone*, *Crawdaddy!* and *Creem*, and who have omitted *TeenSet* and all teen fan magazines. As teen fan magazines have been clearly dismissed, it is evident that the historiography of rock and rock journalism is what one needs to explore to understand the possible reasons why teen fan magazines, specifically *TeenSet*, have been left out. Although it is impossible to present a definitive answer in response to this question, it is important to examine contemporary discourses that reveal the extent to which teen fan magazines have been rejected within the rock canon—beginning with texts written by rock critics[25] to illuminate the degree to which rock journalists have written their own history, and, at times, hagiography, further conveying the omission and the marginalization of *TeenSet* and all teen fan magazines.

The publication of books written by rock critics began to take hold in the late 1960s with jazz/rock critic Ralph J. Gleason's 1968 publication of *The Jefferson Airplane and the San Francisco Sound*. Gleason provides a history of the San Francisco Sound, exploring bands such as the Family Dog, the Grateful Dead, and the Jefferson Airplane. Gleason opens his text by claiming that "looking back now over the incredible three years which saw the predictions come true—San Francisco IS the Liverpool of America now—it all seems to have begun with Luria Castell, the original Family Dog group, and the first dances."[26] While Gleason's text is of importance for many reasons to be discussed beyond this text (for its primary interviews with the Jefferson Airplane and for Gleason being the first jazz critic to steep himself in the San Francisco rock scene), it is significant here as a first historical account of the rock scene written by a jazz/rock critic and mentor to *Rolling Stone* founder Jann Wenner. Moreover, rock critic Richard Goldstein's 1969 book, *The Poetry of Rock*, attempts to place rock not only within the music realm but as important in a literary sense: "I do assert that there is an immense reservoir of power here [referring to rock lyrics], an impressive awareness of language, and a profound sense of rhythm."[27] Goldstein presented rock as more than just a facet of popular music, but as having artistic and literary importance too, thus elevating rock above other forms of popular music, a common theme depicted by rock journalists in this chapter.

In addition to Gleason and Goldstein, British critic Nik Cohn's 1968 book, *Rock from the Beginning*, provides a history of rock. Cohn, a rock critic but also a fan (as they all arguably are), presents an early history of rock, again from a critic's perspective. Shortly after Cohn's text came the publications of rock critic Richard Meltzer's 1970 *Aesthetics of Rock* and Lillian Roxon's 1969 *Lillian Roxon's Rock Encyclopedia*. While Meltzer's book is a cult reader of rock criticism that is still in print and openly explored by the likes of Greil Marcus,[28] Roxon's book provides a detailed description of bands in the rock scene (reissued later with an update in 1971) and an appendix of *Cash Box* Top Singles and *Billboard Weekly* singles. The fame of many of the bands in this encyclopedia did not last, but she provides a documented account of the then-current rock scene including each artist's album or single releases. From an explanation of acid rock to the Zombies, a reader can explore rock subgenres and many now-forgotten bands from the perspective of a rock journalist.

Although the texts above focus more on rock than the rock critics, it is important to include them in the historiography because, by 1968, rock journalism was beginning to transcend the underground and mainstream presses through books published by large publishing houses such as Bantam and Penguin Press. Although these books are of significance as registers of success and possible credibility of rock journalism, the authors and materials are not necessarily reflective of rock journalism history per se, but rather the history of rock culturally and musically. What the world is given is an early history of rock by rock critics and journalists themselves—allowing critics to place themselves within history as they see fit.

In 1969, rock critic Paul Williams, founder of *Crawdaddy!*, released the collected work of his rock writings, *Outlaw Blues*. This text is the first collected work by a rock critic to be published within three years of *Crawdaddy!*'s beginnings. In 1972, *Rolling Stone*'s publication division, Straight Arrow Press, released Jon Landau's collected work titled *It's Too Late to Stop Now: A Rock and Roll Journal* (1972). In Landau's introduction, he justifies himself as an authority and expert on rock, stating, "I met 18-year-old Paul Williams, editor and creator of the original, and, at that time, mimeographed, stapled-together *Crawdaddy!* . . . In due course, I told him his magazine was awful, that no one writing about it knew anything about music, and that I knew just the man he needed: me."[29] Shortly after, *Village Voice* critic Robert Christgau[30] published a similar collected work titled *Any Old Way You Choose It; Rock and Other Pop Music 1967–73*.[31]

While I argue that rock criticism or rock journalism are a faction of popular music journalism, the historical narrative of popular music journalism seems to begin with these publications and an emphasis on rock criticism or rock history told by a rock critic. These specific texts were released as collected works, essentially reflecting an era or the career of an individual, specifically three rock journalists who were writing early in their careers. One must consider Shakespeare's *First Folio*, *The Complete Works of Charles Dickens*, or *The Complete Works of Lewis Carroll*. These compilations were published posthumously or deep in a well-established career, such as for Dickens. The publication of these three collected rock critics' works signifies great work not only within popular music journalism but also within the rock canon. In the field of literature, one is taught what is deemed valuable, and with banned book lists or the omission of certain texts, what is not considered valuable. As literary theorist Andrew Milner argues, "Literature has been the study not of writing per se, but of valued writing."[32] While I am not attempting to compare Dickens to Christgau, Williams, or Landau, the popular music canon arguably presents rock and rock criticism at a similarly exalted level within the rock realm.

Greil Marcus's 1975 *Mystery Train: Images of America in Rock 'n' Roll Music* is a reflection of selected pieces and rhetoric of rock and rock culture from Elvis to Randy Newman. While it does not specifically consider rock criticism history, the title and context are presented as a reflection and criticism of rock from 1955 to the early 1970s written by a rock critic and engages in some criticism through an analysis of musicians. Marcus has continued to write and publish texts with an authoritative voice in rock, such as the more recent *History of Rock 'n' Roll in Ten Songs* (2014), again taking the reader through a "historical" journey through the selected songs.

Furthermore, critic Paul Gambaccini's 1978 *Rock Critics' Choice: The Top 200 Albums* is a text that explores Gambaccini's (and multiple contributors') tastes in rock albums, starting with the Beatles' *Sgt. Pepper's Lonely Hearts Club Band* (1967) at number one. Gambaccini (more modernly referred to as the "Professor of Pop")[33] provides some reason and sentiment as to why these are the best albums. He had (and still has) a reputation as a tastemaker and expert on rock due to his popularity as an American (UK-based) DJ and rock journalist published in *Billboard Magazine* and *Rolling Stone*. However, the final section of the guide consists of multiple critics' top ten albums, from Robert Christgau to Simon Frith. The concept behind using a guide is to help find one's way or to gain more knowledge in a particular place, like walking through a museum with an audio guide, often provided by the institution from which one needs guidance or purchased with a trusted name such as *The Lonely Planet*. The purpose of an album guide functions in the same way; rather than through a physical space, it provides an individual with a guide through a soundscape written by someone with "experience." Gambaccini claims:

> A newcomer to rock music at the end of the decade faces an unprecedented challenge. Building a collection of the best albums available becomes an ever-expanding commitment as additional good records are added to the repertoire and the prices of deleted classics inflate. . . . Enter the experts. . . . We seek guidance for our taste and our expenditures. . . . Without them [the rock critics], we are at the mercy of record company advertising, the squeals of the loudest fans, and that inaccurate barometer of quality, reputation. Without rock critics, there would be anarchy in the browser bins.[34]

Here, critics (referred to as experts) from the late 1960s onward present a guide (continued for several decades by Robert Christgau with his *Christgau's Consumer Guides* and *Record Guides*), one that Gambaccini argues is necessary to prevent poor record choices or too many trail guides and to keep one on the right path. Again, critics have placed themselves as important "experts" or voices of authority as rock's roots are becoming more distant. Motti Regev argues that these texts, as well as others, only enhance the authority of these critics: "In the way they categorize entries (in encyclopedias) and divide chapters, in their choice of musicians and topics worthy of lengthy articles, in their taken-for-granted periodizations, in the adjectives they use, in their ranking of records in terms of quality—these books (and others) contain, and therefore construct, the accepted truths about rock music."[35]

Journalist Malcolm Doney's 1978 *Summer in the City: Rock Music and Way of Life* provides a further narrative on the 1960s and rock. Here, Doney briefly discusses the rock press:

> The Rock press, particularly *Rolling Stone*, did a crucial backup job on the music's image . . . All this background conspired to make the prominent Rock figures into oracles. *Rolling Stone*, for instance, regularly featured a major interview. These had a tremendous influence on the audience. They shaped their idea about what the stars were like, they shaped the reader's own opinions.[36]

While Doney may be questioning the press's ways, specifically *Rolling Stone*, he does contribute to and highlight the growing narrative of *Rolling Stone* and rock journalists as important cultural influencers and tastemakers.

By 1985, critic Dave Marsh published selections of his writings titled *Fortunate Son: The Best of Dave Marsh*. Shortly afterward, *Mainlines, Blood Feasts, and Bad Taste*, a compilation of selections of Lester Bangs's work edited by rock critic, *Rolling Stone* staffer, and *Creem* editor John Morthland was published. Another collection of Lester Bangs's work, *Psychotic Reactions and Carburetor Dung*, was published in 1987 and edited by rock critic Greil Marcus. Ex-*Rolling Stone* editor and journalist Ben Fong-Torres released his biography *Becoming Almost Famous* in 2006 and a documentary titled *Like a Rolling Stone: The Life & Times of Ben Fong-Torres* (2022); Lester Bangs's biography, written by rock critic and Bangs enthusiast Jim DeRogatis, was published in 2000 and titled *Let it Blurt*; and Robert Christgau's (of the *Village Voice*, among others) biography *Going into the City: Portrait of a Critic as a Young Man* appeared in 2015.

Each of these texts discussed or mentioned was written and/or edited by rock journalists (if not by 1960s/1970s rock critics). This chapter conveys that rock critics have shaped and still are shaping their history. Although the origins of the rock journalism narrative have been written by critics themselves, it is not to say historians would have considered it differently. These men were filling a gap in an overall music journalism narrative that rock was once marginalized within—they were attempting to legitimize rock within music. However, as with several events and individuals in history, mythology has developed within many narratives and elements have been accepted as truth. Erin Weber argues that in the case of the Beatles narrative, "it has taken decades for Beatles writers and researchers to begin to separate the facts from the mythology."[37] In the case of popular music journalism, the mythology revolves around how important rock journalists are; as DeRogatis states, "Any damn fool can create art. It's the critic who is really important because without stepping forward to say that this was good art or bad art, who cares?"[38] This claim suggests that critics are more important than what they are critiquing.

With a few exceptions, rock critics outlined their historical discourse, at least from 1966, with the advent of *Crawdaddy!* and until the late 1970s. For this book, the beginning of the serious rock journalism discourse is significant, as it begins in 1966, according to multiple sources who credit Paul Williams and his publication of *Crawdaddy!* as the first "serious" publication to consider rock music, and *Rolling Stone* follows. However, *TeenSet*, as well as *16* and many other teen fan magazines, predates both of these publications. As Dean Biron observes, "The media-based critics who formulated the story of rock music have in turn become a key part of that story, professional connoisseurs whose superior tastes have defined the peaks and boundaries of that field for all time. They also laid the canonical trail for popular music scholarship, which, for the most part, has been only too happy to follow it."[39]

TICKET TO WRITE AND *ALMOST FAMOUS*: THE MYTH, THE LEGEND, THE HISTORY?

The year 2016 provided the first documentary considering rock criticism, *Ticket to Write: A Golden Age of Rock Music Journalism*.[40] Within this documentary, historical accounts are presented, as well as a consideration of what the subtitle of the film refers to as "a golden age of rock music journalism."[41]

The film begins with the premise that the golden age of rock criticism was in the 1970s. The documentary does not present an argument proving that the 1970s was a golden age per se but rather presents stories and memories of experiences with rock stars from rock journalists. While this documentary does provide multiple narratives within rock journalism, it lacks focus; as SpinningPlatters.com's Carrie Khan describes it, "With so much to cover, the film can feel a bit cursory and scattered at times, and the majority of the interviews are, of course, with straight white men."[42] More importantly, *Ticket to Write* glosses over the existence of teen fan magazines. Early in the documentary, DeRogatis claims, "In the beginning, there were two types of publications. There were fan magazines [teen fan magazines] with nice pictures of the stars and their lyrics reprinted, and there were newspaper articles saying this [rock music] was a juvenile delinquent scourge."[43] This is followed by *Creem*'s Bill Holdship briefly mentioning *16 Magazine* and Gloria Stavers. Holdship states that "Stavers was a very hip person, you know, even though she's running this teeny-bop magazine."[44] Although Holdship claims that Stavers is cool, he contrasts her "coolness" with her role in popular music journalism. The film used various clips to briefly mention teen fan magazines but it's poorly presented, an attempt to separate teen fan magazines from the work of rock journalists—feeding into the discourse that teen fan magazines are not of value in the development of rock journalism.

As the documentary discusses the 1960s narrative, it defines the rock critics of the era as interpreters of music for an entire generation:

> Taking their cue from the Lost Generation and the beats, a new young breed of writers emerged, the rock critics, the music journalists who wrote for magazines such as *Rolling Stone*, *Creem*, *Hit Parader*, providing news, information and commentary about the exploding music scene and youth culture. The music was the Revolution's soundtrack and the magazines with their flamboyant rock critics interpreted the music for a whole generation.[45]

I am not arguing that rock critics were not important, but making such a broad claim lacks historical consideration of multiple narratives across a large time period and is impossible to prove.

Furthermore, "unlike journalism, documentary filmmaking has largely been an individual, freelance effort. Documentary filmmakers typically are small business owners, selling their work to a range of distributors."[46]

Documentaries are not necessarily unbiased analytical texts and are "subject to the film-maker's angle, perspective, and artistry."[47] Richard M. Blumenberg, a professor of film, argues that "the problem of truth [within a documentary] is closely associated with the problem of objectivity [in regard to the director and writers]."[48] Here, the "truth" or honesty is not in question, but rock critics' subjective narrative of greatness has been accepted as not only a truth but the *only* truth. *Ticket to Write: A Golden Age in Rock Journalism* (2016) is about the importance of rock journalism and rock critics and features interviews solely with rock journalists (with one exception), thus allowing for a discourse of greatness mostly by men, who themselves are or were rock journalists. The objective is to present a golden age of rock journalism; as historian E. H. Carr reminds us, facts "are like fish swimming about in a vast and sometimes inaccessible ocean; and what the historian catches will depend, partly on chance, but mainly on what part of the ocean he chooses to fish in and what tackle he chooses to use–these two factors being, of course, determined by the kind of fish he wants to catch."[49] The director was attempting to present a specific narrative, thus participants such as rock journalists Richard Meltzer, Ed Ward, Jim DeRogatis, and Robert Christgau were selected in order to advance a specific thesis.

The most famous narrative of rock criticism and rock journalism presented to a mass public audience is Cameron Crowe's 2000 film *Almost Famous*. The film is credited as being based (very loosely) on Crowe's experiences and accounts of working for *Rolling Stone* as an extremely young rock journalist. The film provides a narrative of the struggles and lifestyle rock critics (as well as rock stars and female groupies) are exposed to or create for themselves. While *Almost Famous* was not a box office hit, the film reportedly grossed approximately $30,000,000[50] of the $60,000,000 budget and received multiple awards and acclaim, including an Oscar for Best Screenplay.

Crowe presents the audience with a narrative of a fifteen-year-old boy in the early 1970s attempting to find his place as a rock journalist. The protagonist, William Miller, eagerly consults the editor of *Creem* (and well-known music journalist) Lester Bangs. Within the film, Miller's character has written for small local publications, but his breakthrough begins when Bangs assigns him a piece reviewing an upcoming Black Sabbath concert. He meets Bangs at a local radio station, and the scene quickly changes to Miller intently listening to Bangs over coffee at a diner. Bangs explains to Miller that he "cannot make friends with the rock stars."[51] At this point, Miller begins to

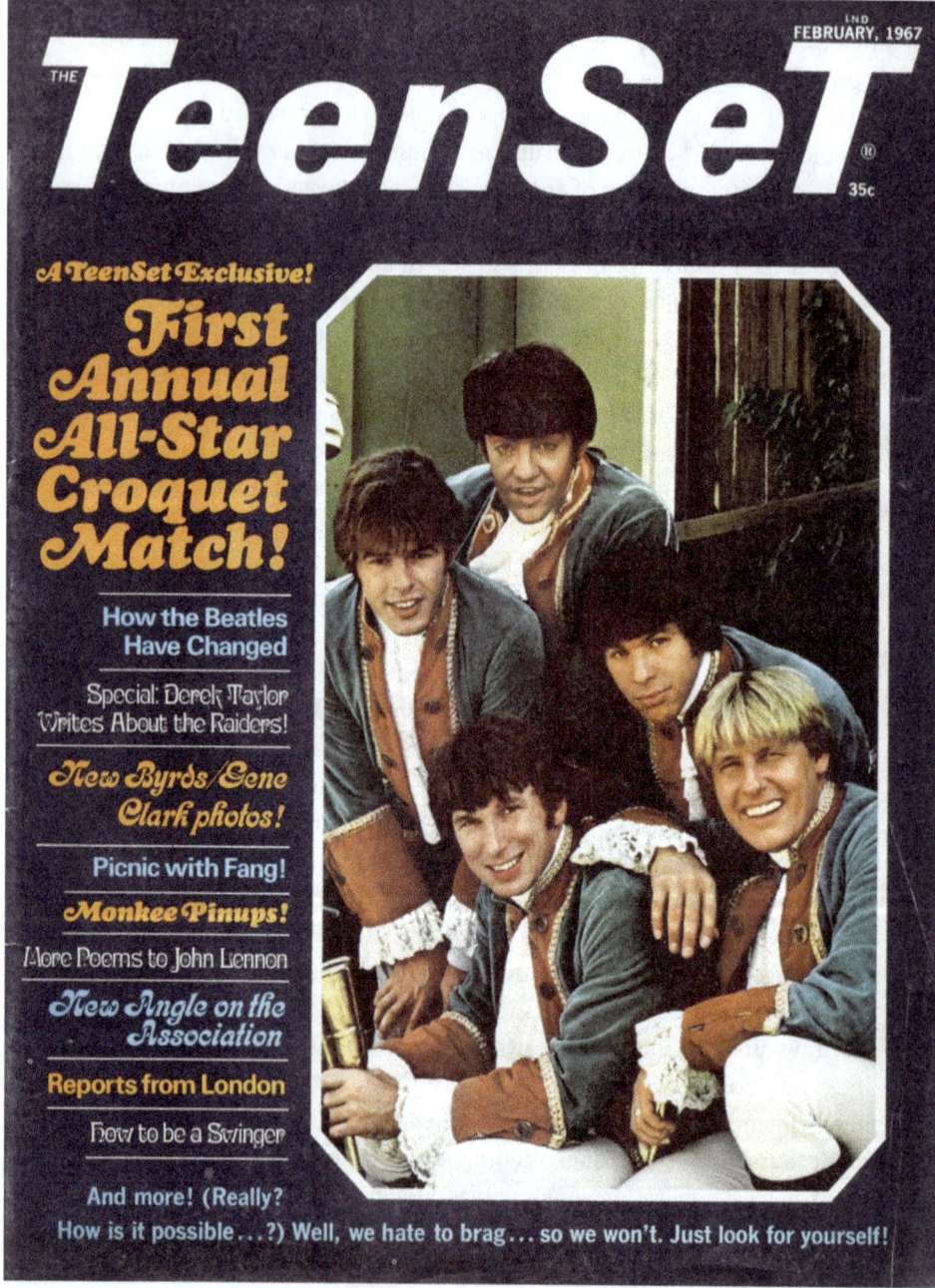

Figure 2.4. Paul Revere and the Raiders black *TeenSet* cover, February 1967. Used by permission of Scholastic Inc.

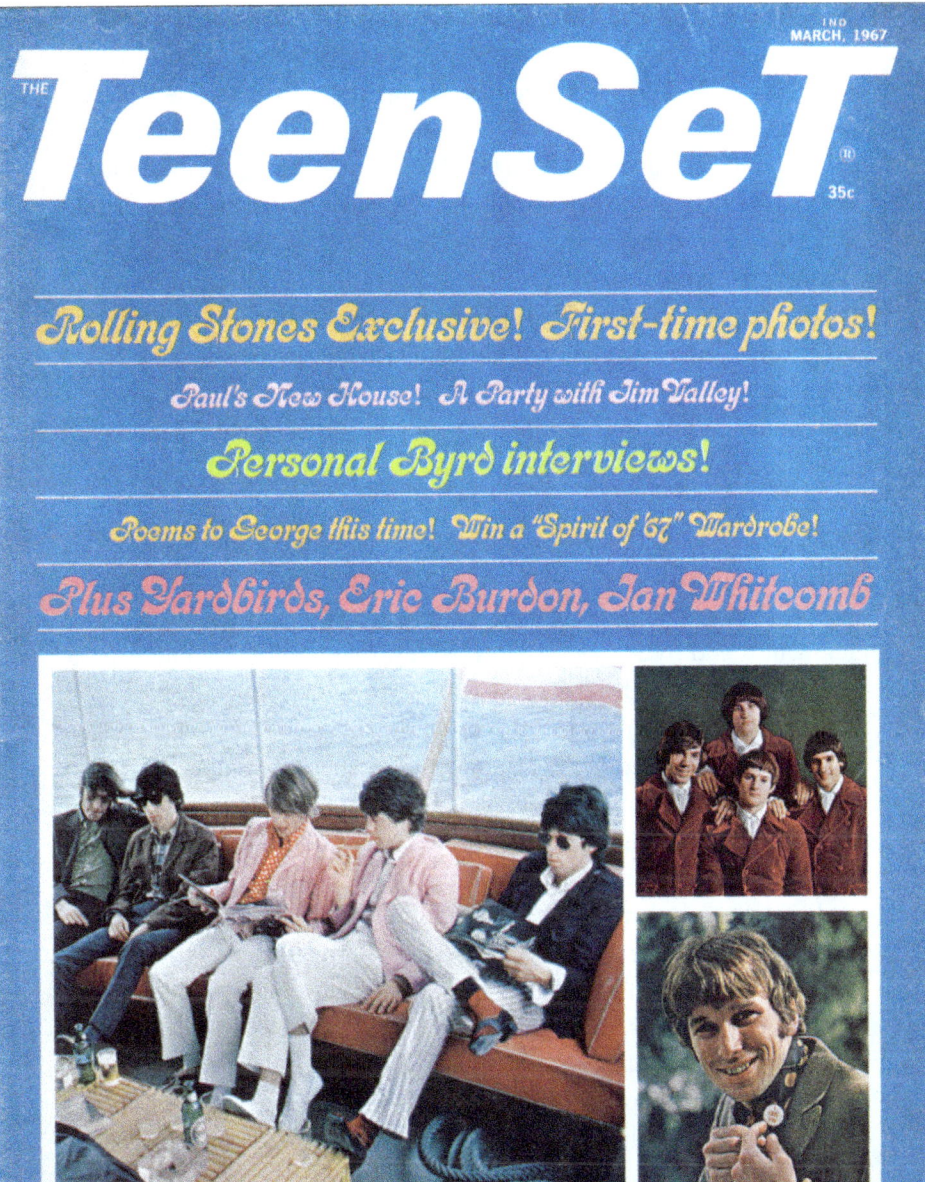

Figure 2.5. Rolling Stone *TeenSet* cover, March 1967. Used by permission of Scholastic Inc.

write down key concepts Bangs shares. He explains to Miller that rock is not what it once was, and he "should just turn around, go back and be a lawyer or something."[52] Miller's face convinces Bangs that he is up for the task. This scene ends with Bangs advising Miller, "You have to make your reputation on being honest and unmerciful."[53] The final scene shows Miller having difficulty writing his piece on the band Stillwater. He calls his mentor (or, as argued here, his sage) for advice and comfort. Bangs suggests that "while women will always be a problem for guys like us, most of the great art in the world is about that very problem."[54] He proceeds to state, "Great art is about guilt and longing,"[55] thus suggesting to the audience that rock criticism is an art form. The final words from Bangs to Miller consist of his original advice: "Be honest and unmerciful."[56] This advice was not taken at first, but it will be the second time around.

Crowe presents Bangs as a sage-like character that fits the confines of the literary archetypal sage. Here, an archetype is defined as "the original pattern or model of which all things of the same type are representations or copies."[57] A sage is also said to be "a mature or venerable person of sound judgment"[58] and to be "sage-like" as "wise through reflection and experience."[59] Specifically, archetypal sages "often seem mysterious, possessing great power and wisdom that reveals itself as they guide an adolescent protagonist across the threshold from the presumed innocence of childhood through the perils of adulthood."[60] While Bangs is not specifically taking William through the plot and sharing experiences, he is available when needed to advise him through his difficulties, a prevalent characteristic of the archetypal sage. Bangs's character does this through sharing past experiences or wisdom and his understanding of rock stars and the rock world, as well as being a journalist with a young man who is coming of age. He is reachable, but the audience does not know when he will appear, and Miller is to go forward on his own. Miller does not heed the original advice to be aware of friendships with the subjects or to "be honest and unmerciful"[61] but will be reminded by Bangs when struggling to produce his piece for *Rolling Stone*. This mentorship could be compared to other cinematic or literary sages such as *Star Wars* character Obi-Wan Kenobi, *Happy Gilmore*'s Chubbs, or *Harry Potter*'s Albus Dumbledore.

Renga and Lewis find the archetypal sage problematic in young adult novels as the majority are white males. Although *Almost Famous* was not a novel or specifically written for youth, the portrayal of Lester Bangs in his midtwenties guiding a fifteen-year-old boy molds within the argument. They argue that the presentation of the male as the sage guiding the young adult is dangerous because, in the case of the young adult, it "furthers a paternalistic narrative."[62] *Almost Famous*'s portrayal of Bangs in the case of rock criticism feeds into the narrative that the rock critic is a wise, white male whose knowledge of rock and rock culture is beyond his years.

Although this argument mostly focuses on Bangs, the objective is to highlight the depiction and the mythology that is snowballing around him and rock journalism years after his death. As Michael Stanford argues, "The characteristic of myth, fictitious or not, is the hold that it has on our minds."[63] Unlike fictional literary sages, in this text, the character of Lester Bangs is attempting to portray a past living being, not a fictional individual. This is not to say that multiple texts do not present real-life sages to the world or a reimagined figure rather than a factual portrayal, as multiple films present reimagined figures or events. Yet historically, this is the first filmic presentation of rock journalism, and at the time, the only portrayal of a real-life rock critic. Thus, what the audience is presented with here is an interpretive essence of Bangs, not the real man. The first presentation of Lester Bangs beyond his writings and just after the release of his biography is in *Almost Famous*, a film written and directed by an ex-rock critic who received a breakthrough from Lester Bangs, an elaborated memory far removed from the origin. In his review of *Almost Famous*, critic Roger Ebert is drawn to the "power and pervasiveness of these 'moving pictures' media"[64] as discussed with the illusion of Stillwater as a nonfiction band:

> William's other angel is the legendary rock critic Lester Bangs (Philip Seymour Hoffman), then the editor of Creem: "So you're the kid who's been sending me those articles from your school paper." He ignores the kid's age, trusts his talent and shares his credo: "Be honest and unmerciful." During moments of crisis on the road, William calls Bangs for advice. Lester Bangs was a real person, and so are Ben Fong-Torres and Jann Wenner of *Rolling Stone*, played by look-alike actors. The movie's sense of time and place is so acute it's possible to believe Stillwater was a real band.[65]

Historian Anthony Brundage argues that "whenever we ponder past events, it's not only a set of historical facts that comes to mind but a rich array of images. Not only are these images an inseparable and necessary component of historical knowledge, but they are hard-wired into the way we think."[66] This suggests that if we are presented with a particular image of a historical figure, whether or not the image is true, individuals will place it within their understanding or image of the figure, as Ebert clearly notes.

To further this, Ben Fong-Torres's website biography claims that he is "a real-life character in *Almost Famous*, the 2000 film by Cameron Crowe,"[67] and the end of the webpage claims "Almost famous since 1969."[68] The statement is not followed by any commentary as to whether the portrayal is or is not accurate, leaving the reader to believe Crowe's presentation of Fong-Torres is most likely accurate or at least a pleasing representation of Fong-Torres.

Even though there is no claim that *Almost Famous* is historically accurate, the blending of fictional legend and historical figures blurs the lines, arguably mythicizing rock journalism through hagiography. Mythology or legend is often accepted by hagiographers as part of their truths, and when they are blended, it is difficult to decipher fact from legend. Scholar Jennifer Otter Bickerdike uses the concept of hagiography, "the study of saints,"[69] and applies it to the consideration of mythicized dead rock stars, specifically Kurt Cobain and Ian Curtis. She analyzes the mixing of myth/legend and history, finding that "with each passing year since their deaths, the human elements of saints are overshadowed by the ever-changing legends surrounding their lives and work, fiction and reality combining into a new identity for each individual."[70] What Crowe presents is his own legend or hagiography to the world of rock journalism and a canonization of Lester Bangs. Bangs's death makes it easier to canonize (as the other famed critics are still alive): "For death creates a simultaneous 'real event,' providing authenticity and meaning while allowing images alone to evolve and be manipulated in the marketplace."[71] This is not to say that through other means, living critics are not attempting to create their own mythology, but the dead cannot openly disagree with future portrayals of themselves by others. Thus, it is possible to believe every detail of the portrayal of Lester Bangs, the overarching claims from *Ticket to Write*, and that rock journalism is an art form that is culturally more valuable in comparison to other narratives within popular music journalism.

I am not attempting to critique *Almost Famous*, but these two concepts of the literary archetypal sage and rock criticism and critics being presented within popular music hagiographies have contributed to the historical discourse of popular music journalism, which again privileges an accepted narrative of rock journalism, a male-dominated firmament presented as a form of high art.

THE ACADEMIC HISTORICAL DISCOURSE: BUYING-IN AND CHALLENGING

In addition to the press's growing contribution to its own history, the academic discourse, beginning in 1981 with Frith's accessible publication *Sound Effects: Youth, Leisure, and the Politics of Rock 'n' Roll*, and a small amount of consideration through to the 1990s, has significantly grown from the early 2000s (after the release of *Almost Famous*). These inquiries within the field of rock journalism have focused beyond the happenings and cultural commentary of the critics and consider aesthetics, Bourdieu's field theory, gender, genre conflicts, and multiple other concepts. However, these studies consider the critics and rock criticism as much as the nonacademic texts have, and they still heavily focus on the seeming faction of historical rock criticism rather than popular music journalism as a whole. While the academic discourse is diversifying and is now exploring historical contributions of jazz criticism within rock journalism (see Brennan), growing considerations of women and, more generally, modern rock journalism, the discourse continues to present an argument and myth that *Crawdaddy!* and *Rolling Stone* are "patient zeros" and maintains the idea that teen fan magazines should not be considered beyond recognition of their existing as part of the celebrity gossip arena.

The academic discourse on the history of the rock press begins with the development of "serious" consideration of rock by the underground and rock press. Within this narrative, the advent of *Crawdaddy!* followed by *Rolling Stone*, *Mojo Navigator*, *Creem*, *Circus*, and other specialist magazines and fanzines[72] marks the historical beginnings of serious rock consideration and criticism as found in the scholarly work of Frith, Lindberg et al., Jones, Regev, and Powers. Regev argues, "The late 1960s also saw the emergence of periodicals devoted to a 'serious' treatment of rock—as opposed to the 'entertainment'- oriented press. *Crawdaddy!*, *Creem*, and other publications appeared, but the one which researchers commonly agree has been the most important and influential is *Rolling Stone*" (Frith 1981; Denisoff 1975; Taylor 1985).[73] Although I am not challenging this statement, Regev does not credit any form of teen fan magazine and appears to be categorizing it as entertainment. For him, the beginning is *Crawdaddy!* Frith argues that "America's rock press emerged from two other sources. First, there was the underground press proper. This had its origins in the *Village Voice*, but its real foundations were laid by the *Los Angeles Free Press* and *Berkeley Barb* in 1964 [1965]."[74] While Frith does predate *Crawdaddy!*, teen fan magazines or jazz magazines are not considered but rather a style of writing, such as the development of New Journalism[75] and newspapers that did not solely focus on all things popular music.

Additionally, the ideology of rock or rock aesthetics[76] has been presented historically as being established or disseminated from these texts by rock critics. Frith, as a forerunner in the popular music academic community and again, as a former critic, claims:

> that underground papers were important as the source of what became the dominant ideology of rock. This ideology was confirmed and developed by a second American event, the creation of new, specialist music magazines: *Crawdaddy!* began publication in 1966 and was followed over the next few years by *Mojo-Navigator*, *Fusion*, and *Creem*. These magazines varied greatly in their format, style, success, and concern, but they had in common the serious treatment of rock as a cultural form, and they made, from their side, the same connections between rock and life-style [sic] that the underground press made from theirs.[77]

Rock critics have earned a place in history as the champions of rock aesthetics (principles of rock) and are argued to have elevated rock music and culture to a high art status across many fields.

These critics are continuously discussed and acknowledged as not only establishing but forwarding rock ideology. Regev argues, "[Greil] Marcus is representative of a larger group of critics, scholars, and fans of popular music who subscribe to the belief that the music of the Beatles, Bob Dylan, the Rolling Stones, and Jimi Hendrix—to name the most obvious examples—constitutes 'real art,' no less real than any serious music might be."[78] Frith furthers this argument:

> The ideology of rock—the arguments about what records mean, what rock is for—has always been articulated more clearly by fans than by musicians (or businessmen). In a sense, rock matters more to fans—rock as fun and pleasure is a more difficult idea to negotiate than rock as a career or business. The paradox is that rock, for all its emphasis on community and culture, is, for most of its fans, most of the time, a personal experience—people listen to their records at home, develop private fantasies about their stars—and they need all the help they can get. Hence the importance of the professional rock

fans—the rock writers. Music papers, indeed, are important even for those people who don't buy them—their readers act as the opinion leaders, the rock interpreters, the ideological gatekeepers for everyone else.[79]

By late 1970s, the early rock critics were being positioned (and were continuing to position themselves) as ideological gatekeepers, and in 2001, this claim is affirmed: "As a particular type of gatekeeper, rock critics play a significant role in shaping the representations of artists for an admittedly small, but influential, population, as well as establishing an artist's place in music history."[80] Kembrew McLeod argues that the rock critics establish a place for an artist in history, possibly as Landau is credited with "discovering" and "popularizing" Bruce Springsteen. This claim, again, places a rock critic on a pedestal with a very powerful voice of authority. This suggests that, historically, this is not solely a matter of rhetoric but that rock critics have (had) a reach that can (could) make or break artists. This also implies that the record companies and advertisers did not influence what was written and that individuals were not able to listen to the radio or a record and make a decision for themselves. As discussed previously, the early rock critics wrote and still write companions to the "best" music, such as Dave Marsh's 2014 *New Book of Rock Lists*. This is not to suggest that the rock critics are not important and do not influence, but it would be impossible to gauge their contributions and influence beyond what is written about them. However, history has presented a discourse that suggests they are responsible for making or breaking artists.

A large part of the discussion of rock criticism focuses on the ideology (also known as "rock aesthetics") of the critics and the music; these tropes include authenticity, consistency, and otherness, meaning that rock supposedly encompasses these and, implicitly, as conveyed in the introduction, "pop" does not.[81] As Biron argues, "The rock-centric dialogue that seeps into popular music criticism is too easily accepted as a natural and permanent phenomenon somehow representative of the aesthetic in its entirety, with figureheads such as the Beatles as intrinsic to its telling as Beethoven, Bach, and Mozart are to the classical equivalent."[82] These values are not necessarily based on production or even the artist's original intent but rather on the above-mentioned tropes. For example, authenticity is arguably the driving principle within the rock aesthetic, but authenticity is vague, and as Kevin Featherly describes, "Authenticity is probably simultaneously the most invisible and most opaque of the concerns that occupy popular music critics, yet

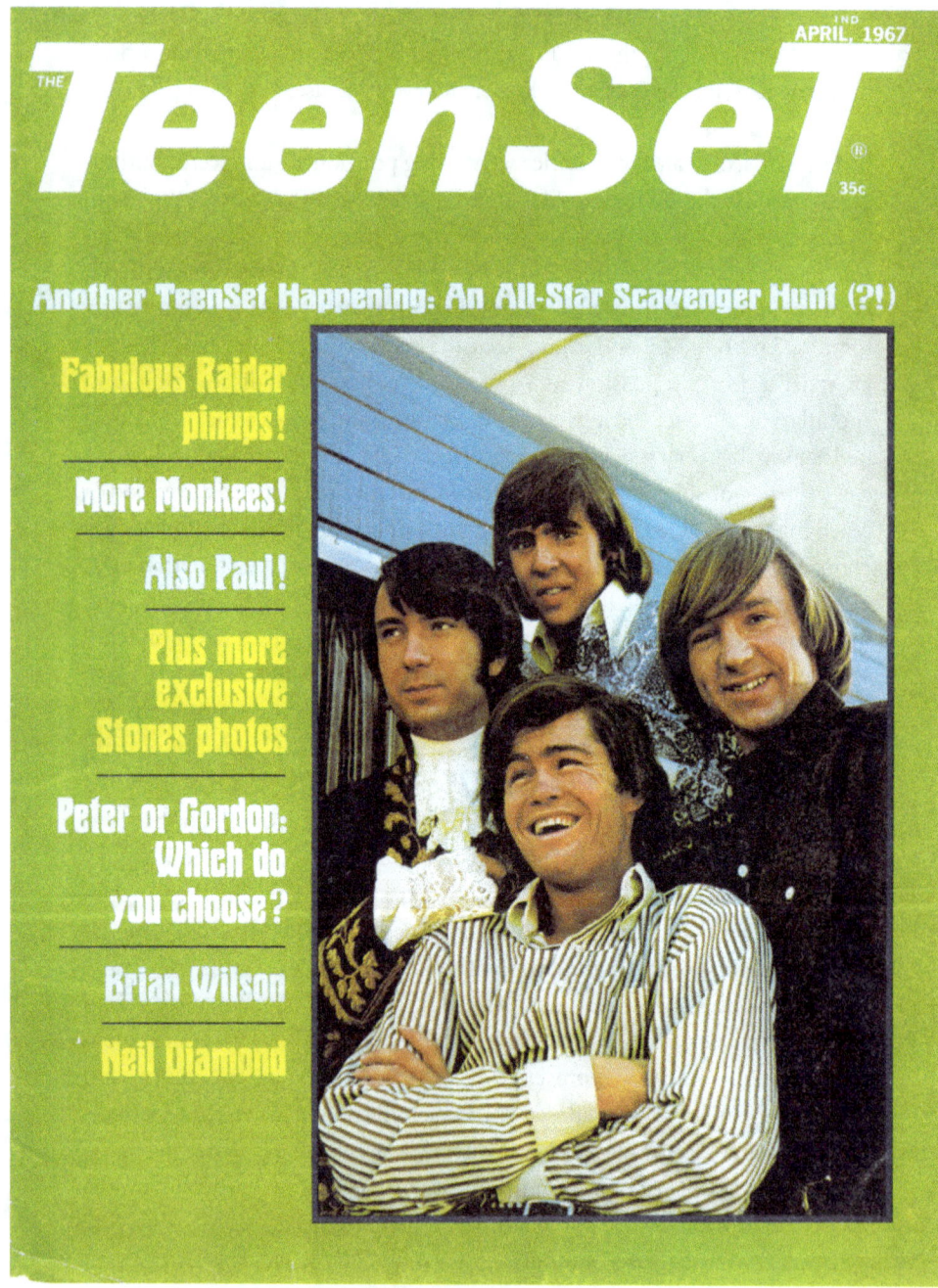

Figure 2.6. Monkees green *TeenSet* cover, April 1967. Used by permission of Scholastic Inc.

Figure 2.7. Monkees red *TeenSet* cover, May 1967. Used by permission of Scholastic Inc.

it is referred to or implied in almost all popular-music criticism."[83] Critics do not provide a schema explaining what is and is not worthy of being considered authentic or high art within the field of rock criticism, yet as they praise and criticize, the reader is provided with a notion of what the critic deems to be authentic (and inauthentic) within rock.[84]

Academic texts have considered these tropes in depth as rock criticism is now recognized as a field. Jones, Regev, Lindberg et al., and Chris Atton, along with acknowledgments from Powers and Brennan, have applied Bourdieu's explanation of field theory to rock criticism. Linberg et al. provide an extensive consideration and application of field theory, arguing that rock criticism itself is a field; they pose this dilemma: "One might also question the exclusion of other rock journalism in favor of criticism on different grounds. It could be argued that this introduces or cements a high/low divide and that this divide might have dire consequences in terms of, say, gender and/or ethnicity."[85] Regev previously proposed a similar dilemma:

> The implication here is that it might be hypothesized that artistic hierarchies, which rank producers according to their aesthetic or expressive value, as judged by "experts" in the field, are becoming a central structuring force in a growing number of fields of production. In light of this examination of popular music, it seems that the cultural field is currently characterized not so much by an abandonment of the belief in hierarchies based on this ideology but rather by a struggle over the content of the hierarchies.[86]

What we find in this placement is the struggle between high and low, as field theory allows itself. As art music (classical) was (and is still) considered a high form and popular music (such as jazz and rock) a low form, there are high and low forms within popular music, too, and this is evident to Lindberg et al. and Regev. In this case, other forms of popular music journalism have been, are, and can be considered lower forms in comparison to rock journalism. While rock journalism in *Rolling Stone*, *Creem*, and from other rock critics in the mid-1960s attempted to gain credibility, the end result was to mimic the jazz hierarchy in which rock was not taken seriously.

As discussed previously with *Almost Famous* (2000), the rock journalism narrative is shrouded in hagiography and, at times, this is also true of academic considerations of rock critics. Lindberg et al., while providing an extensive consideration of rock criticism as a field based on Bourdieu's field theory, use terminology that canonizes early rock critics by discussing critics as crusaders. They state, "If the forefathers of rock criticism were crusaders, discovering a new Promised Land, their followers were those who colonized it and won the battle as creators of different distinct positions, evolving within a few years (1967–1972) into a field with its own criteria, discourse and 'clergy.'"[87] The terminology above only contributes to the canonization of rock critics. While Lindberg et al. do find faults within the discourse that argues critics alone allowed for rock to be taken seriously (by seriously, I mean more than just entertainment), they still advance the mythology with phrases such as "crusaders." Below, they compare the likes of Dave Marsh, Jon Landau, Greil Marcus, Robert Christgau, and Lester Bangs to the puritans establishing American colonies and as "founding fathers" of serious rock journalism—equating early rock journalism to essential foundational democratic governing documents such as the Constitution.

> As we will see, they [rock critics] are all deeply involved in American cultural mythology, and while America had been the promised land of Puritans and other refugees from Europe, these critics entered rock writing at a time when rock was widely seen as the promise of a new generation. It became their task to secularize this promise and write the Declaration of Independence and the Constitution of the new Republic of Rock. Therefore, they are the founding fathers of rock criticism.[88]

However, the Declaration of Independence or Constitution of the United States is not taught as a sole act of the American founding fathers but rather as influenced by John Locke, Rousseau, Baron de Montesquieu, Voltaire, and others before their time. As an academic text, it is surprising to see such canonization of rock critics, as Lindberg et al. even briefly address mythology within the historiography of rock criticism and note that rock critics have written rock history. While they rightfully consider the often-neglected criticism of the 1980s and 1990s as well as women rock journalists such as Ellen Willis and Ann Powers, they again lack the consideration of precursors such as teen fan magazines.

Through these texts, the reader is presented with a narrative and consideration of the same white male critics, although the narrative is beginning to expand. For fifty years, the discourse has focused on the same "founding fathers" and others such as the deceased Ralph J. Gleason and Nat Hentoff;

Figure 2.8. Peter Tork *TeenSet* cover, June 1967. Used by permission of Scholastic Inc.

however, they were jazz critics first who crossed into rock criticism. What is found is that when considering rock journalism, it is easy to find oneself trapped in a historical loop from 1966 to the mid-1970s. It is understandable that these men are written about and should be discussed, and some are attempting to expand *this* narrative, such as Devon Powers's 2013 insight to early critics such as Ellen Willis and Richard Goldstein, but the narrative has mostly discussed the aforementioned "founding fathers" in relation to whatever argument authors are presenting. Females who should be discussed, such as Stavers, Willis, Roxon, Weinstein, and *TeenSet*'s Judith Sims, are often left out of this narrative. Thus, we are presented with a repetitive narrative that contributes to a canonization that is hard to challenge or allow for conflicting or contributing information to be a part of. Dean Biron argues that the narrative of rock and rock journalism within popular music history has become an "exhaustion narrative":[89]

> It seems that the rock canon, if only by dint of the extensive dialogue it generates, now holds sway as the supreme measure of musical achievement. This sacred list [referring to preferred rock music by many critics], instigated by a select coterie of journalist critics who, in cementing in place the official history of the form, sought to unearth their own Vindications [sic], casts a shadow across the entirety of contemporary music.[90]

It is important to consider the discourse at hand, and academia is slowly considering more narratives than nonacademic authors are, partially due to the notion that non-rock journalists are challenging this repetitive narrative presented by the critics themselves. Even in the field of rock criticism, the narrative is limited. It is not that there are too many academic texts solely considering rock criticism, as rock criticism should be and is still being explored, but what is lacking within the rock criticism academic discourse of this time period are more case studies of critics' work and the artists they are considering. While it is claimed multiple times that what they have done is important and reflective of an era, they were writing about music, and this is something that should be explored more. Who and what they were writing about should be considered, rather than the sheer accolades of writing about rock seriously.

As texts like Brennan's are paving the way for diversification of consideration of popular music extending beyond the historical examinations of the beginning of rock criticism, they are also encouraging the examination of popular music journalism as a whole. For example, Brennan has reconsidered jazz journalism as a precursor to rock journalism (as well as jazz critics' responses to rock). He argues that "it is worth noting that it suits the first generation of rock critics to claim that rock criticism was an entirely new way of writing about music because it bolsters an ideology that positions them firmly as pioneers. My view is that rock writers and rock writing were not without precedent."[91] Brennan's stance openly acknowledges precursors to rock criticism and journalism and is the first to examine jazz as popular music along with rock, thus exploring a relationship that is often denied. While the early academic texts examining rock journalism embraced the historical synchronic narrative of rock criticism from 1966 to 1972, the discussion of rock journalism is diversifying (as conveyed in the introduction).[92]

CONCLUDING REMARKS: THE PROBLEMS WITHIN THE CURRENT HISTORICAL DISCOURSE

The elite historical status of rock criticism has made it difficult for other contributing and differing popular music narratives to be considered or taken seriously in rock journalism history. The legend of the rock critics is ingrained within popular music history as depicted through a multitude of texts presented throughout this chapter. While these critics and the early rock press have rightfully earned a place in history, it is time to consider other historical narratives.

As presented, academics are beginning to consider different historical narratives, slowly expanding and reconsidering the discourse. However, the historiography has not changed significantly, as the critics themselves are continuing to perpetuate a specific history, with some academics, to an extent, still following. Understanding the current monopolization of the discourse allows for *TeenSet* to shine on its own, not only as a precursor and contributor to rock journalism but also as historical documentation from another perspective of the 1960s within popular music journalism that is often rejected in favor of a history written by rock critics.

CHAPTER THREE

SHOW ME *TEENSET*!

TeenSet as a Valuable Source in Popular Music

As discussed in chapter 2, part of the reason *TeenSet* is dismissed, in general, is that teen fan magazines are not seen as serious rock music media outlets. However, the value of *TeenSet* (as well as other teen fan magazines) is not only in its existence in the 1960s but also in its continued use as a primary source to further historical narratives. *TeenSet* articles, images, and interviews have been quoted or mentioned in over thirty texts, including multiple biographies from a consideration of Neil Young, Jimi Hendrix, the Association, Buffalo Springfield, Laura Nyro, Pete Best, and the Beach Boys, and discussions in academic texts examining David McCallum, rock criticism, and *Hair*. The utilization of *TeenSet*'s content conveys not only the number of times the magazine has been sourced but also how this utilization contributes to shaping how popular music and popular culture are represented in the present. Thus, selected textual examples will be analyzed[1] to illuminate critical considerations of authenticity and value in popular music and culture. This chapter shows how *TeenSet* is an authentic source that provided knowledge and valued perspectives of popular music and culture during the mid to late 1960s and is currently shaping our present historical understanding of the past—contributing to the present historical perception of popular music.

TeenSet Shaping Historical Narratives

Two texts examining musician and songwriter Laura Nyro,[2] one academic, the other nonacademic, utilize *TeenSet*'s content to further their arguments in

Figure 3.1. Paul Revere and the Raiders tan *TeenSet* cover, July 1967. Used by permission of Scholastic Inc.

various ways. First, Michele Kort's biography of Nyro, *Soul Picnic: The Music and Passion of Laura Nyro*, quotes *TeenSet*'s commentary of the Monterey Pop Festival to help combat a later negative memory of Nyro:

> Right after the festival, *TeenSet* magazine wrote simply that "Laura Nyro staged one of the more unusual acts." But as one concertgoer harshly characterized her performance thirty years later, Nyro was "a dreadfully pretentious woman offering up exactly the sort of formulaic pop-music piffle we had expected to avoid by gathering in Monterey." Of course one man's piffle is another's artistry. *Rolling Stone* magazine's historians were much kinder when they concluded that Nyro simply "seemed to try too hard for the laid-back audience." [3]

This reference to *TeenSet* is used to convey the response to Nyro's performance at the Monterey Pop Festival. The other two sources quoted above were from a later period, as *Rolling Stone* was not in existence for four more months and covering the festival would not be news. Jann Wenner and Ralph J. Gleason were at the Monterey Pop Festival, but *TeenSet* was the only magazine to display an image of Laura Nyro in regard to Monterey Pop (*Tiger Beat* had a two-page Monterey Pop spread in their September 1967 issue). Kort seemingly considered *TeenSet*'s comment as fair, and at this time, there is no evidence of Nyro in *Rolling Stone* in the 1960s. It could be argued that *TeenSet* may be utilized here because the author lacks other primary sources,[4] but in fact, Kort is using *TeenSet*'s reaction to Nyro's performance to combat a negative memory of the performance. It was not until the 2017 rereleased, uncut version of the *Monterey Pop* documentary that her entire performance was featured. In 1967, Judith Sims of *TeenSet* felt the need to include Nyro in its photographic coverage, as Nyro was of note.

Patricia Spence Rudden's 2007 chapter, "Stacking the Wax: The Structure of Laura Nyro's Studio Albums," also sourced articles considering Laura Nyro from *TeenSet*'s February 1969 issue. Rudden argues that Laura Nyro albums are structured, and not merely, as others argued, Nyro's memories of a bad acid trip. She sources *TeenSet*'s 1969 article "Purple, Tuna, and Laura Nyro" by Peter Johnson:

> In February 1969, Pete Johnson, a West Coast rock writer, wrote that ETC "is a concept album. Each of the songs relates to the others, though the

relationship is not a simple one." He recognizes what he calls "a progression . . . from innocence to knowledge and back to innocence" and unpacks the meaning of the title in terms of the number of songs and the titles of the songs that conclude each side. Other writers retold, in less detail, the story of the bad trip . . . and only Van de Horst and Johnson comment on the album's structure.[5]

Rudden not only uses *TeenSet*'s content to support her argument but shows that this article attempted to "unpack" the meaning rather than retelling a story that Johnson, in *TeenSet*, was providing the readers with another perspective and has enhanced a critical understanding of Nyro as a musician. While Rudden credits Johnson, rather than *TeenSet*, the article was approved by Judith Sims, and *TeenSet* featured multiple articles that provided critical discussions of music and performance rather than merely recounting information already in existence. Thus, in Nyro's case, *TeenSet*'s interview and consideration of Nyro and her work have contributed to how one currently perceives Nyro in the present.

Like Nyro, our understanding of Neil Young has also been furthered by *TeenSet*, as two texts have quoted or discussed Neil Young's interviews from within *TeenSet* as factual information that attempts to teach readers about Young's musical progression. For example, in Sharry Wilson's *Young Neil: The Sugar Mountain Years* (2014), Wilson examines an interview between Young and Sims: "In a 1968 interview with Judith Sims for *Teen Set* magazine, Neil mentioned his ukulele: 'I learned three chords on it; really went wild and learned "Blueberry Hill" and "On Top of Old Smokey" . . . all those neat songs.'"[6] *TeenSet* is sourced to enhance the narrative of Neil Young's musical development and progression, providing a reader with a glimpse into Young's playing of a folk instrument and folk songs, enhancing Young's persona as authentic through folk connotations. Wilson claims, "A reference to Neil's little-known earlier time with his family in Winnipeg can be found in the April 1968 issue of *Teen Set* in the article 'Neil Young Profile' by Judith Sims."[7] In popular music biographer Jimmy McDonough's *Shakey: Neil Young's Biography* (2002), musician Ken Viola recalls *TeenSet* and their features on Buffalo Springfield.

> Despite the band's misgivings over the production, Buffalo Springfield would gain them a loyal following beyond Los Angeles and in the burgeoning rock

press, where Paul Williams at *Crawdaddy!* and Judith Sims of *TeenSet* spread the word. Ken Viola was obsessed by *TeenSet*. "I'd be at the candy store at six a.m., waitin' for them to snap those bundles open so I could get the latest issue and read about the Springfield."[8]

McDonough not only provides credit for the growing popularity of Buffalo Springfield to *TeenSet* along with *Crawdaddy!* but also conveys the importance of *TeenSet* as heavily featuring, valuing, and progressing the career of not only Buffalo Springfield but also Neil Young and the other individual Buffalos. He makes it clear that the burgeoning rock press is Paul Williams with *Crawdaddy!* and Judith Sims with *TeenSet*. There is no hierarchy implied; McDonough presents Sims and Williams as equals. To validate Viola's comment, *TeenSet* covered Buffalo Springfield over sixty times in twenty-three out of the thirty-four issues published (see appendix 1). The only musical acts that surpassed the frequency of Buffalo Springfield's mentions/discussions were the Beatles and the Monkees. *Rolling Stone* was still in its infancy and did not exist in time to cover Buffalo Springfield for over half of the band's existence, and Judith Sims adored Buffalo Springfield, thus, an extensive amount of coverage of the band is found in *TeenSet*.[9]

While texts about Neil Young and Buffalo Springfield utilize *TeenSet*'s content (articles and photographs) to provide knowledge and understanding of, say, Neil's musical origins, three Hendrix biographies source a *TeenSet* interview titled "Jimi Hendrix, Black Power and Money"[10] by Jacoba Atlas that conveys Hendrix's political leanings. This article has been used multiple times in consideration of Jimi Hendrix. In *Jimi Hendrix and Philosophy: Experience Required* (2017), Daryl Hale uses Atlas's article to argue against the 1960s accusation that Jimi Hendrix had no "soul" as the article titled conveys the Black community's disappointment in Hendrix. "'Hendrix has no soul,' they say. He just ain't no James Brown.'"[11] Hale argues:

> Jimi's music crossed over so many musical boundaries—his influence from the folk blues masters like Robert Johnson and Muddy Waters; his driving hard-rock sounds, such that Clapton and Cream were in awe of his expertise; and his drifting off in jazz directions as drew in Buddy Miles. Add on to that his amazing technical mastery of extracting sound from a Stratocaster (especially in that upside-down signature Hendrix performance motif), never quite executed before, and it is no surprise that his music was hard to cat-

egorize. When militant critics insisted that whites could not play blues, Jimi gently coerced some "brothers" simply to sit and listen to a Cream album. The reaction (as given by an interviewer in *TeenSet* magazine): the listeners were amazed at how three white boys got all that done. Jimi saw the power of music as one for healing divisions and transforming cultural differences and attitudes.[12]

Hale uses *TeenSet* to forward his narrative and shape the way in which readers consider Hendrix's philosophy in music as "transforming cultural differences and attitudes."[13] The *TeenSet* interview is used to promote Hendrix's feelings toward race and the possible power of music.

Journalist Mick Wall's 2019 biographic *Two Riders Were Approaching* and Glebbeek and Shapiro's 1995 *Jimi Hendrix: Electric Gypsy* both consider Hendrix's comments from the same article by Jacoba Atlas. However, Wall focuses on a narrative rather than analyzing the content:

> Six months before the Toronto bust, an interview with Jimi had come out in radical youth-culture magazine *TeenSet*, headlined Jimi Hendrix, Black Power and Money. Jimi, talking about black militancy, quoted as follows: "Then get your Black Panthers . . . I know it sounds like war, but that's what's gonna have to happen, it has to be a war if nobody is going to do it peacefully. . . . You have to fight fire with fire." Mike shit the bed when he was told about it. *What the fucking fuck, Jimi? You wanna kill your audience stone dead overnight?* The Feds took it even more seriously. But the Feds, led by Evil Edgar, didn't grasp the fact that no self-respecting American black kid would be caught dead reading crapola white hippy jive like *TeenSet*.[14]

Wall begins by calling *TeenSet* a "radical youth-culture magazine" (which suggests that *TeenSet* is culturally and politically engaged in the late-1960s zeitgeist) and ends with a "crapola white hippy jive" magazine (he is not himself dismissing the magazine, but rather attempting to refer to the Black perspective on the matter). By using the term "hippy" to describe *TeenSet*, he connotes *TeenSet* as countercultural, and Wall inadvertently argues that *TeenSet* was making an impact; whether this coverage was good or bad for Hendrix, people were paying attention, reading, and reacting.

Glebbeek and Shapiro requote Hendrix's same interview to further their historical understanding of Jimi Hendrix. They also end the discussion by noting that "whatever Jimi was trying to get across here, one thing was for sure—he was saying it to the wrong magazine. No black kid on the streets was likely to be reading *TeenSet*."[15] Like Wall, Glebbeek and Shapiro question the article's placement within *TeenSet* magazine; however, their rationale for this judgment has nothing to do with the fact that it was in a "teen fan magazine" but because they assumed that *TeenSet* would not have many Black readers; the same was probably true of *Rolling Stone* or *Crawdaddy!* However, it is important to note this article was in *TeenSet* because the staff and editor took an interest and Hendrix felt comfortable speaking with reporter Jacoba Atlas.

Steven Roby's *Hendrix on Hendrix: Interviews and Encounters with Jimi Hendrix* (2012) includes fifty-seven selections from 1966 to 1970. Within the preface, Roby argues that "this book includes some of the most important Jimi Hendrix interviews that took place from 1966 to 1970—the peak of his career.... Together, they represent Hendrix's story in his own words."[16] Roby's extensive collection features Hendrix interviews with Flip Wilson and Dick Cavett alongside then-*TeenSet* reporter Jacoba Atlas's "Jimi Hendrix, Black Power and Money." Including this interview only confirms the argument that not only has *TeenSet* been sourced to promote or question Hendrix narratives, but that *TeenSet*'s content is of value, and as Roby argues, represents Hendrix "in his own words,"[17] thus contributing in multiple ways to shaping our historical understanding of Hendrix's political views, popular music, and culture. Roby provides valuable information about the limited lifespan of Hendrix's career, and again it is found in *TeenSet*.

In the academic world, Dr. Mary Rizzo utilized the 1969 *TeenSet* review of the musical *Hair*. Throughout her argument, she sources *TeenSet*'s review as equal to reviews within *Rolling Stone*, the *London Sunday Times*, the *Wall Street Journal*, *Time*, and the *New Yorker* (among multiple others). Her discussion places *TeenSet*'s review on the same level as other reviews and uses *TeenSet* to argue that *Hair* felt as if it transcended normal theater but also codified the counterculture.

The chart in figure 3.2 contains all the texts that source *TeenSet*'s content. There are other texts that discuss *TeenSet*, but those specific texts discuss *TeenSet* historically (Armstrong, Spizer, etc.).

None of the sources above specifically discuss *TeenSet*'s impact but rather utilize *TeenSet*'s content to advance or shape a narrative, an argument, or a persona within popular culture. To further their arguments, the authors in figure 3.2 have all quoted *TeenSet*'s content in some fashion (from images and

Mary Rizzo, *Consuming Class, Buying Identity: Middle-class Youth Culture, 'lower-class' Style and Consumer Culture, 1945-2000*, Phd diss. (University Of Minnesota, 2005), 211.	Searles, Malcolm C. *The Association 'Cherish': The Story of America's First Folk-Rock Band*. Leicester: Troubador Publishing Ltd, 2018.
Borst, William A. *The Scorpion and the Frog: a Natural Conspiracy.* Bloomington, IN: Xlibris, 2004.	Shapiro, Harry, and Caesar Glebbeek. *Jimi Hendrix: Electric Gypsy*. New York: MacMillian, 1995.
Wiener, Allen J. *The Beatles: the Ultimate recording guide.* Holbrook, MA: B. Adams, 1994.	Shipton, Alyn. *Nilsson: The Life of a Singer-Songwriter*. Oxford: Oxford Press, 2013.
Harry, Bill. *Paperback Writers: The History of The Beatles in Print.* New York: Avon, 1986.	Winn, John C. *That Magic Feeling: The Beatles' Recorded Legacy, Volume Two*, New York: Three Rivers Press, 2009.
Hale, Daryl. "Quicker Than A Wink Of An Eye." In *Jimi Hendrix and Philosophy: Experience Require*, edited by Theodore Theodore, Chicago: Open Court Publishing, 2017.	Wilson, Sharry. *Young Neil: The Sugar Mountain Years*. Toronto: ECW Press, 2014.
McDonough, Jimmy. *Shakey: Neil Young's Biography*. New York: Random House, 2002.	Riordan, James, and Jerry Prochnicky. *Break on Through: The life and death of Jim Morrison*. New York: William Morrow, 1991.
Savage, John. *1966: The Year the Decade Exploded*. London: Faber & Faber, 2015.	Heylin, Clinton. *The Act You've Known for All These Years: The Life, and Afterlife, of Sgt. Pepper*. Edinburgh: Canongate Ltd., 2007.
Linenthal, Peter, and Abigail Johnston. *San Francisco's Potrero Hill*. Mount Pleasant, SC: Arcadia Publishing, 2005.	Anolik, Lili. *Hollywood's Eve: Eve Babitz and the Secret History of L.A*. New York: Scribner, 2019.
Wall, Mick. *Two Riders Were Approaching: The Life & Death of Jimi Hendrix:* The Life. London: Orion Publishing, 2017	Kort, Michele. *Soul Picnic: The Music and Passion of Laura Nyro*. New York: Thomas Dunne Books, 2016.
Swenson, John. *Stevie Wonder*. London: Plexus, 1986.	Miles, Barry. *Frank Zappa*. London: Atlantic Books Ltd, 2014.
Brown, Stacy and Love, Dennis. *Blind Faith: The Miraculous Journey of Lula Hardaway, Stevie Wonder's Mother*. New York: Simon & Schuster, 2002.	Kubernik, Harvey. *Canyon of Dreams: The Magic and the Music of Laurel Canyon*. New York: Sterling, 2009.
Potash, John L. *Drugs as Weapons Against Us: The CIA's Murderous Targeting of SDS, Panthers, Hendrix Lennon Cobrain, Tupac, and Other Activists*, Waterford, OR: Trine Day, 2015.	Constantine, Alex. *The Covert War Against Rock: What You Don't Know About the Deaths of Jim Morrison, Tupac Shakur, Michael Hutchence, Brian Jones, Jimi Hendrix, Phil Ochs, Bob Marley, Peter Tosh, John Lennon, The Notorious B.I.G*. London: Feral House, 2000.
Kane, John. *The Last Seat in the House: The Story of Hanley Sound.* Jackson: University of Mississippi Press, 2020.	Curley, Mallory. *Beatle Pete, time traveller: annotated instructions for a cartoon book*. N.p.: Randy Press, 2005.
Rudden, Patrica S. "Stacking the Wax: The Structure of Laura Nyro's Studio Albums." In *Singing for themselves: Essays on Women in Popular music*, edited by Patrica S. Rudden, 25-37. Cambridge: Cambridge Scholars Publishing, 2007.	Barrett, Thomas M. "The Unidentified Agent: Illya Kuryakin: Making the Russian (In)Visible in The Man From U.N.C.L.E." In *James Bond and Popular Culture: Essays on the Influence of the Fictional Superspy*, edited by Michele Brittnay, 107. Jefferson, NC: McFarland & Company, Inc, Publishers, 2014.
Roby, Steven, ed. *Hendrix on Hendrix: Interview and Encounters With Jimi Hendrix*. Chicago: Chicago Press, 2012.	Lyons, John F. *Joy and Fear: The Beatles, Chicago, and the 1960s*. New York: Permuted Press, 2021.

Figure 3.2. Utilizations of *TeenSet*.

articles to many interviews) equating *TeenSet* to other reputable and established sources such as the *New York Times* or, in the case of authentic sources in rock, *Rolling Stone* magazine. *TeenSet* interviews with Jim Morrison, Richie Havens, Frank Zappa, Jimi Hendrix, Laura Nyro, the Grateful Dead, Arthur Brown, the Rolling Stones, Janis Joplin, Jack Bruce, and Neil Young (among many others) advanced a critical understanding of these artists and were conducted during the height of their fame.

THE PHOTOGRAPHS AND FILM

This chapter, thus far, has illuminated how *TeenSet* presents and shapes our historical understanding of popular music through articles and interviews used as research sources by subsequent authors. Many young women and men were not able to attend popular music gatherings in the late 1960s for multiple reasons, such as geography, limited touring (as the Beatles highlighted, limited venues were available for large acts and were not made popular until Peter Grant booked college venues), racial bias, and reputations of rock groups (drugs, sex, and rebellion). Thus, *TeenSet* played a pivotal role in presenting and curating popular music for a large audience (up to 250,000 were in circulation, not including shared or in-store readings). The focus of this section is the photography of Jim Marshall and, later, Bob Bonis and Marc Weinstein, as well as Oliver Stone's film *The Doors* (1991), thus continuing to convey how *TeenSet* presents popular music and the impact of such a presentation.

JIM MARSHALL: SHOW ME THE *TEENSET* PICTURES

While it is evident that *TeenSet* did purchase or receive photographs through its connection to Derek Taylor, Capitol, Brian Epstein, and NEMS (North End Music Stores),[18] it is also on record that *TeenSet* hired or collaborated with photographers, and the most famous collaboration was with Jim Marshall—who was already known in the music photography scene for his photos of John Coltrane, Thelonius Monk, and other musicians. While featured photography by Gene Trindl, Gino Rossi,[19] Chuck Boyd,[20] and Bruce McBroom

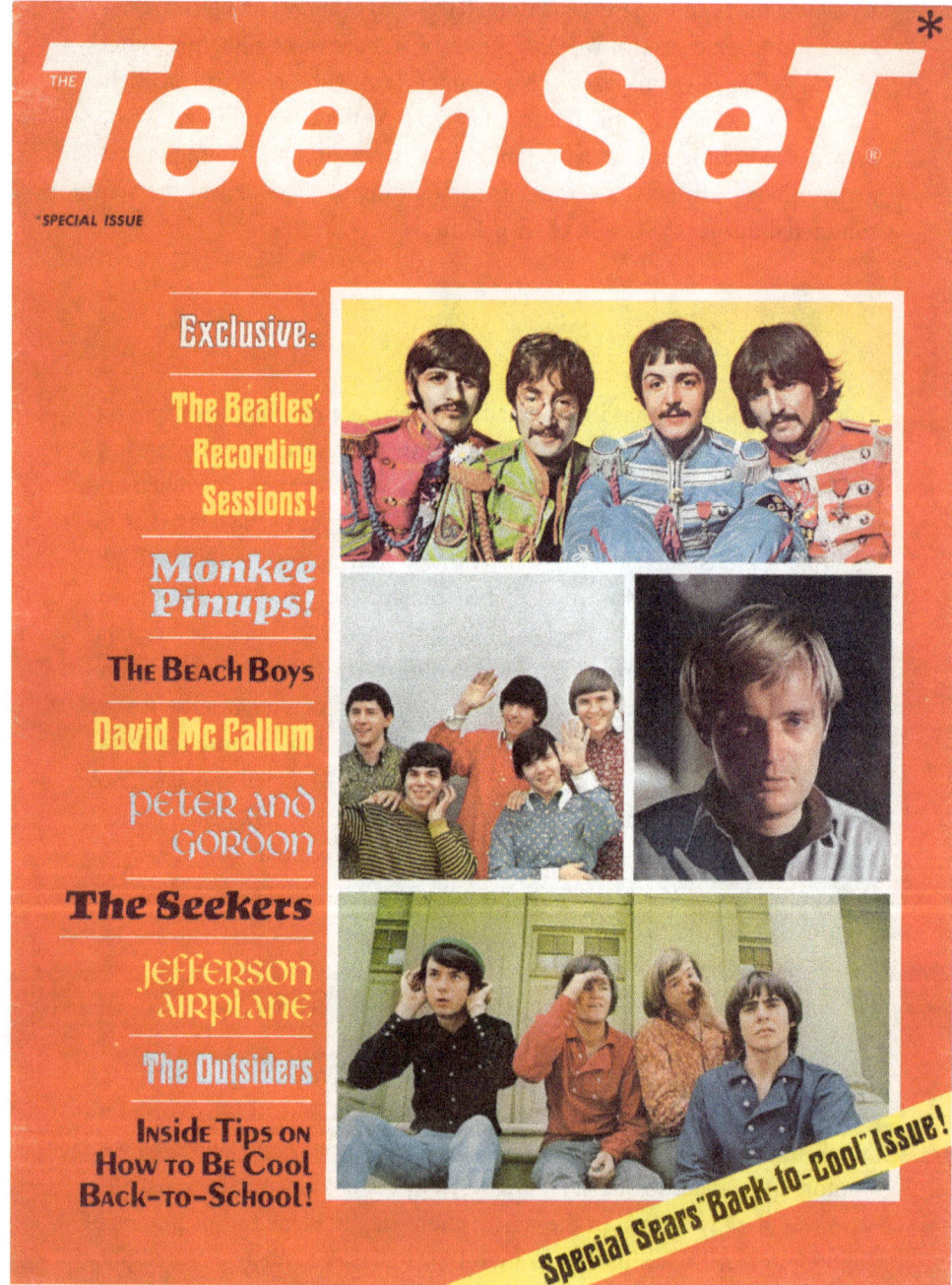

Figure 3.3. Sears's "Back-to-Cool" Issue, *TeenSet* cover, Summer 1967. Used by permission of Scholastic Inc.

Figure 3.4. Paul McCartney *TeenSet* cover, August 1967. Used by permission of Scholastic Inc.

needs to be examined in more detail, Marshall's music-focused photographs have become recognizable and, in many cases, iconic.

TeenSet featured over 250[21] of Marshall's photographs (see appendix 2) and continued featuring his photographs within the short-lived *AUM*. As evidenced below, many of Marshall's iconic images were exclusive to *TeenSet* until the publication of Marshall's photography books years later. As the majority of his photographs published in *TeenSet* do not (and did not) originally have captions, with two exceptions, *The Two Queen Bees of San Francisco Rock* and *Dylan with Tire*, here, photographs without captions will be referred to by a created caption based on the context of the image.

In 1967, a first-of-its-kind pop music festival, the Monterey Pop Festival, was held and captured by Jim Marshall exclusively for *TeenSet* magazine. These photos have been used in reconsiderations of the Monterey Pop Festival multiple times.[22] In *Jim Marshall: Show Me the Picture*, Michelle Margetts states, "I bet that if you were somehow able to poll the collectors of Jim's work, shots made at Monterey would be in the majority of those hanging on walls around the world."[23]

Joel Selvin and Jim Marshall's 1992 book *Monterey Pop* presents an account, through description, narrative, fact, and photographs, of the Monterey Pop Festival. Some of the photographs within the 1967 *TeenSet* article are featured in this text but not attributed to *TeenSet*. The only mention of *TeenSet* is in the caption of a photograph of Judith Sims (figure 3.5).

This *TeenSet* photo spread not only highlights multiple performances but also photographs of the crowds and the musicians around the festival. It provided readers with images of the performances and also a feel for the Monterey Pop Festival (and the developing counterculture) which, in many cases, would have been inaccessible to most readers. Some of the photographs have been reprinted in Selvin and Marshall's *Monterey Pop* and also in multiple other sources including books such as *Jim Marshall: Show Me the Picture* (2019); *Trust* (2009); *Proof* (2004); *Not Fade Away* (1997); and the 2019 film *Show Me the Picture: The Jim Marshall Story*, and they were featured in galleries and multiple unlicensed shares on the internet.

In addition to the Monterey Pop Festival, Marshall's photography was unique within *TeenSet*. *The Two Queen Bees of San Francisco Rock* (figure 3.6), featured in the May 1968 *TeenSet* issue, is a rare coupling of Janis Joplin and Grace Slick. Here, one is presented with two rock stars together who exist in the same category as their male counterparts: Grace Slick, the lead singer of

Figure 3.5. Judith Sims in the press section at the Monterey Pop Festival. Photograph by Jim Marshall. Courtesy of © JIM MARSHALL PHOTOGRAPHY LLC.

Jefferson Airplane, and Janis Joplin of Big Brother and the Holding Company. This image presents not only two women of the San Francisco scene but also two very different women. While both are rock stars, Grace Slick's previous career was in modeling, and Janis Joplin was cruelly nominated[24] "the ugliest man" at the University of Texas in the campus newspaper, the *Daily Texan*.[25] As Sheila Whiteley noted in the rock press, Joplin was often criticized for not being the idealized frontwoman.[26] This is brought to attention not to contextualize the photograph as a juxtaposition but because this photograph's rhetoric does not highlight the differences in the women or even suggest anything of the sort; rather, the photograph presents the women as equals with stern faces. This and other photos accompany an article titled "Positively San Francisco" by Robert Courtney that focuses on the history and development of the San Francisco sound and culture and ends by encouraging the readers to listen. "The San Francisco sound—the sound that swallowed Brooklyn and all the rest of the country as well. Pick up on it now."[27] Joplin and Slick are the only two females to be presented among other San Francisco groups, such as Blue Cheer, Quicksilver Messenger Service, Dino, the Grateful Dead, and Steve Miller. Here, Marshall's *The Two Queen Bees of San Francisco Rock* is featured first in color on its own page. The rest of the photographs follow, but the first image is of two women. The photograph presents readers with a representation of women not only in popular music but also as leaders of the San Francisco scene.

This photograph is also considered important as it is a rare occurrence of Grace Slick and Janis Joplin being photographed together. Marshall recalls the photo shoot in his text *Trust* (and later reprinted in the 2019 *Jim Marshall: Show Me the Picture*):

> It was in 1967 for *TeenSet* magazine for an article on the two *Queen Bees of San Francisco Rock* [this statement furthers that he knew about the article]. That morning, I went over to Grace's house and then had to pick up Janis. Janis wasn't in the mood to do any pictures that day, but I begged her and she came along. Everyone always thought there was a huge rivalry between Janis and Grace, but they were dear friends. This is the only time they were photographed together.[28]

TeenSet also printed a photo spread of Marshall's photographs of Bob Dylan called "Look Back." Unlike the others, this particular photo spread was of older photographs of Dylan. The objective of this very short article was to convey the changes not only that Dylan went through but arguably highlights changes in popular music and culture more broadly. The article's opening photograph is of Bob Dylan playing his acoustic guitar with a crowd of people in the background, most notably Pete Seeger. These photographs are from a walk around Greenwich Village in 1963 and the Newport Folk Festival, two years before Dylan went electric.[29] The article begins: "Two years ago? Or was it three? Dylan at the Newport Folk Festival, with less hair, more weight (above and opposite page), baggy jeans and work shirts, Pied Pipering a whole generation down his road . . . until it gets too crowded."[30]

These photographs were first released three to five years later in *TeenSet*. One particular image has moved beyond the rest to become more recognizable, not only as Marshall's work but as a symbol of Dylan's authenticity as a folk musician. While all feature recognizable elements of folk from Joan Baez, beat poet Allen Ginsburg, and Pete Seeger spending time in New York's Greenwich Village, the image that has gained the most fame is *Dylan with*

Figure 3.6. *The Two Queen Bees of San Francisco Rock*, TeenSet, May 1968. Photograph by Jim Marshall. Courtesy of © JIM MARSHALL PHOTOGRAPHY LLC.

Tire. It is often presented as an important piece in Marshall's body of rock photography and shows Dylan in an "everyday" manner. Dylan is picking up a tire and rolling it on the street, possibly something a young, bored individual would do. He is conveyed (as in all these photographs) as authentic, not as a star, but possibly as an auteur walking around a dirty street playing with a dirty tire and finding some inspiration in the mundane. The photograph is captioned in *TeenSet* as "a typical New York street (near left) was made untypical by his presence."[31]

Michelle Margetts states:

> "Dylan with Tire" is one of what Jim called his "hero shots," and it (plus the proof sheet or a vertical of the same moment) has been published in three of his books and included in nearly every article and interview that was ever done with Jim. It's an image so iconic and mysteriously compelling that it became much bigger than itself from the moment it was first printed; people have been trying to imbue it with meaning since *The Saturday Evening Post*[32] ran it more than four decades ago.[33]

While the image is not credited here as first being published in *TeenSet*, it refers to it as "iconic" and "compelling," which resonates with *TeenSet*'s original caption calling it "untypical." The photograph may have reached a larger and different audience when it was featured later in Marshall's books or documentary, but it was first published in *TeenSet* as the focal point in the two-page spread. In *Jim Marshall: Show Me the Picture*, Margetts further states, "Inarguably, Jim's most famous Bob Dylan shot is the one he called 'Dylan with Tire.' It captures such an optimistic and ebullient and inspiring time in Dylan's life—and also Jim's."[34]

It must be significant that Jim Marshall chose to sell these specific Dylan photographs to *TeenSet* first rather than a competing mainstream magazine. Dylan's popularity at the time would spark interest in the photographs. This also suggests that Marshall sold them to a magazine that would print them, that he trusted (as will be considered later in this chapter), and that valued the photographs.[35]

In addition to Dylan, within the February 1968 issue, *TeenSet* offered a double-sided poster featuring a Monterey Pop image of Jimi Hendrix by Jim Marshall on one side and John Lennon on the other (*TeenSet* began releasing these large 2' by 3' posters for their readers in December 1967, beginning with

Figure 3.7. *Dylan with Tire* by Jim Marshall, featured in *TeenSet*, February 1968. Photograph by Jim Marshall. Courtesy of © JIM MARSHALL PHOTOGRAPHY LLC.

George Harrison). This poster contains no writing, and the only indication that the foldout poster is within is noted on the cover of the magazine: "Extra! Extra! *TeenSet* spectacular #3 John Lennon & Jimi Hendrix! (It's reversible!) (It's 2' by 3'!)"[36] Although the issue contains articles discussing Lennon, there is no mention of Hendrix beyond the cover.

Unlike the John Lennon image on one side, Marshall's photograph is full of emotion and of a musician performing (of the five 2' by 3' posters, this is the only one within *TeenSet* that shows an artist performing). Considering Marshall's image of Hendrix more closely, it is clear the focal point of the image is Hendrix's face; however, his emotional expressions force one to explore the photograph to see what is causing such feelings. Hendrix lets the note ride as his arm windmills into a fist into the right-hand corner of the photograph. His facial expression conveys an emotion that is between a man and his guitar as he feels the sounds he is producing; perhaps—as

Figure 3.8. Image of Jimi Hendrix featured on pull-out poster, *TeenSet*, February 1968. Photograph by Jim Marshall. Courtesy of © JIM MARSHALL PHOTOGRAPHY LLC.

Paul Williams argues—the closeness of sex can be a similar closeness personified in rock.[37] The medallion on his neck looks like a piece worn by royalty, which he has arguably become in popular music history, but at this time, he was still growing in popularity. His open, American colonial-style jacket projects an image of casualness but not conventional, possibly a homage to Sgt. Pepper, as a contributing author of *Show Me the Picture*, Joel Selvin, describes: "All by himself, Marshall wandered around the stage that morning, taking pictures of Hendrix face-to-face . . . wearing that Sergeant Pepper military coat."[38] Rather, Hendrix's persona is captured, a persona that conveys the aesthetics of rock—that what he is playing is emotional and meaningful, something authentic and "in the moment," as if one could hear the elongated note ripple from the page to the ear. The angle of the photograph allows for a frontal view of Hendrix as if the recipient of the poster is sitting in the front row of the concert and part of the experience.

Ultimately, the angle provides a closeness to more than just Hendrix, but a performance deep in emotion, that the readers were there and a part of this event. While other photographs of Hendrix throughout the late 1960s feature Hendrix up close, only a few feature him performing this close and clear (a consequence of Marshall taking this photo during the soundcheck before nightfall).

Marshall's work for *TeenSet* overall has "played a pivotal role in the public perception of"[39] these musicians, not only from 1967 to 1969 when the photographs were printed in *TeenSet*, but up to the present day. Not only do they illuminate the body of work of photographer Jim Marshall, but they are important historical documents in relation to figures such as Jimi Hendrix, Janis Joplin, Grace Slick and Jefferson Airplane, Jim Morrison, and the Who, and, more broadly, to the Monterey Pop Festival, rock, and the 1960s. As historian Joshua Brown argues in the case of Frederick Douglass's portrait, "These portraits do more than simply document what Douglass looked like; they offer insight into his political choices, his self-presentation, and his attitude toward popular culture."[40] Considering the Hendrix photograph (figure 3.8), it is not a portrait per se but of Hendrix performing (even if warming up), and it is representative of more than an image of Hendrix but offers insight into Hendrix's emotions. *TeenSet*, in turn, by printing this image as a large centerfold poster, not only recognized the rhetoric this image personified of Hendrix or rock but made a statement that this was to be celebrated and appreciated as rock.

Furthermore, one uses one's cultural knowledge to attempt to decode or interpret such an image. While the October 1967 *TeenSet* Monterey Pop spread contains captions that allow for a guide to interpreting the images, this image of Hendrix first presented in *TeenSet*'s February 1968 issue is not accompanied by a caption, signifying that readers do not need one. The implication is that the interpreter of the text would understand who Jimi Hendrix is/was or could read the text through context and that Hendrix was recognizable. Additionally, this poster is of an African American male, and if argued that *TeenSet* was mostly white female readers, it would be an unusual choice for a 1960s white teen girl's bedroom. This is not to say that single-paged pull-outs or posters of the Supremes would not deck bedroom walls, but Hendrix, as a rock 'n' roller with his open coat, may be considered sexual and objectionable in some homes. Thus, the decision to create a large poster of Hendrix is a statement in itself and one that is representative of

Figure 3.9. Davy Jones *TeenSet* cover, September 1967. Used by permission of Scholastic Inc.

Figure 3.10. Mama Cass Monterey Pop *TeenSet* cover, October 1967. Used by permission of Scholastic Inc.

how *TeenSet* contributed to the way rock is considered today. This argument is enhanced by *TeenSet*'s decision to publish articles featuring images of bluesmen such as Howlin' Wolf, Muddy Waters, Lou Rawls, and Lightnin' Hopkins (figure 4.10).

Today, these photographs have been used to rightfully focus on Jim Marshall's achievements and legendary status as a photographer and document his presence within the popular music/rock world, but they also have multiple connotations. The *Hendrix Warming Up at Monterey* image is the photograph chosen for the publicity of the biographical documentary of the life of Jim Marshall. Yet some of these photographs exist as we understand them because *TeenSet* collaborated (on many occasions) with Jim Marshall, and the images were presented to the world originally in *TeenSet*. *Show Me the Picture: The Story of Jim Marshall* (2019) displayed many of the images within *TeenSet*; however, it did not mention *TeenSet*.

Marshall has received recognition for his work over the years and published many of his photographs in narrated collected works such as *Monterey Pop* or *Trust*. His fame in popular music photography, not including jazz, began with *TeenSet*. As Joel Selvin shared in *Show Me the Picture: The Story of Jim Marshall*:

> He sported an aggressive, in-your-face attitude at odds with the tenor of the hippie community. Still. He recognized the deep musical roots of musicians like Jorma Kaukonen of the Airplane, Jerry Garcia of the Grateful Dead and plunged himself into this exciting new music.
>
> Marshall's photos from the Monterey Pop Festival in June 1967 sealed the deal. His color image of Jimi Hendrix bent over his guitar after he set it on fire with lighter fluid was a stunning evocation of not just the event but the entire new rock movement. Ironically, the mainstream media at the time paid so little attention to the event that Marshall covered the show for *TeenSet* magazine. He shot a ton of photographs for that magazine of bands like the Byrds, Buffalo Springfield, the Who, Cream, and other teen pop stars on their way through San Francisco, long before the mass circulation magazines showed interest in the new music.[41]

Selvin suggests that Marshall's choice to photograph the Monterey Pop Festival was crucial to his future role, later described as "the godfather of rock photography,"[42] as his participation "sealed the deal" in his involvement in the popular music scene. Selvin also differentiates *TeenSet* from mainstream media. He places value on *TeenSet* as distinct from the common mainstream magazines and unequivocally states that Marshall's photographs were in *TeenSet* first. In correspondence with Selvin, he stated Marshall "shot Monterey Pop on her [Judith Sims's] dime. That classic Hendrix shot was on *TeenSet* assignment."[43] It was and is not surprising that, at the time, mainstream media and other music magazines such as *DownBeat* would be uninterested in this first-of-its-kind pop event. *TeenSet* should receive credit for both utilizing Marshall's photography and taking popular music seriously and also wanting to present the Monterey Pop Festival, the music, musicians, and the feel of the overall festival. Whether or not mainstream media would have covered the Monterey Pop Festival does not mean that Marshall would have been invited to or presented his photographs to another outlet, and if he did, our perception of the Monterey Pop Festival might be different.

Marshall opens his book *Trust* by specifically noting his time with *TeenSet*:

> There was a magazine in LA called *TeenSet* that I did a lot of work for. I'm not really known for studio work, but I did some studio portraits for them. I generally worked with five bodies, mostly Leicas, especially for black and white; the colour was usually with a Nikon. The approach was the same for me: try and get what you want from the artist. Sometimes a writer would do the story or interview and I would take photos but not usually at the same time.[44]

In this text, Marshall lists only *TeenSet* among the magazines and newspapers he provided services for, and later in the book, he features a photograph of the Who that he took and explains it was for *TeenSet*: "The Who in February '68. They were due to play the Fillmore West, and they were staying at a motel in San Francisco. I made them get up and come outside to have their photograph taken for *TeenSet* magazine. This was their fifth trip to the US, and they were just starting to break here."[45] Without going in depth, he mentions *TeenSet* in some context in almost every book he has published, and he specifically states that he took "portraits for them."[46] There is no doubt that without *TeenSet*, some of the photographs that contributed to Marshall's fame and portfolio as a rock photographer may not exist, or at least would not be as well known. Amelia Davis[47] did not argue that *TeenSet* advanced Marshall's career but did say that "Jim would pitch a story to them [magazines or newspapers], and if they liked it, Jim would shoot and decide what pictures they could use. Sometimes, the magazine would come to Jim and ask if he had any shots of certain musicians."[48] Yet this implies photographs that were taken could have been a collaboration between Marshall and Sims or Sims's idea(s) and that some photographs may not exist without *TeenSet* and this collaboration. In Sims's 1996 obituary, *Rolling Stones*' Ben Fong-Torres furthers this argument: "To photograph the San Francisco music scene, which she loved, Judith Sims called on the singular Jim Marshall, who credits her with some of his best-known portraits, including the one with Grace Slick and Janis Joplin together."[49] In my correspondence with Fong-Torres, he felt that even though Marshall was known for some earlier music photographs, *TeenSet* was helpful in advancing his career. Considering figure 3.5, it is evident that Marshall knew Sims before the Monterey Pop Festival, and the fact that it is included in the *Monterey Pop* book suggests that Sims was of value to Marshall not only in 1967 but in 1992 and worth including alongside Hendrix, Brian Jones, Ralph J. Gleason, and Joplin, among others.

With the collaboration of *TeenSet*, Marshall's photographs have contributed to how rock and specific musicians and events are personified. If this concept of collaboration is questioned, one must consider that Marshall covered the Rolling Stones' 1972 tour, and while not necessarily "hired" by *Life*, he did apply to take photographs of the tour, and although he had artistic license, the general subject matter was already selected by *Life*. It should, of course, be acknowledged that Marshall also helped Sims achieve the rock imagery desired for *TeenSet*, and without him, *TeenSet* would not have been the same. As a large part of Marshall's persona is built on the concept of gaining the trust of artists and trusting them in return, his consistent work with *TeenSet* shows not only did Sims trust Marshall, but Marshall trusted Judith Sims and art director Nancy Chester to present his work to readers. Selvin stated that Marshall "adored Judith and never thought *TeenSet* was beneath him. He thought she gave him great play and accorded him full respect."[50] In correspondence with Davis, when asked, "Would Marshall put his photos in a magazine or print that he did not trust or value in some fashion?" Davis responded, "Jim would never allow his photos to be used if he did not trust the user. He pulled his photos from many stories from bigger publications than *TeenSet* magazine if he felt the publication was misrepresenting the photos."[51]

Marshall's images have become extremely recognizable in the popular music realm and in popular culture more widely. The Marshall images focused on above have become iconic within the rock/popular music canon and context as they are well known and easily recognizable and contribute to the persona of a musician or comprehension of an event. Scholars Hariman and Lucaites argue that iconic photographs "reflect social knowledge and dominant ideologies, shape and mediate understanding of specific events and periods (both at the time of their initial enactment and subsequently as they are recollected within a tableau of public memory), influence political behavior and identity, and provide inventional (figurative) resources for subsequent communicative action."[52] While all the photographs presented in this chapter have grown in fame and recognizability in the rock and popular music realm, Marshall's photo of Hendrix has arguably grown to iconic status and contributes to shaping not only our understanding of Hendrix, the Monterey Pop Festival, and Jim Marshall's abilities, but of popular music. "By saying a particular image is iconic, one supplies a context that includes sharing,"[53] and *Hendrix Warming Up at Monterey* has been shared, with the development of social media, a multitude of times that cannot be accounted for. However, as discussed above, the recent use of *Hendrix Warming Up at Monterey* to promote the *Show Me the Picture: The Story of Jim Marshall* documentary and to commemorate Marshall's death in 2010 has contributed to the iconic status of Jimi Hendrix (and Marshall). Within the documentary, Selvin claimed, "The Hendrix pictures from the soundcheck and Jim standing face to face with this guy. Those photos are indelible"[54]—which, again, Selvin candidly credited these photos to Marshall's *TeenSet* assignment. These photographs have made a mark that cannot be unseen. They create a reaction and represent events not only in the time they were originally presented but in the present day and, no doubt, in the future as well.

As Hariman and Lucaites observe, "For some, iconic images offer ready examples of how social phenomena are aesthetic, emotional, embodied, material, performative, and mediated, while also confounding such binaries as high and low culture, official and vernacular discourse, and sacred and profane signification."[55] *Hendrix Warming Up at Monterey*, as I have analyzed, represents raw emotion and authenticity and embodies not only Hendrix but the aesthetics of rock. While it was not a well-known photograph when it was released as a poster in early 1968, *TeenSet* was presenting its readers with an image (among others) that is still used today to evoke emotion and an understanding of rock and popular music. At the time of writing, this particular poster had not been included in any February 1968 *TeenSets* currently for resale, suggesting that the posters were removed and hung.[56]

Figure 3.11. Beatles *TeenSet* cover, November 1967. Used by permission of Scholastic Inc.

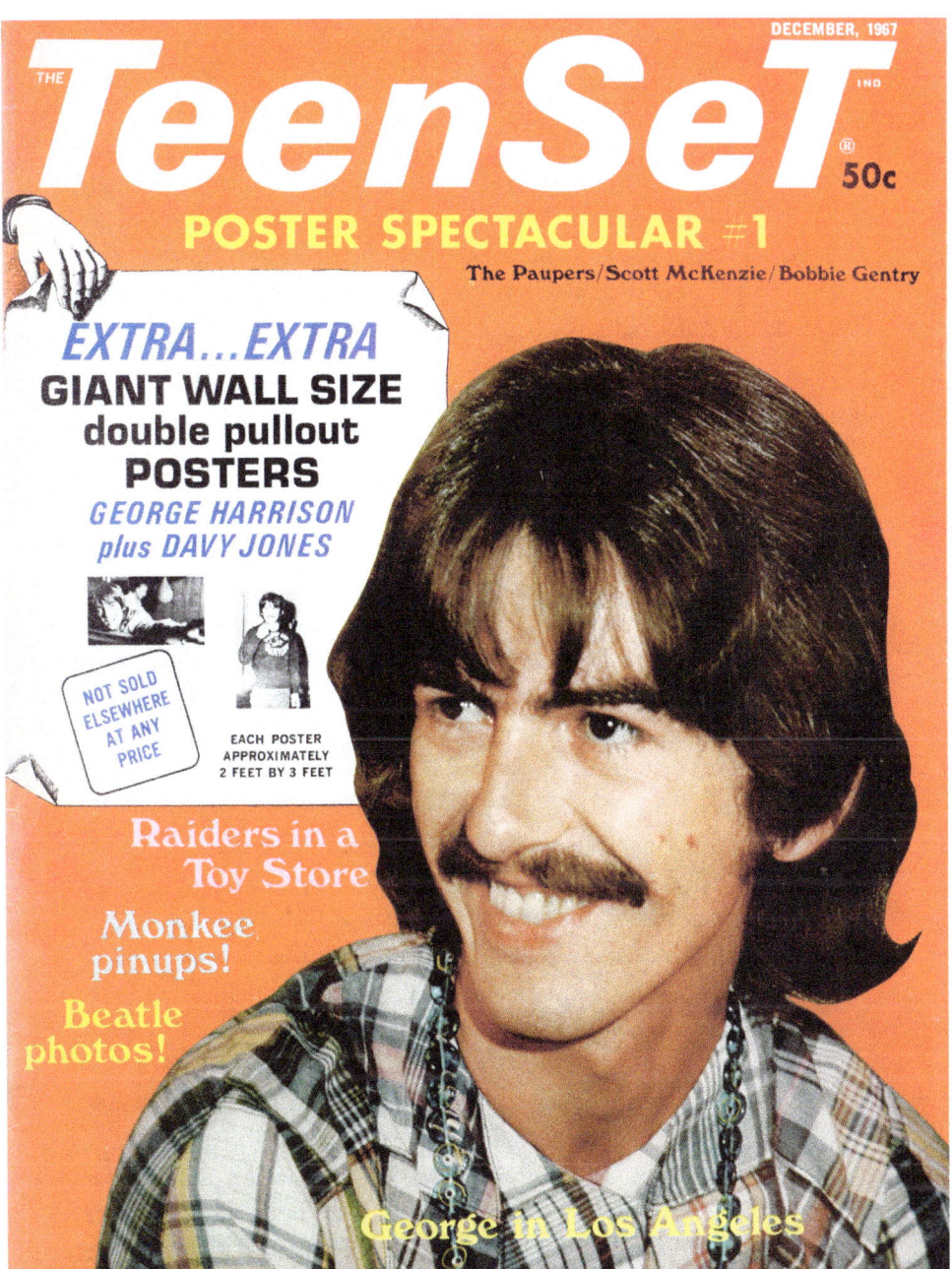

Figure 3.12. George Harrison *TeenSet* cover, December 1967. Used by permission of Scholastic Inc.

Moreover, more claims to the artistry of Marshall have been made throughout the years. SFGATE.com claims, "Marshall is almost as well known for his aggressive and abrasive character as for his photographs of musicians such as Bob Dylan, Jimi Hendrix, and Janis Joplin. His work, however, speaks for itself. The stunning shots in *Not Fade Away: The Rock and Roll Photography of Jim Marshall* (Little, Brown . . .) are images that helped define the artists they portray."[57] These now-iconic photographs have come to represent and shape conceptions of rock, authenticity, and personae (as considered previously with the canonization of Lester Bangs).

THE "LOST" PHOTOGRAPHS "HIDING" IN *TeenSet*

In 1965, young Beatle fan Mark Weinstein posed as a photographer and "used a fake press pass to get backstage at the Beatles' biggest show. The historic New York concert drew more than 55,000 fans, but there was only one other photographer present—and he ran out of film."[58] At that moment, Weinstein assumed the role of an official photographer and took photos of the Beatles. In an interview with *The Daily Beatle*, he shared his account and described sending the photographs he took at Shea Stadium to NEMS Enterprises:

> For the duration of the concert, I took photos from different angles and different sides of the stage. At one point, the Beatles' staff photographer, Robert Whitaker, ran out of film, and I actually gave him one of my rolls! I only did it so I could make a future connection with the Beatles. A couple of weeks later, I sent some shots to him at NEMS Enterprises Ltd. reminding him of who I was. Instead of hearing back from him, I received a letter from Tony Barrow, the Beatles' publicist, and some autographed promotional photos of the Beatles.[59]

The photographs taken by Weinstein were published in *TeenSet*'s June 1968 issue, accompanying Beatle fan poetry (figure 3.13).

In 2013, Marc Weinstein's rare Beatles negatives were auctioned for $46,700.[60] The photographs were originally published in *TeenSet* but were discussed in the media as if they had never been seen before. The high price placed on these photographs conveys their cultural significance. While it is likely that Weinstein is not aware that his photographs were published in *TeenSet*, the rights to his photographs of one concert became, over a long period of time, very valuable and recognizable, not just because of the publicity surrounding the sale but also because of their content. If they had not been good photographs, Weinstein would have an interesting story to tell but nothing to place a monetary value on. Whether or not their placement in *TeenSet* added value does not particularly matter, as *TeenSet* used the images to represent the Beatles, and no other magazine had access to these images. Again, *TeenSet* provides a deeper narrative in which only its readers, for over forty years, had pictorial access to the Beatles from another perspective.

Between 2010 and 2011, Bob Bonis's photographs of the Rolling Stones and the Beatles were published in two separate books titled *The Lost Rolling Stones Photographs: The Bob Bonis Archive, 1964–1966* and *The Lost Beatles Photographs: The Bob Bonis Archive, 1964–1966*. Bonis acted as a tour manager for both groups and took photographs of the bands as a hobby and for his own personal collection.

Bob Bonis's *Lost Rolling Stones* and *Lost Beatles* archives are presented as representing the Rolling Stones and the Beatles and documenting a period of time that is of value in popular music and rock history. In both texts, these photographs are advertised as never seen before, yet this is not entirely true, as some were published in and on the cover of *TeenSet*. Sims explicitly discusses the value she found in Bonis's photographs within *TeenSet* in 1966:

> I can't tell you much about the [Beatles'] Boston taping session because I was busy trying to take photographs, which will no doubt turn out to be blanks. After that attempt, all photographers have my profound respect; anyone who can understand all those little dials and meters . . . fortunately, Bob Bonis of GAC (who was with the tour on weekends) was snapping pictures just for the fun of it. I managed to convince him that one could take photographs for fun *and* profit. (And besides which, Paul had recommended him).[61]

The Bob Bonis Archive website states that the archive is "the most important, never-before-seen archive of rock 'n' roll photos ever discovered."[62] Yet all these photographs were not lost, but were simply not remembered, and were not discovered, but rediscovered. However, one must consider what makes the photographs important. The photographs are not only important because of the subject matter but also because of the intimate relationship the photographer has with the Beatles and the Rolling Stones on tour. The *BeatlesBible.com* argues that:

Figure 13. *TeenSet* poetry article including Marc Weinstein's 1965 photograph of Paul McCartney from Shea Stadium, *TeenSet*, June 1968. In the author's collection.

WAS IT REALLY JUST THREE YEARS AGO?
A BEATLE-LOVER'S MEMORY

BY AFAN

WORDS AND MUSIC BY LENNON & McCARTNEY

August is so many things
to so many people.
Seasons turning
leaves burning
romance ending
another beginning
sunsets rusty
schoolbooks dusty
tall corn stalks drying in the
  fields
  apples heavy with the taste of
late-summer sun
the end of something
the beginning of something else
Do you measure your time in
  August too?
And is your August spelled
  B-E-A-T-L-E-S?

RICHIE

That
boy
takes
your heart
away.

BEATLES FOUR EVER

1965...
Their magic year.
They had been here before.
(A hysterial first tour.)
They would be here again.
(A harried finale.)
But those years were ours.
1965 was theirs.
Shea Stadium...
Their magic place.
Their triumph of triumphs
as a hundred thousand
tiered like noisy layers in a
cake of kaleidoscope colors
came to say the word
(to shout, scream and cry or
  whisper it)
and the word was love.
On this third anniversary of
  their year
we remember that concert
and the other times and places
  we have seen them.
Remember them here on these
  pages.
Not to mention forever.

Shea Stadium. Three years ago. The Beatles.

PHOTOS BY MARC WEINSTEIN

The Beatles were already unfazed by the presence of photographers by the time they arrived in America in February 1964 and were happy to play up to the cameras before eventually tiring of the attention. Candid shots of them at work or play, however, are less common. The Bonis archive offers a true behind-the-scenes glimpse of the Beatles as they relaxed, played, rehearsed and performed.[63]

The photographs are regarded as "rock 'n' roll" and reviewed and sold as valuable, not only because they were branded as "unseen" but also because of their intimate behind-the-scenes nature. They provided an audience with not only images of the Beatles and the Stones but also an intimate and in-depth negotiation of them as stars and as musicians without a high awareness of a camera. While these images made interesting pull-outs, *TeenSet* also provided the readers with a different narrative of the Beatles as multiple photos from Bob Bonis were featured on the December 1966 and January 1967 covers (figures 2.2 and 2.3) and accompanied Sims's 1967 and 1968 *Beatlemania 1966!* articles reporting from the 1996 Beatles tour. For the Rolling Stones, also in the March 1967 issue (figure 3.14), Bonis's photographs enhanced the photo spread attributed to Bonis titled "As Time Goes By . . . The Rolling Stones."[64] The article acknowledges Bob Bonis's role with the Stones and boasts that *TeenSet* is the first place these private photographs were published. "Bob Bonis traveled with them [the Rolling Stones] for almost two years as road manager-coordinator, taking photos wherever and whenever he could, just for his own enjoyment and for the Stones' personal use. Here, for the first time in any publication, are some Bonis photos taken while on tour with Mick, Keith, Brian, Charlie, and Bill. Enjoy."[65]

The book jacket notes of *The Lost Rolling Stones Photographs: The Bob Bonis Archive, 1964–1966* state:

> Documented in these photos is this seminal period when the Stones made their transformation into the world's greatest rock 'n' roll band. And during that time, few were closer to the Stones than Bob Bonis, the tour manager for their US tours between 1964 and 1966. While on the road with the Stones, Bonis, a passionate amateur photographer with a keen eye, an innate sense of composition, and a deep love for his subjects, snapped some 2,700 photographs of the band—a remarkable collection that until now has only been known to family and close friends.[66]

Figure 3.14. The Rolling Stones as portrayed in both in *TeenSet* March 1967 and *Bob Bonis: The Lost Archives*. Photograph by Bob Bonis. Courtesy of © The Bob Bonis Archive.

While the text states that "he allowed only a handful of his photographs to be published in teen magazines"[67] and "almost all of the photographs in this book are being seen here for the very first time,"[68] it does not mention which photographs were seen or that they were specifically published in and on the cover or *TeenSet*, but only that, in general, these photographs have never been seen.

The *BeatlesBible.com* adds to this argument. It states, "With Beatles photography books becoming more common with each passing year, it takes something special to properly stand out. *The Lost Beatles Photographs* is, in every sense of the word, outstanding. That these pictures were unpublished for forty-five years remains mystifying, but their release is truly something to treasure."[69] I found it interesting that archive holder Larry Marion did not include the fact that these photographs were first published in *TeenSet* magazine in 1966 and 1967 (or rather that a dedicated Beatles source such as *BeatlesBible.com* did not note they were in *TeenSet* first). However, in correspondence with Marion, he felt "it wasn't specifically necessary to the point I was making,"[70] and he clearly valued *TeenSet* and teen fan magazines. In general, not crediting *TeenSet* may be attributed to its ephemerality, but

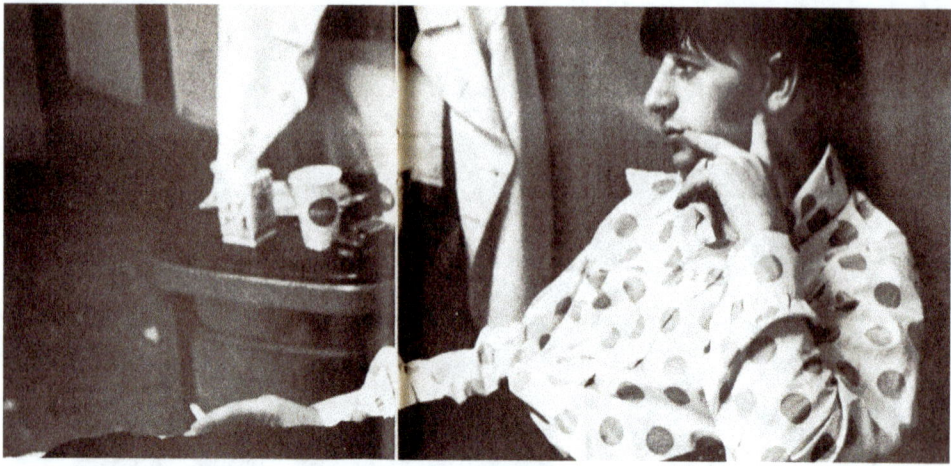

Figure 3.15. Bob Bonis's photograph of Ringo Starr accompanying the article "Beatles Mania 1966," *TeenSet*, December 1966. Courtesy of © The Bob Bonis Archive.

it also reflects the fact that *TeenSet* has not been preserved in the public eye. Yet to counter the concept of ephemerality, *TeenSet* has become a collector's item in multiple fan circles. The Bonis collection is remarkable; however, some of these photographs were seen by many readers and contributed to shaping an intimate understanding of both bands. Marion noted that "Bob always declined any requests to publish his photographs during his lifetime, with a very rare exception, *TeenSet* being one of them. Even when members of other bands on the tours requested his permission to use his photographs in their books (autobiographies), he refused permission."[71] This suggests, as in the case with Marshall, that Bonis trusted Sims and her editorial role with *TeenSet*. Ultimately, no other teen fan magazine had photographs quite as intimate,[72] and the use of *TeenSet*'s content is discussed as being important in archiving rock.

THE DOORS (1991)

In addition to text and photography, Oliver Stone's *The Doors* (1991) also utilized *TeenSet*'s 1968 June issue to further a musician's persona and help shape a narrative. The Morrison Hotel Gallery notes that "in 1967, photographer Joel Brodsky took a series of black and white portraits of the Doors and Jim Morrison, known as 'The Young Lion' photo session.[73] The movie's

Figure 3.16. Donovan *TeenSet* cover, January 1968. Used by permission of Scholastic Inc.

Figure 3.17. *TeenSet* featured in *The Doors* (1991). Screen grab.

portrayal of this event uses a female photographer to capture these images. During the shoot of the film, she tells Jim he is a 'rock god.'"[74] Jim begins to daydream about his fame. Within this scene, magazine covers featuring Morrison's image float over his face, ascending toward him (figure 3.17). Out of the six magazines to be displayed, the June 1968 *TeenSet* magazine (with Val Kilmer's Morrison character replacing the real Morrison on the cover) is the most prominently centered magazine at the beginning of the scene. On the left of *TeenSet* was *Jazz and Pop* and on the right, *Song Hits*, shortly followed by a floating sequence of *Crawdaddy!*, *Pop Music*, and *Hullabaloo*. No other magazine with the word "teen" in the title is included here.[75]

Morrison goes into a trance, and to emphasize his popularity, magazines that consider him (among others) are in the foreground. *TeenSet* is being sourced to solidify the comment that Morrison is a "rock god."[76] This signifies that *TeenSet* was seen as a contributor to the rock 'n' roll persona of Jim Morrison that is perpetuated throughout the film.

CONCLUDING REMARKS

TeenSet has been utilized as a trusted source to enhance our understanding of popular music and culture of the 1960s. Considering multiple texts that have sourced *TeenSet*'s content over the years, mostly biographic but some academic, it is evident that *TeenSet* has affected and influenced a historical discourse and has perpetuated the persona of authenticity for specific artists through articles, texts, and later, images.

As noted, *TeenSet* ceased to exist in 1969. The rock journalism discourse does not include *TeenSet* as a serious contributor to rock journalism. However, the texts and images (read as texts) considered here counter *TeenSet*'s omission. The multiple utilizations of *TeenSet* magazine within popular music sources solidifies *TeenSet*'s growing contribution to considering, unpacking, and understanding facets of rock and popular music, whether politically through Hendrix's politics, conceptually through the structure of Nyro's albums, or emotionally through photographs. No other magazine collaborated with Marshall as *TeenSet* did, and these photographs have become bigger than Marshall or *TeenSet* itself. Indeed, they have come to represent an era and many musicians. Bob Bonis's photographs have become more recognizable and have also contributed to shaping our perception of the Rolling Stones and the Beatles, and Sims had the insight to publish these photographs. *TeenSet* is an early repository of and contributor to what is now considered valuable rock photography. *TeenSet* celebrated and considered artists that it considered authentic and of value within popular music. To say that 1960s rock or popular music was *only* taken seriously by rock critics or magazines such as *Rolling Stone*, in turn, would be to ignore the clear contributions that *TeenSet* has made as we reconsider and revisit the past. In other words, *TeenSet*'s utilization (knowingly or not) is of value itself, as it reveals *TeenSet* as not only a serious source but also an authentic one that is still advancing, in multiple ways, our understanding of the 1960s musical landscape.

CHAPTER FOUR

TAKING POPULAR MUSIC SERIOUSLY

JUDITH SIMS AND THE WOMEN ON THE SCENE

I just presented good people in a kind of semi-gushing, appreciative atmosphere. But then in those days there was so much to appreciate.[1]
—JUDITH SIMS

Magazine scholar David Abrahamson argues that magazines are not merely a reflection of a period and culture but also convey values, rhetoric, and attitudes—which, in the case of *TeenSet*, were led and conveyed by peer editor Judith Sims and freelance staff such as Carol Gold. These values and this rhetoric have been illuminated throughout the development of *TeenSet* through Sims's editorial persona (her values and influence) and constant presence within the magazine and on multiple music scenes. Not only did she steer *TeenSet* in a direction that considered popular music and culture in a unique way, but she was featured in many of the photographs within *TeenSet* alongside the Beatles, the Beach Boys, Frank Zappa, Buffalo Springfield, Paul Revere and the Raiders, and more—many of which she kept in her personal collection until her untimely death.

Although the current discourse would lead one to believe the majority of popular music editing, writing, and scene coverage was executed by men and men alone, this strong narrative is grossly inaccurate. As discussed previously, women writers considered the early 1960s popular music scenes first, and many females wrote for *TeenSet*. Although Sims, as editor, was the guiding force of *TeenSet*, more broadly at work was a majority female freelance

Figure 4.1. Nancy Chester's John Lennon *TeenSet* cover, February 1968. Used by permission of Scholastic Inc.

staff that focused on the music and the scenes and cultural politics encoded within them. While not all the authors were women (and the number of male authors grew in 1969), specifically, her freelance staffer Carol Gold's involvement and coverage of the London music scene was invaluable to the magazine, introducing new rock acts to America before they broke.

Considering *TeenSet*'s audience, the majority of readers were estimated (by Sims herself) to be female, but the content, and, at times, the advertising, challenges the notion that "serious" popular music coverage is only conveyed by male-dominated publications. Therefore, below, I argue that *TeenSet* seriously considered popular music through the leadership of Judith Sims and female freelance staffers such as Carol Gold, and through its content and advertising, it was the first magazine to consistently consider music scenes—undermining what has been stereotypically conceived as a male-dominated rock canon.

JUDITH SIMS'S EDITORIAL PERSONA

An editor is often heavily involved in all aspects of the magazine they edit, which signifies that an editor has the ability to set the tone and values of a specific publication. Abrahamson argues that a specialty magazine is often successful due to what he refers to as "the editorial persona."[2] He defines this as "the voice through which the publication spoke to its readers, and it set the tone for the entire editorial contents."[3] Here, Sims is argued to have guided the direction and set the tone of *TeenSet*, and to understand Sims's role within *TeenSet*, one must consider the role of a magazine editor. Although she did not create or own *TeenSet* and she makes it clear, at times, that she did not always have absolute control over the magazine (especially under Regensteiner), this chapter will illustrate the ways in which she set the tone of the magazine. Indeed, *TeenSet* was ultimately reflective of Judith Sims's musical and cultural interests and values, with Sims being the only constant between the changing of publishers. Abrahamson also found that the editorial "persona of the magazine [any specialty magazine] was slightly older, somewhat better educated and more affluent, more widely traveled, and certainly more worldly [than the readership]. . . . As a result, the editorial persona was ideally suited for the role of guide, counselor, friend, and adviser to the reader."[4] Sims was slightly older than her readers, university educated, and knowledgeable about popular music and music scenes.

TeenSet provided something that the other competing teen fan magazines lacked,⁵ a consistent editorial persona.

Sims took an approach that many other rival teen fan magazines did not fully embrace, as she included an editorial column that she authored at the beginning of each issue. This editorial acted as an introductory point to the magazine, often containing whatever pressing concerns Sims felt needed to be vocalized, whether fan, musician, or whether it was magazine-specific or about cultural issues. This editorial was a constant that, with one exception,⁶ was always written by Sims. In this column, Sims spoke in an attempt to inspire, encourage, calm, reason, update, and, at times, criticize the reactions of the audience at hand. For example, Sims addressed angry fan mail, her own challenges, *TeenSet*'s direction, drug use in popular culture, and protest. Her "individual voice or persona also represented a set of values and attitudes with which the magazine's intended readership could be expected to sympathize."⁷

An example of Sims addressing her readers and setting the tone for the magazine is seen in an early editorial in her "ETC. ETC." editorial column (this column was presented with lower-case letters, "Etc. Etc.," until August 1967). Her first two editorial columns are an array of thank yous from the readers to publicist Derek Taylor, but in December 1966, she began addressing her audience directly. Here, Sims boldly addressed the "more popular than Jesus" scandal that caused many Beatles items to be destroyed by Southern American Christians:

> As I write this column, it's the eve of the 1966 Beatles tour. By the time you read this column, the tour, the excitement, and, hopefully, the controversy will have become history. But at the moment—7 p.m., August 6, 1966—the controversy is very much with us and serves to effectively dampen that happiest of annual invasions, the Beatles tour of America. Does it really matter what John Lennon thinks of Christianity, Jesus, and his disciples, or the future of the Christian religion? It shouldn't—he's one individual expressing one opinion. The public outcry almost proves his point: one little statement from a Beatle is enough to put almost the entire Christian community of America into a state of outraged panic. It would seem that Christians needed John Lennon's endorsement to function effectively. The Christians in Britain, oddly enough, feel no such outrage. They read that statement by John months ago, and there were no subsequent campaigns to burn Beatle records and books

or ban Beatle performances. But then, perhaps Europeans aren't afraid of the Beatles. They probably realize that Beatles are Beatles, and the mere fact that one of them (or perhaps all of them) doesn't follow the same religious code of ethics is hardly cause for panic. There's really nothing to worry about—we very seriously doubt that John Lennon is out to replace Jesus.[8]

The scandal began shortly after *Datebook* reprinted Maureen Cleave's *London Sunday Times* article, "How Does a Beatles Live? John Lennon Lives Like This."[9] As discussed in chapter 2, Unger was continuing to position *Datebook* as culturally progressive, even if using a sensationalist tactic of placing a racist word on a magazine cover. However, Sims did not address the possible sensationalism but rather shared her position on the matter, and *TeenSet* did not consider the pressing issue beyond an editorial, a fan letter, and a response to the fan letter.

The printing of the fan letter shows a different opinion than the editor's, which allowed Sims to respond to the controversy, furthering her expectations of readers and possibly sympathizing with the Beatles fans who were combating hatred toward the Beatles. The fan letter to the editor states:

> I've always enjoyed listening to the music of the Beatles and also enjoyed their movies. . . . I hope on the behalf of the many "Beatle fans" in the world this statement is not true, because if it is, I'm afraid the "Beatles" will go down in popularity very, very much. I hope you will print my letter, and also I hope you have an answer to why John Lennon made such a statement. I thought I was a "Beatle fan."[10]
>
> —Barbara Pannell, San Pedro California

Sims consistently responded to between six and ten of the letters in the Mail Scene department aside from the personal responses she mailed in return,[11] and in her editorial, responded to Barbara Pannell:

> If John Lennon made that statement—and he did—what possible bearing does it have on the Beatles' success? They are world famous for their musical, acting, and composing talents: they have never pretended to be devout Christians. They have never pretended to be anything but "rock and roll musicians." Is this how you and others reward an honest statement of opinion?[12]
>
> —Editor [Judith Sims]

Sims suggested that readers should value the musicianship (as Pannell wrote she did) rather than focus on one contentious opinion voiced by Lennon, and her responses establish *TeenSet*'s position on this issue.[13] She also encouraged teens and other readers to keep an open mind, a stance that reflects her values as an editor and, by extension, those of *TeenSet*. Sims's reactions to her readers also signify that she was taking her audience seriously, whether or not she was reassuring them or disagreeing with them. She made it very clear throughout the many issues of *TeenSet* that she was not interested in sensationalism (even if it was meant to encourage thought) by including articles that spoke out against it: "The few honest publications for teenagers are having enough trouble on the newsstands as it is, bucking the ever-popular rubbish like 'Mark's Wild Nights of Forbidden Love' or 'Paul Begs You to Be His Girl.'"[14] It is evident in *TeenSet* that her fandom and enthusiasm for music and culture were valued over tabloid stunts.

In the very same issue, Sims also presented herself as someone a reader could sympathize with through her retelling of when she received the news she was to tour (as press) with the Beatles in her article titled "Beatle Mania 1966: Or, Life Aboard the Yellow Submarine":

> I realize that the position of editor requires a certain amount of poise, decorum, and maturity if one is to function at all in the so-called business world. Still, there are moments when decorum, poise, etc., have no place in the life of a fan magazine editor; such a time was the night I learned I would be traveling with the Beatles during their 1966 tour of America. I didn't actually scream; I settled for a restrained yell, some broken chairs, and a very animated dance. And immediately started worrying about what to wear.[15]

While her editorial and responses to Pannell's fan letter conveyed guidance and advice, here she provided a scenario that readers could relate to as Beatles fans, a stance that is consistent throughout *TeenSet*'s entire run. For example, author Carol Tyler highlights in her 2018 interview on *Something About the Beatles* how important selecting the outfit she wore to see the Beatles was to her.[16]

Magazines in the 1960s labeled "teen" were known for providing sensationalized information and were continually accused by their readers, throughout the 1960s, of fabricating stories. Sims attempted to establish *TeenSet* as not only a popular music magazine that provided interesting perspectives but also as an honest and factual popular music source. Twice, Sims dedicated her editorial column to assurances for her readers, who questioned *TeenSet*'s honesty, that *TeenSet* was not fabricating information. In her June 1967 editorial column, Sims addressed readers' claims that *TeenSet* was lying about Paul, Smitty, and Harpo, members of Paul Revere and the Raiders, being married.

> The girls who wrote to us in anger declared that TeenSet lied: they "know for a fact that only Paul is married." I'm sorry, girls, but you are wrong and I am right (it's nice to be right for a change!). The discouraging note in this whole episode is the fact that an explanation is required. Teenagers are so used to reading "lies" that they automatically assume something they don't want to believe is a lie. That attitude doesn't say much for fan magazines in general. . . . I suppose I object to this because the same reading public that distrusts other magazines also distrusts *TeenSet*—in spite of all our efforts to present only the truth. I can't say that we don't make mistakes. . . . We did get a few letters from girls who asked, "Is it really true?" Their minds were not so closed that they automatically assumed it was a lie; they first tried to investigate it a little.[17]

Sims openly acknowledged that there were magazines that were possibly untrustworthy; as previously emphasized, other magazines were not printing such information, as they often presented a star as single, and Hollywood sensationalism was utilized somehow, in varying degrees, in the majority of teen fan magazines. However, her primary objective appeared to be to present *TeenSet* as a purveyor of honesty and authenticity as well as encouraging young women to be proactive.

In the same issue, the article "Truth or Fiction" appears with the heading "It's hard to tell with some fan magazines. This article is the first in a series which will hopefully make you aware of the difference."[18] The unnamed author (later announced as Janey Milstead[19] in August 1968) started to work for another teen magazine, thus the name is withheld. The article claimed that even Brian Epstein controlled information when marketing the "image" of the Beatles.[20] Yet fundamentally, the article argues that *TeenSet* is honest, and Sims stood by *TeenSet*'s claims (even if she noted that some misinformation may have been provided in the past).[21]

As the popular music landscape and counterculture rhetoric evolved, Sims eventually stopped addressing the concept of honesty in teen fan magazines as *TeenSet* became more interested in popular music and culture (such as alternative lifestyles) and stopped concerning itself with other teen fan magazines. For example, in an editorial piece considering the Grateful Dead, she praises their break from societal norms:

> They rejected society long before society retaliated and rejected them. They look outrageous—awful, even—and they're not about to change because the majority of the population says things like "but why would anyone want to look like that? What's the point?" And that's the point. No one else would, so it's a simple method of distinguishing them from those. (They are incorrigible, you see.) They don't even live like other people because they all live together, in a big house, wherever; and what's really weird is that they all get along. They like each other. Some say they even love each other, but we can't believe that because we know that we couldn't live with 12 other people and love them all. Terrible people, the Grateful Dead. Too bad there aren't more of them.[22]

Sims welcomed alternative burgeoning counterculture views and lifestyles and encouraged her readers to open their minds to the novel trends in popular music, such as the San Francisco scene and the Grateful Dead. Sims presented the Dead not only as musicians but as nonconformists in popular music. At this time, nonconformity was becoming more evident within rock music and the growing counterculture. Her final statement in the quotation above acknowledges the value in the Dead's nonconformist ways, and this value becomes evident in subsequent *TeenSet* issues.

TeenSet continued to project and reflect revolutionary rhetoric within the editorial column while the magazine was in the midst of changing its name. This was not only reflective of the rock and revolutionary rhetoric but of *TeenSet*'s position within the politics of the counterculture:

> I keep reading about young people having their heads bashed in. At San Francisco State, at Columbia University, in Chicago, Paris, Prague, and I'm reminded that a few of my older friends still believe that these same young people storming the ramparts of the Establishment, for better or for worse, will eventually become "mature" and will settle into the mundane responsibility of their parents. Fat Chance. . . . . And these same students and rebels who have let their blood, sat in cells, made their demand heard . . . these students will automatically become "respectable" and docile and suburban when they leave the college fray? They will walk away from the barricades, straight up to baby carriages, and will assume the attitudes of their parents? Surely you

jest, my friend. The speed of change is advancing geometrically. It isn't frightening. It's exciting, especially to one who spent her student years with the placid Eisenhower administration, to one who thought beards were radical and Hayakawa just a clever semanticist. Obviously, the times aren't the only thing "changing." People are. Young people are.[23]

Sims spoke (or possibly affected to speak) as a voice of her generation. Her voice not only resonated with the idyllic hopes of the counterculture that young people were changing, but she (alongside her freelance staff) was the one who brought these ideas to her readership, which was dominated by young people in their teens and twenties. She enthusiastically projected the actions and changes she perceived as exciting, instilling and introducing these concepts within the confines of *TeenSet*, as well as including sarcasm using quotation marks (as seen above) to challenge ideas. Implicit in her comments is the recognition that her readers are aware of what is happening in protests across the country and possibly in the world through various media. Thus, instead of only discussing popular music with her readers, she made it clear that, as the editor of *TeenSet*, she found value in these protests (and thus the revolutionary rhetoric residing in rock music and the counterculture).

Collectively, these editorials served as a constant reminder to the reader that the magazine was led by the same editor and contributor of many articles from when they first encountered *TeenSet*. Nancy Furlong remembers *TeenSet* as Judith Sims's vision: "*TeenSet* under Judith Sims's stewardship was the best the USA teen market had. I credit Judith with the ethos and vision."[24] Richard Morton Jack furthers this sentiment by claiming that the first issue of *TeenSet* was impressive due to Sims. "All in all, it [*TeenSet*] was an impressive piece of work—and its quality was down to its new editor, an Iowa native [she was not an Iowa native; she was born in Illinois and went to college in Iowa] and former schoolteacher, Judith Sims Canon."[25]

Through the "ETC. ETC." column, letters to the editor, and articles, Sims cultivates not only the values but the overall tone of *TeenSet*, which transitions from Capitol's promotional intentions at its inception to its subsequent reveling in revolutionary and rock rhetoric. She kept an open line of communication and always projected her thoughts and ideas, thereby working to establish a tone for *TeenSet*. She continued to do this throughout *TeenSet*'s existence and transition into *AUM* magazine. These values and attitudes considered revolutionary rhetoric, fashion,[26] sound,

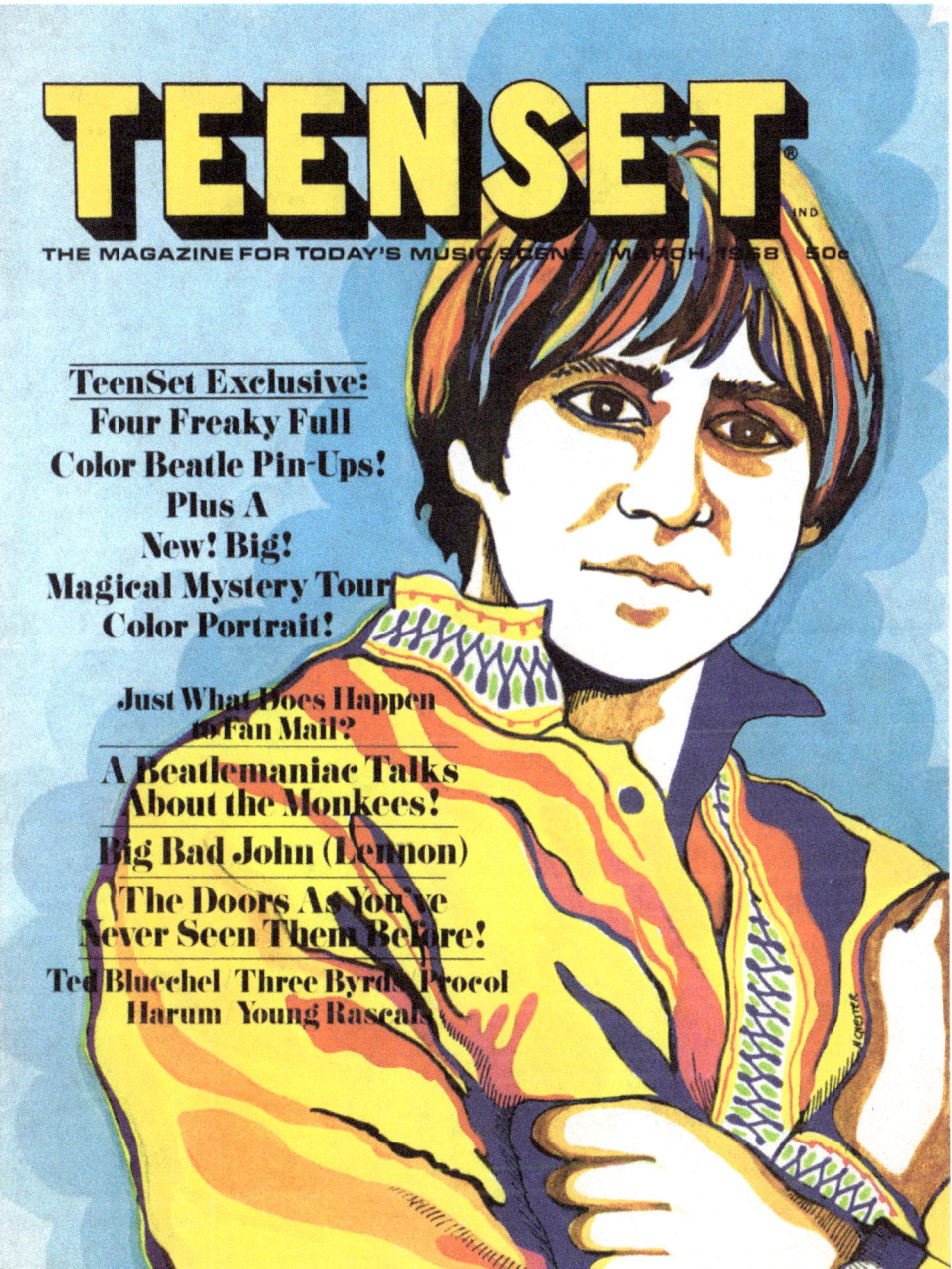

Figure 4.2. Nancy Chester's Davy Jones *TeenSet* cover, March 1968. Used by permission of Scholastic Inc.

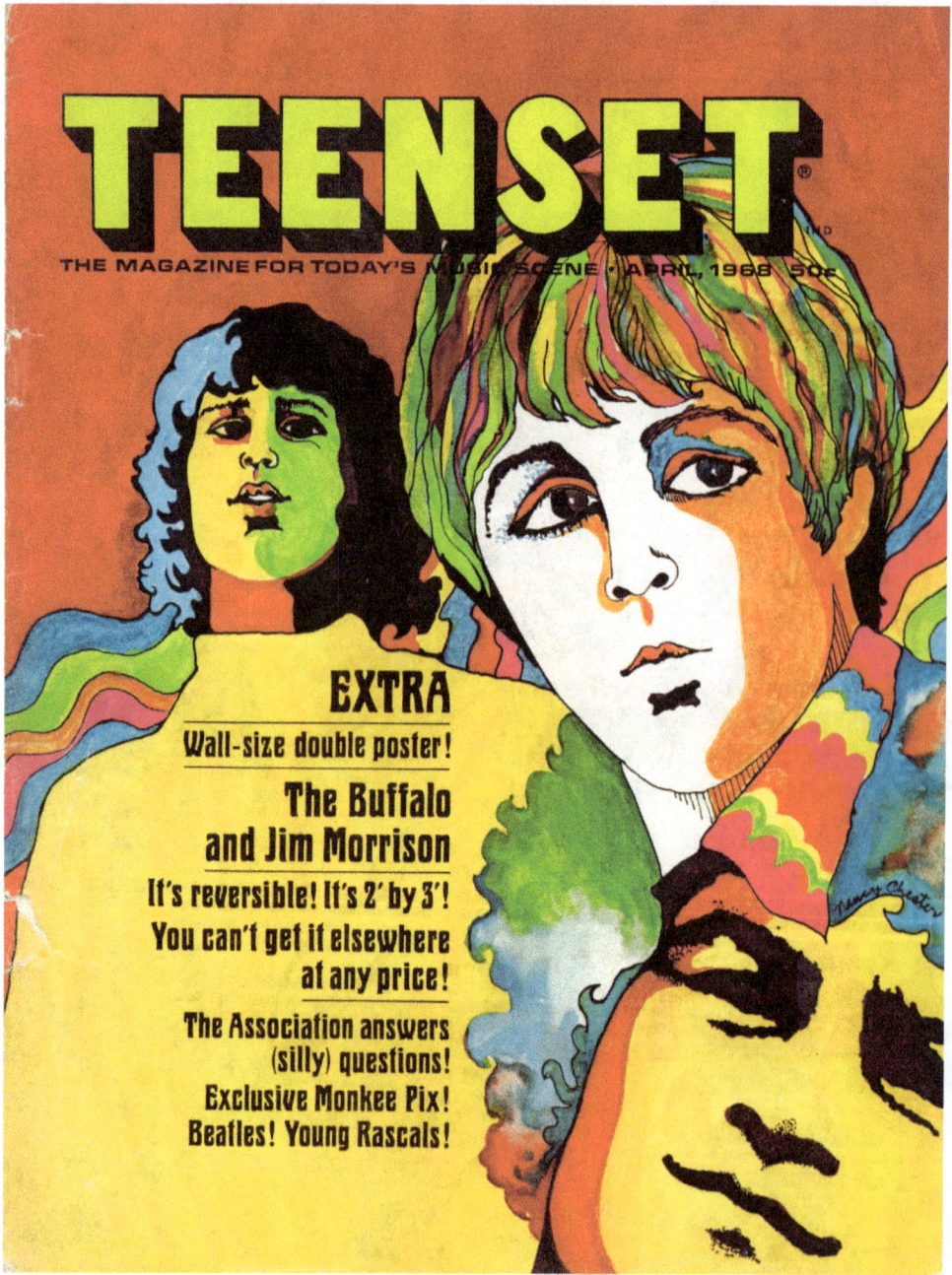

Figure 4.3. Nancy Chester's McCartney, Dolenz, and Morrison *TeenSet* cover, April 1968. Used by permission of Scholastic Inc.

lifestyles, race, and politics and were represented and reflected in articles, editorials, and commentary.

FURTHERING HER PERSONA: SIMS'S PRESENCE AND CONSIDERATION OF UP-AND-COMING ARTISTS

It is evident that Sims was vigorously involved in all aspects of *TeenSet*, as all other staff, other than her and art director Nancy Chester, were freelance.[27] Through her editorial role, she had the ability to arrange (at times, with the help of Derek Taylor) and participate in various events that gathered well-known and up-and-coming musicians together. The events, consisting of an "All-Star Scavenger Hunt,"[28] "Go Fly a Kite,"[29] "All-Star Croquet Match (figure 4.4),"[30] and "TeenSet's First Annual Christmas Party and Ice Skating Debacle,"[31] were heavily documented and published in the magazine, and Sims was always a featured participant. More often than not, there were several artists and groups involved, from Buffalo Springfield to Frank Zappa.

The first of the activities was arranged by publicist Derek Taylor[32] and freelance writer Michael Vosse. It was presented in the February 1967 issue with the subtitle "The First Annual *TeenSet* Grudge Croquet Match and Free-for-All." Although this article did not specifically consider the topic of music, it was a gathering of musicians such as the members of the Beach Boys, Buffalo Springfield, Chad and Jeremy, Frank Zappa, Van Dyke Parks, and their significant others[33] in the LA area—signifying a grouping of stars in one location (often considered part of the fading "Hollywood scene").

When asked about this particular event (as well as others), Buffalo Springfield's Richie Furay recalled:

> When the invitation came out, if your schedule permitted, you were excited to go. They were always fun events and they showed a comradery among the groups in LA at the time—some were very well known (the Beach Boys) and others, up and coming. The fun part was just getting together with one another, enjoying each other from a different perspective than the stage.[34]

In correspondence with Van Dyke Parks, he suggested the croquet match images featured in *TeenSet* were important: "All the pictures are confirming

Figure 4.4. *TeenSet*'s Croquet Match including Judith Sims, Van Dyke Parks, Fang, and Jeremy Clyde, *TeenSet*, February 1967. Photographer unknown. Print originally in Judith Sims's collection. Author's collection.

images of the 'Counter Culture'—a social work in progress, branding 'the sixties' with LA's emergence as *the* seat of a musical and socio-political force"[35] that Sims was part of and would convey with *TeenSet*. This presence allowed her voice of authority to grow in her editorial role within popular music.

Her authority is illustrated in December 1966 and January 1967 in her lengthy and detailed report of accompanying the Beatles on tour across America. While her reporting of the tour is significant, it is in the August 1967 issue that Sims shares her time spent in EMI Studio 2 during the recording of the Beatles' *Sgt. Pepper's Lonely Hearts Club Band*. Here, she reports on multiple aspects of the recording process, the Beatles' presence and interactions with each other, and various observations from her time in the studio. *The Beatles Book* photographer Leslie Bryce took photos of her time in EMI (figure 4.5); many were featured in *TeenSet*. These photographs placed Sims as present in popular music and presented *TeenSet* as part of the popular music arena.

Figure 4.5. Paul McCartney and Judith Sims, EMI Recording Studios, *TeenSet*, August 1967. Photography by Leslie Bryce. Printed with permission from *Beatles Book* photo library.

The photographs not only convey her editorial persona as an "unequivocal source of reliable and expert authority"[36] but also show her as "tuned-in" and present. When asked what she remembered about Judith Sims, Apple Scruff Nancy Furlong instantly remarked that "Judith was on the Beatles 1966 tour and covered that in *TeenSet*."[37] Judith Sims was on the entire (American leg) 1966 Beatles tour as part of the press entourage that traveled with the band. Debbie Gendler also remembered Sims in regard to her presence among the Beatles: "She went to Abbey Road Studios when it was still called EMI Studios. I was jealous of her ability to be close to the Beatles!"[38] This was the only thing Gendler said about Sims specifically. Sims's personal Beatles coverage was unrivaled in any type of magazine. This is yet another instance of Sims's presence within the popular music firmament of the period, and no other teen fan magazine or popular music magazine editor can make this claim.[39] I

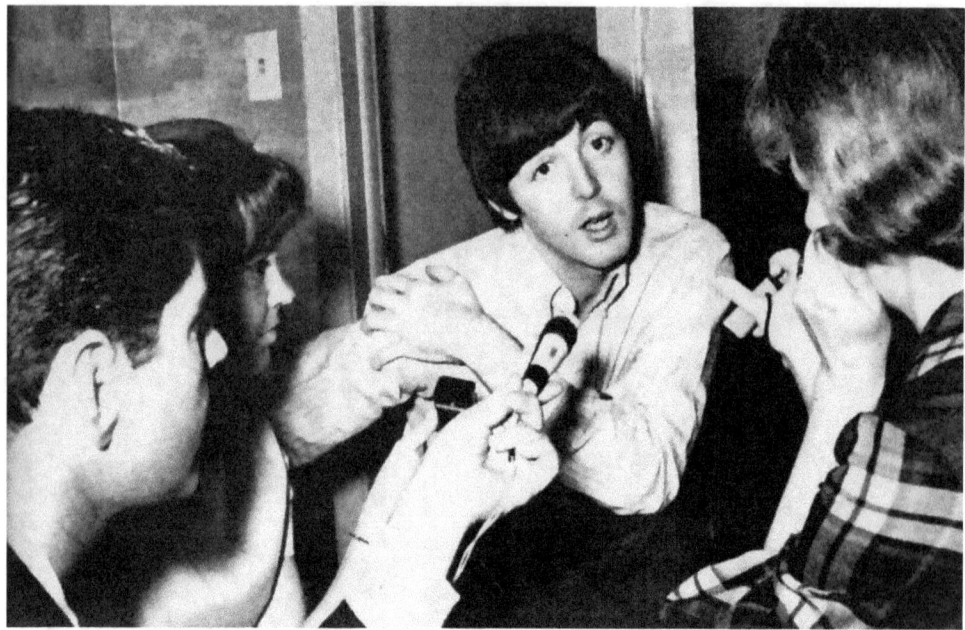

Figure 4.6. Judith Sims, Marilyn Doerfler, and journalist Jerry G interviewing Paul McCartney during a taping session on the 1966 Beatles tour, *TeenSet*, December 1966. Courtesy of © The Bob Bonis Archive.

argue that she not only conveys authoritative rhetoric but, by putting herself within the scene constantly and as the editor of the magazine, she had the ability to offer her readers experiences and knowledge from her perspective. In conversation with first-generation reader Steve Kern, he claims, "Judy was one of the most wonderful and essential writers/editors of the mid-sixties music era because Judy was there with the artists, completely engaged in the pop music world, and spectacular in her coverage of anything that was cutting-edge and important in the pop world. Especially in LA."[40] The images she was in were not of her posing face-forward with the musicians as a fan may take, but usually in a moment that positioned her as part of the scene as "close" rather than merely obtaining one-time smiling snapshots of her with the musicians.

In the early to mid-1960s, it was not uncommon for authors' names in teen fan magazines to be excluded, but by 1968, Sims's presence grew within *TeenSet* as she began including her name in all articles penned by her. For example, in October 1968, Sims is not only credited for writing the editorial and responding to letters to the editor, but she was also listed as the author

Figure 4.7. Judith Sims and Frank Zappa. Photograph by Malcolm Lubliner. Courtesy of Malcolm Lubliner.

of five articles, including a profile on Jorma Kaukonen of Jefferson Airplane and an interview with Mick Jagger (thus increasing her presence within *TeenSet*). Besides herself, the majority of the articles in this issue were written by women. At this time, *Rolling Stone* and other magazines were attributing almost all writing to male authors, writers such as Jon Landau were becoming more recognizable, and writing about popular music was growing as an art form. Crediting herself more (deservedly) signals that Sims felt what she was doing was noteworthy, and it also afforded the opportunity to express more of an editorial voice. In contrast, as *Rolling Stone* gained popularity, editor Jann Wenner wrote less, if at all. Moreover, in 1968, Sims began writing the "Hollywood Scene" for British *Disc and Music Echo* magazine. Each column featured her photograph. She was gaining status in the popular music journalism world in the late 1960s, and her presence was internationally known. Her future position at *Rolling Stone* only validated her presence, knowledge, and authority within popular music journalism.

In addition to building her presence, Sims provided a platform for many up-and-coming artists who would not necessarily sell a magazine, including Buffalo Springfield (a band that *TeenSet* covered before any of its rivals). She did so through *TeenSet*'s regular music profile section and events. Richie Furay confirms this:

> Judy was outgoing, very friendly. She took her role as editor of *TeenSet* seriously; not in any way as a "groupie" but as a professional. The groups that she liked, she made sure they had exposure in a very competitive print market. In a way, she was alone in who she presented to the public; some stayed with the "happening acts" who were sure to sell magazines and make money for them—whereas she didn't shy away from making sure new groups had a visual presence in her magazine as well.[41]

Furay's comments also further the view that *TeenSet* was reflective of Sims's vision, not that of the publisher. When asked if *TeenSet* was unusual in any way, Nancy Furlong replied, "Thanks to Judith, *TeenSet* championed new bands, which other teen magazines rarely did, nor did they focus on the youth culture scene."[42] While Furlong openly acknowledged she did not know *TeenSet*'s background or ownership, she strongly felt, after consuming many teen fan magazines, that Sims was the one who shaped *TeenSet*, included new bands, and considered the youth culture of the time. Kern remembers that *TeenSet* (and *AUM*) first covered new groups as well, even if they had famous members: "I like to remind people that *AUM* had the very first in-depth article on Crosby, Stills, and Nash . . . before their first album was released. When no one yet knew what a Crosby/Stills/Nash was. But of course, Judy knew."[43]

Journalism scholar Carolyn Kitch argues that "magazines offer a blend of authority and interpretation,"[44] and in addition to her authoritative persona,

Figure 4.8. Nancy Chester's Gibb, Slick, and McCartney *TeenSet* cover, May 1968. Used by permission of Scholastic Inc.

Figure 4.9. Jim Morrison *TeenSet* cover, June 1968. Used by permission of Scholastic Inc.

Sims also provided interpretations to her readers. Yet she presented certain artists in a less critical way than other magazines or journalists did, particularly Janis Joplin. In September 1968, Sims placed Janis Joplin[45] on the cover to accompany her article titled "Janis Joplin and the Boys in the Band": "I approached the Columbia rehearsal studio with no small amount of trepidation. After all, I had never confronted a female superstar before. With male superstars, there's no real problem because I'm female and that seems to establish some basis for a comfortable verbal exchange. With Janis, there'd be none of that Tarzan-Jane stuff."[46]

While this may suggest that Sims was submissive among male rock stars, it should be considered that her comment possibly suggests that she knew how to handle male rock stars, who were the norm in comparison to female rock stars. Yet as Sims notes in her opening, Janis was different. Many male rock stars had a "hard-drinking" or drug-using reputation, but it was unusual for a female musician to have such an openly disclosed reputation. Sims even refers to Janis and the boys as boozers: "I was way out of my element. Janis, Sam, and Jim Gurley (lead guitarists) and even Peter are boozers, you see, and I am a mere novice at that sport. A rank amateur led astray by hardcore professionals."[47] Sims did not seem fazed by the drinking, as she openly admitted she had been part of the festivities (reflecting the direction of the magazine at the time). While Sims witnessed and acknowledged Janis's ability to hold her own, she shared *her* impression of Janis with the readers: "The heated discussion was ended with bleary affection by Janis, who is a sentimentalist hiding behind a Southern Comfort image, turned to me and gurgled. 'I love these guys. I really do.' And I really believe her."[48] Throughout the article, Sims recognized and sympathized with Joplin's sentimental side. What Sims brought to her readers was a recognition that Joplin was a representative of the counterculture on an equal footing to her male counterparts and provided a more intimate profile of Joplin while still considering some aspects of "rock" lifestyles. The way Sims framed Joplin is how current female scholars are framing her today (see Whiteley and Holly George-Warren), unlike how *Rolling Stone* referred to her as the "Judy Garland of Rock and Roll"[49] in the same era (see Coates for further discussion).

Sims openly acknowledged *TeenSet*'s role when seemingly compelled to in her editorial of the very same issue:

> Oh, it's been one of those months again. Friends, acquaintances, even strangers have come up to me and asked, "Hey, you have such a groovy magazine, why don't you make it heavier?" What they mean by "heavier," I think, is a concentration of articles with in-depth musical exploration, hard-hitting no punches-pulled editorials, and more of the Real Truth (translation: more sensationalism). Like who smokes dope, and what really happens between pop stars and groupie-teenyboppers. Well, I'm not so sure that's valid for *TeenSet*. You can read the Real Truth, plus good in-depth musical coverage, in underground newspapers. All of these are aimed at the hip, older audience and give a good report of what happens. They don't, for obvious reasons, reflect a feminine appreciation[50] of pop groups: they don't feature excellent clear color photographs; they assume that anyone reading the material knows as much as does the oh-so-intelligent interviewer.... I'm more interested in pop stars as people than as manifestations of the "revolution" or as musical geniuses. Since in many cases a pop star fits into all categories, why shouldn't there be several publications covering the various categories? In other words, I just want to do my own thing (man). I like it, and while it may not qualify for the Literary Hall of Fame, it serves a purpose and hopefully gives as much enjoyment as I gain by doing it.[51]

Sims also made an important observation. *Rolling Stone* and others did not have many female employees nor any female staff writers; "obviously," as Sims remarked. As mentioned in chapter 1, women reporters struggled to earn reporting jobs. The implication Sims addressed here is that a hierarchical or "rockist" interpretation and way of reporting about popular music is the only one of worth. Her response illustrates the rock rhetoric she was combating: the idea that in order to be "serious," coverage of rock music must be from a male publication. The perspective within *Rolling Stone* was not necessarily reflective of female fans (as the majority of the writers were male). Sims acknowledged the "boys intellectual" club, as certain popular music outlets expected the reader to be knowledgeable about rock music. This gestures to the fact that there was a developing hierarchy within the rock press that was not welcome to *all* levels of fandom but rather was representative of the growing rock aesthetic. Sims suggested that the rock press was sensationalist, in contrast to the approach of *TeenSet*, reflecting the fact that it did address up-and-coming groups and scenes that other publications were not consistently considering.

This is not to say Sims did not value or celebrate the growing rock press trend. If anything, by the late 1960s, she began to hire more writers who wrote for publications like *Rolling Stone*. In 1969, she featured an examination of the then-growing rock press, which appeared in *TeenSet*'s final March issue. Dave Swaney's article, "The Rogue's Gallery of Rock Writers," acknowledges the rise in rock reporting and profiles critics such as Ralph J. Gleason, Jann Wenner, Robert Christgau, Richard Goldstein, Pete Johnson, Tom Nolan, and Jerry Hopkins, among others:

> Generally speaking, the rock press is, at best, amusing to record manufacturers, who ignore bad notices and mail good ones all over the world. . . . But the importance of the rock press is growing as writers build careers and reputations and readers begin to realize that rock and rock journalism is more than just a passing phenomenon. . . . The delightful thing about the rock press today, something to enjoy now and treasure later, is its individualism and lack of flackism.[52]

While the "individualism" did not last into the mid-1970s due to advertising pressures and jet-setting,[53] *TeenSet* acknowledges the value of rock journalism as it was developing and before many famous critics gained fame for their writing. For example, famed critic Lester Bangs's first *Rolling Stone* review, *Kick Out the Jams* (see Bangs), was published shortly after this particular article. At the same time, *Creem Magazine* also released its first issue. This particular article recognized that rock journalism was growing, evolving, and male-dominated as the content page referred to the article as "ROCK WRITERS/Men who shape our opinion"[54]—arguably a first examination of rock criticism.

Finally, the article highlighted critics Pete Johnson, Tom Nolan, and Jerry Hopkins, all of whom contributed articles to *TeenSet* in 1969.[55] This open acknowledgment of the consideration of rock journalism in *TeenSet* and recognition of three freelance *TeenSet* contributors only advances the view that *TeenSet* was a contributor to the then-growing rock press and the actual beginnings of the historical discourse. This also solidifies that while *TeenSet* felt the newly developing rock critic was of interest, and even if it hired some freelance rock critics, it had its own approach to considering popular music. Sims, thus, places *TeenSet* in a liminal role between the underground and teen fan magazines.

Ultimately, Sims did steer *TeenSet* in a direction Capitol did not plan for but also did not pay attention to. In conversation, Fong-Torres claimed that "to buck Capitol Records' interest in yet another fanzine, only a sponsored one, required strength and guts."[56] However, it is evident that Sims did not have full control over the magazine, as she openly lamented in her "ETC. ETC." column:

> My first ETC. column for this month was a long tirade against the Powers That Be and how they keep thwarting me in my crusade for new and different articles—but I threw that one out. After all, you have better things to do besides read about MY problems . . . and you (out there in readerland) don't have to be convinced of my purpose. The Powers That Be have to be convinced. And they probably wouldn't read or understand anything I said about them.[57]

When Regensteiner Publishing Enterprises took over the magazine's production, Sims was met with challenges from the older men (most likely "the Powers That Be"). Sims told Chester Flippo in 1974, "Both men were assholes [referring to Dick Ray and Sheldon Widmer], always trying to tell me what to do since they both had teenage children, which made them authorities."[58] Sims not only was accused of not being heavy enough (in comparison to male-dominated publications) but, in turn, was challenged by the men who were assigned to oversee the magazine production (but clearly, as with Capitol Records, men who paid little attention to the contents of the magazine). She was attempting to put out a popular music and culture magazine and fought to keep it from being solely a projected "teen" perspective, thus, as part of her editorial persona, she set a tone and established the value of a female voice within popular music journalism. Conclusively, Sims's approach helped her to obtain closeness to musicians and artists that allowed for special "get-togethers" and helped present popular music in a way that all fans could enjoy.

Taking Popular Music Seriously: A Consideration of Race

As noted in the introduction, women, especially young girls, were seen as passive—not serious consumers or producers of music. Thus, the contents of what they read about, in regard to popular music, have also been dismissed. As argued throughout this book, *TeenSet*, through generalization, is classified as a young girls' magazine that must have reported on big stars' favorite foods and colors, but the content of the magazine challenges the accepted discourse that *TeenSet* and teen fan magazines were devoid of any serious "rock" journalism or that only male-led magazines of the time took popular music seriously.

An early example to consider is female freelance writer Lee O'Dill's two articles, "Color It Blues" (December 1966) and "Rhythm and Blues" (January 1967), both concerning the development and origins of blues/rhythm and blues. The first in the two-part series contained images of Muddy Waters, Howlin' Wolf, and Lou Rawls on the front page of the article, and the second page displayed Lightnin' Hopkins, Eric Burdon, and the Paul Butterfield Blues Band (figures 4.10A and B). The physical aesthetics of these particular articles are striking, as in 1966, *TeenSet* prominently placed middle-aged Black men on its pages (notably as controversial as the shirtless Hendrix poster in a still-segregated America). By including this article, Sims (as well as O'Dill) challenged the "safe" status of all teen fan magazines with the consideration of race in popular music.

Within the two articles, O'Dill presents the origins and current influences of the blues and rhythm and blues to *TeenSet* readers. These articles were published the year after the signing of the 1965 Civil Rights Act, but still in the midst of civil unrest and systemic racism. O'Dill provides insight and consideration of racial politics embedded in popular music:

> To a five-year-old child, the blues are several different colors: his own eyes, Mother's favorite dress, Daddy's new car. To a forsaken lover, the blues mean the pitiless empty feeling in the depths of his heart. To the American Negro, the blues are, have been, and will be a way of life, and more importantly, a way of communicating the undeniable hardships that race endures.[59]

While O'Dill does not delve further into these hardships faced by Black Americans, she does set the tone of the article and signals to the reader that the blues is rooted in an oppressed cultural history.[60] The title also suggests consideration of race, as at this period in history, the term "colored" was a commonly used term to refer to Black Americans, even if here it may seem to be an attempt to refer to the color blue.

Howlin' Wolf

Muddy Waters

COLOR IT BLUES

BY LEE O'DILL

To a five-year-old child, the blues are several different colors: his own eyes, Mother's favorite dress, Daddy's new car. To a forsaken lover, the blues mean the pitiless empty feeling in the depths of his heart. To the American Negro, the blues are, have been, and will be a way of life, and more importantly, a way of communicating the undeniable hardships that that race endures.

The blues developed from the African rhythms slaves brought over to America and from America's first original brand of music, the gospel tune. It has been cross-bred with European styles into folk, country-western, jazz, rhythm 'n' blues, and rock 'n' roll.

Until just a few years ago, real blues singers were appreciated only in the deep South, in parts of Chicago, New York and other cities with large Negro populations, and by a few scattered folk-blues enthusiasts who eagerly and diligently scoured record shops for the early recordings of Tampa Red, Muddy Waters, Little Walter, Howlin' Wolf, Lightnin' Hopkins, Sonny Boy Williamson, Big Bill Broonzy, Memphis Slim and John Lee Hooker.

While American youngsters were digging the blues-tinged sounds of Bo Diddley, Chuck Berry and the Everly Brothers and the soft sounds of Bobby Rydell, Brian Hyland and Connie Francis, a few scattered youths in England were digging *up* those old blues records, listening and learning, then putting this knowledge to use. Soon the English invasion swamped Europe and America, bringing along with the fresh, young sounds of the Beatles, some hard, fran-

Lou Rawls

Figures 4.10A and B. "Color It Blues" by Lee O'Dill, *TeenSet*, December 1966. Author's collection. Used by permission of Scholastic Inc.

Lightnin' Hopkins

Eric Burdon of the Animals

The Paul Butterfield Blues Band

tic rhythm 'n' blues, or perhaps more correctly, blues with a very rhythmic backing. The Rolling Stones, Animals, Kinks, Manfred Mann, Zombies all recorded albums full of songs credited to blues composers and mercilessly recreated the vocal and instrumental tracks of the originals, adding far superior recording techniques and quite different personal appearances – which all added up to the American teenager's complete and absolute acceptance of this, to them, new musical form.

What in this hitherto unknown style touched the hearts (or more properly the "soul") of young people?

The sadness, most likely. This emotion has a particular appeal to these half-children, half-adults, who are just getting their first tortuous taste of heartbreak (other than that experienced when one can't have another piece of candy or go to a third matinee this month or learns that there is no Easter Bunny or Great Pumpkin). This quality, added to the physical charms of the performers, endeared these records and artists to girls.

And all of a sudden, boys started taking a vital interest in this music, too. It was not saccharine sweet or "sickeningly mushy" like so many songs girls adore (all the better to moon over an idol or boy-next-door). Here was a hardness, ruthlessness that appeals to every male mind. And so the blues were accepted by both sexes in this new, hipper, wildly clothed, long haired form.

But little by little, single by single, fan by fan, the real, down-home, earthy, authentic Chicago and Alabama blues captured the fertile minds and tapping feet of the youngsters, too. Primarily older (say 17 years and up) record enthusiasts, hearing "Little Red Rooster" or "Got My Mojo Workin'" or "I'm a Man" became curious about where these tunes came from. They heard the original versions and flipped out.

Suddenly, young blues singers appeared from all corners of the U.S.: John Hammond from New York with just an acoustic guitar and Hohner Band harmonica; Paul Butterfield from Chicago with that city's influences; Captain Beefheart and His Magic Band from Southern California with the strange name, but strictly down-home sound.

And the old bands, still in existence after twenty years of playing in half-filled bars, surged to popularity, performing now in folk clubs. Muddy Waters and His Chicago Blues Band hit the road, Junior Parker drew bigger crowds in the East. Something was

CONTINUED ON PAGE 57

In her second article in the series, "Color It Rhythm and Blues," O'Dill presents to *TeenSet* readers a consideration of race again: "But Motown does not suit everyone's taste. . . . Discerning listeners label this brand of music Negroes singing white music—this upsets music purists. Actually, they have fans of both races."[61] Here, O'Dill considered the concept of authenticity within music and a debate that considers what is Black music and what is white music—a topic that still occupies general and scholarly works (see Barker). Yet O'Dill argues that it did not matter, as the sound was popular and influenced many, from Paul McCartney to Neil Diamond. Her objective in both articles was to solidify an understanding of the origins and influences of the then-current and popular sounds and style within popular music, attempting to further an appreciation of the music inspired by the blues, but by considering race, O'Dill presented not only a serious consideration of popular music but also racial politics and a question of authenticity within popular music and culture.

She challenged gender norms, not only being a woman writing about the blues but also by acknowledging that girls welcomed the blues' musical influence before boys did:

> The sadness, most likely. This emotion has a particular appeal to these half-children, half-adults, who are just getting their first tortuous taste of heartbreak (other than that experienced when one can't have another piece of candy or go to a third matinee this month or learns that there is no Easter Bunny or Great Pumpkin). This quality, added to the physical charms of the performers, endeared these records and artists to girls. And all of a sudden, boys started taking a vital interest in this music, too. It was not saccharine sweet or "sickeningly mushy" like so many songs girls adore (all the better to moon over an idol or boy next door). Here was a hardness, ruthlessness that appeals to every male mind.[62]

While O'Dill did claim that girls liked the "mushy" sound more than the boys and thereby furthered the then-growing rock rhetoric, she gave girls credit for recognizing the power of the blues at their core, the emotion of the blues. O'Dill was not the first published woman to write about the blues and rhythm and blues, as in the 1950s Ruth Cage[63] and in the 1960s Barbara Gardner (of Vee-Jay Records) had briefly written for *DownBeat*. Yet in 1966, the story of the origin of the blues would have been largely out of reach to young females, and O'Dill and *TeenSet* presented a consideration of race and the origins of music to young readers across the nation. O'Dill, whether inadvertently or not, challenged an accepted norm that magazines in the category of "teen" did not take popular music seriously as the origin of the then-current popular sound was explained and considered. The existence of these articles and advertisements further solidifies the view that Sims was setting the tone early on of what type of information is meaningful to *TeenSet*, articles that encouraged an understanding and appreciation of all aspects of music.

FIRST RESPONDERS: WOMEN ACTIVE IN AND REPORTING ON THE THEN-CURRENT, UP-AND-COMING, AND FADING MUSIC SCENES

> As the editor of *TeenSet*, a teenage rock magazine, I frequently pointed my pink VW convertible north to San Francisco to check out the real action. The drive took seven hours on US 101, and by the time I pulled into the Hyde Park Suites on North Point, I was not tired: I was ready to roll.
> —JUDITH SIMS, reflecting twenty years later, *Los Angeles Times*, 1987[64]

In the last twenty years, music scenes have become a popular subject for academic study, as "music scenes not only foster local musical culture and experience; some have also launched national and even global musical careers and trends."[65] Music scenes vary in time and place, but "in the 1960s, certain cities were well known as breeding grounds for rock bands, particularly San Francisco."[66] One of the most notable aspects of *TeenSet* was that it was the first periodical (teen fan or rock press) to provide constant cultural and music scene coverage from Hollywood, San Francisco, and London. Sims and her freelance staffers (such as London's Carol Gold) reported on what was happening and where. Sims herself even considered the possibilities of other up-and-coming scenes. As *TeenSet* was based in LA, it was easy for Sims to keep up with the growth and changes in Hollywood, as well as San Francisco, which was in close proximity. Sims, Gold, and her freelancers were the first to bring consistent scene coverage and introduce bands to the US that were not yet national, beginning to break, or whose debut album was not yet released. Their efforts considering a music scene were unique to *TeenSet*;

Figure 4.11. Nancy Chester's Ringo Starr *TeenSet* cover, July 1968. Used by permission of Scholastic Inc.

Figure 4.12. Cream *TeenSet* cover, August 1968. Used by permission of Scholastic Inc.

that is not to say *16 Magazine* did not mention scenes such as San Francisco, but it was not concerned with growing cultural and geographic music scenes.

TeenSet had considered music scenes since June 1966. The recurring sections all feature the "In" in quotation marks, as in "what's happening" in that scene. The three scenes that *TeenSet* consistently considered were Hollywood, London, and San Francisco (as they developed and faded). These mostly monthly scene considerations were listed within the Departments section of the table of contents and usually consisted of one page with a brief commentary on music, venues, style, and anything that *TeenSet* felt was of interest within the scene. In its first consideration of music scenes, *TeenSet* presents the Hollywood scene rather briefly, introducing readers to the Sunset Strip, "Hollywood's Hippie Hangout": "The Sunset Strip's scene for the 'street scene' is 'The Trip,' a nightclub of 'nitery' where any night you can celebrity-gaze at visiting performing pop artists or take in the latest dance and farther-out clothes anywhere this side of London."[67]

TeenSet continued to introduce what was happening to its readers in Hollywood as various things developed. In October 1966, *TeenSet* mentioned the closing of The Trip, the temporary closing of which drove business to the Whisky A Go Go. This would be new to readers, who did not (and most likely would not) have access to the Hollywood scene, and it presents the importance of clubs within music scenes. *TeenSet* introduced a developing popularization of jug bands and recognized the growing popularity of the Nitty Gritty Dirt Band,[68] which did not release their debut album until 1967:

> The Strip-hippies have a new soul brother from nine to midnight: Harvey Miller[69] ("Humble Harv") on KBLA, who racked up fantastic ratings in Philadelphia and was the first in LA to air the Stones' 11-minute 35-second "Goin' Home.". . . The Trip nitery was closed for several weeks because of internal management problems, so the long-hair set migrated up the strip a few blocks to the Whisky A Go Go. . . . Jug bands are beginning to hit (thanks to some songs done by the Spoonful), with the Jim Kweskin Jug Band and the Nitty Gritty Dirt Band.[70]

In November 1966, *TeenSet* began providing more in-depth descriptions of the Hollywood scene at the time in a similar one-off article titled "Hollywood Group Scene" by reporter Sue Cameron, thus continuing a trend of introducing artists who were not yet known nationally, such as Buffalo Springfield,[71] the Mothers of Invention, and Captain Beefheart and His Magic Band, as well as introducing clubs that were part of the scene:

> There are many clubs that are frequented by top executives in the music business.... Among these clubs are The Trip, The Whisky A GO GO, Bido Lito's, The Brave New World, and Gazzarri's.... Without a doubt, the wildest of the groups is the Mothers, who recorded for MGM Records. They have made a name for themselves playing back and forth between Whisky and The Trip.... Pick up their album *Freak Out* and you'll really know what's happening.... The Buffalo Springfield probably does not ring a bell at this moment. But look out, because this group has got to be one of the biggest.[72]

This article discusses Captain Beefheart and Buffalo Springfield before their album debuted nationally (or internationally, for that matter). *TeenSet* continued to encourage its thousands of readers to listen to Buffalo Springfield: "In December 1966, the Buffalo Springfield, mentioned in last month's *TeenSet*, are slamming home with a fantastic song—one of several originals, all great—called 'Nowadays Clancy Can't Even Sing.' We hope their next will be their 'Sit Down, I Think I Love You.'"[73] *TeenSet* consistently covered Buffalo Springfield and encouraged their growth from their debut at the Whisky A Go Go to providing an editorial column upon their demise; as previously argued, *TeenSet* provided a platform for many bands. "'In' Hollywood," as well as many of the articles, continued to be featured on and off as bands, such as the Doors, developed.

TeenSet continued to consider and navigate what a scene consisted of as San Francisco developed, and the Hollywood scene was questioned as it was redeveloped. *TeenSet*'s first "'In' San Francisco" appeared in the January 1967 issue:

> This is normally (if anything is "normally" in this magazine!) the "In" Hollywood column, but we abandoned the Sunset Strip last weekend and headed due north for San Francisco.... And that town is, if you'll pardon the expression, groovy! We (meaning my new assistant, Ginni Ganahl, and mutual friend Tracy Thomas of Derek Taylor's office) (and your wandering editor, of course) inhabited Haight (pronounced "hate") Street for hours, visiting the Psychedelic Shop (books, records, cards), In Gear (sweaters, purses, authentic 1920s fashions).... San Franciscans don't merely advertise pop music performances on the radio, by the way. Art nouveau posters (or just plain

weird posters) were everywhere, beckoning us to dances, concerts, shops, or freakouts. Mouse Studios has been busy: several such posters were credited to the Mouse (a quiet little man with a bushy beard and violent imagination). Saturday night we grooved with hundreds at the Fillmore where LA's Byrds flew in five formation again.... Jefferson Airplane members were backstage at the Fillmore visiting the Byrds.[74]

Sims considered multiple aspects while reporting on the San Francisco scene. She brought San Francisco to many who, as with LA, had no access to the scene. The passage highlights the extent to which she and her staff were taken with the city, and their return for more scene experiences introduced the psychedelic growing poster art form and the art of Stanley Mouse and Mouse Studios (which, at the time of writing, has a cult-like following of avid collectors of not only Mouse but Grateful Dead memorabilia; see Mouse Studios). By May 1967, *TeenSet* (or, most likely, Judith Sims) mentioned that the Sunset Strip was declining, but San Francisco was a flourishing scene:

By now, *TeenSet* readers should know that the once-fabulous Strip scene is no longer fabulous. In fact, it no longer is. We sit around a lot and mope about that, but when we aren't moping, we're in San Francisco, where the scene is getting more fabulous all the time. The Sunset Strip was Hollywood's hippie scene, but unfortunately, there were other interests involved in the Strip. The "freaks" were edged and nudged and "encouraged" to leave the Strip.... San Francisco apparently has less fear and more tolerance of their "freak" element. To prove the point, San Francisco's pop-music-freak-out sub-culture [*sic*] staged a "Human Be-In" on Saturday afternoon at the polo ground with an estimated 25,000 people attending.... It was a peaceful gathering with no political purpose; it simply demonstrated the existence of the subculture.... There were *three* police at the SF Be-In.[75]

TeenSet told its readers that the Sunset Strip had been destroyed by those who did not understand the scene, illuminating out-of-touch commercial developers. The article argued that San Francisco was welcoming to "freaks" who lived a different lifestyle and/or had values that did not reflect the accepted norms, unlike what was becoming of the LA scene. Again, *TeenSet* considered and projected what it, or rather Sims, valued in a scene.

Furthermore, Sims spent time in Boston to consider whether the rumors of a Boston[76] scene were just hype or were, in fact, happening:

Suddenly, there were all these articles in the trades . . . about the fabulous Boston sound, the great new Boston pop music scene. . . . So we went to Boston to check it out. Surprise! There is no Boston "scene" to speak of. There is no Boston "Sound" as such. There are a lot of good groups there, but they're stifling from a lack of work and interest.[77]

She introduced clubs, groups, and, most importantly, discussed the definition of what a scene consists of:

1. Groups. Good ones, and a wide variety. Boston certainly isn't lacking in this category.
2. Physical environment—clubs, dance halls, parks—places where groups can perform comfortably and frequently to a large audience.
3. A hip audience. A large bunch of people who know what's going on, like it, and do something about it (like pay admission, clap, dance, buy records, etc.).
4. A relatively permissive attitude on the part of the local Establishment. There can't be much of a scene where local police and merchants restrict new clubs and harass long-haired musicians and fans.[78]

While Sims made it clear a scene did not exist in Boston, she also exhibited her expertise and understanding of what made a music scene by defining it for her readers. In addition, as previously mentioned, she provided the reader with context about the fading Hollywood scene, which most likely influenced her fourth guideline. This is the only time an East Coast scene is considered in *TeenSet*, but Sims's journey to and investigation of the possible growing scene signifies that Sims was attempting to hear and see the next up-and-coming scene rather than just considering the Top 40. She emphasized that her interest was in more than just the musical hits, but where the sound was coming from and what was causing it: "Where artists come together around shared musical experience that has a particular meaning in their common local experience."[79] Her Boston investigation deepened her editorial roots by setting the standard for what a scene was to her and her staff, further solidifying her presence and voice of authority within the popular music press. Beatles and second-generation *TeenSet* reader and collector Jeff Hoganson noticed this: "I loved how Judy immersed herself in the music scene at the time. Even though she was based in LA . . . she was completely switched on to the entire California music scene and beyond!"[80]

TeenSet went beyond LA and San Francisco to London. This column is presented in a similar fashion, covering nightclubs, musicians, and events. Freelancer Carol Gold, the permanent London correspondent, kept the readers up to date with London. In an interview with Richard Morton Jack, Gold recalled her role at *TeenSet*:

> In 1966, I decided to move to London for a while, so Judy asked me to be *TeenSet*'s British correspondent, as well as writing features and interviews for them. They paid me a decent retainer, and I'd type out my copy and mail it off to them each month. It was a whole lot of fun. I gained the trust of the musicians because I approached them as a professional writer, not a fan, never wrote anything that wasn't true, and respected it when I was asked to keep things off the record.[81]

However, Gold did more than just provide insight into the music scenes; she was, in fact, *part of the scene* and introduced future British invaders to *TeenSet* readers. Gold first appeared in November 1966 with an article titled "How to Swing in London without Even Trying." Here, Gold introduces herself as a "London-loving American."[82] Her introduction to London included the concept of different "in" crowds and scenes in London, and she introduced the world to "The Regulars" (later referred to as Apple Scruffs) in 1966:

> There's an "in" crowd of fans—an elite group of hardy pop followers who haunt the stars' homes and pursue their idols through work and pleasure. It was this fan "in" crowd that first heard "Paperback Writer" while it was being recorded . . . they were standing on a twenty-foot wall outside the EMI recording studios in St. John's Wood. . . . The stars know these fans and call them "The Regulars."[83]

She navigated the concepts of the "in" crowd and conveyed to the readers that her goal was not to be a fan but a friend to the musicians: "We wanted to be friends, not fans, and it's a hard rule that you can't be both."[84] Gold's article, while an introduction to the "in" crowds in London, set a tone for the reader that she would not report as a fan but as an insider on the scene. Her insider role became more evident throughout *TeenSet* as she was photographed with multiple musicians such as Jeff Beck, Jimi Hendrix, the members of Cream, and Rod Stewart. Gold illustrated the London scene to American readers

Figure 4.13. Janis Joplin *TeenSet* cover, September 1968. Used by permission of Scholastic Inc.

who might not have had any other outlet, just as Sims did with Hollywood and San Francisco. Gold claims that "you'd think after reading the millions of words written about England in just about every magazine and newspaper in the world ever since the Beatles exploded into prominence, people would know all about the music scene here. Well, 'tisn't so. This really is a world of its own, and the rest of the world sees only the surface."[85] Gold delivered this to thousands of readers, and in Apple Scruff Nancy Furlong's case, the news was highly anticipated: "Her news on trends, bands, and the general London scene was avidly looked forward to and read."[86]

The "'In' London" column became a regular piece that appeared in multiple issues as well as other articles authored by Gold. This column first appeared in the February 1967 issue. In this same issue, Carol Gold had two other articles covering Alan Price, as well as an article that would eventually become known as "Carol's Crisis" (with variations of this title such as "The Continuing Saga of Life in London"). The "'In' London" column not only kept the readers up to date with who was playing where and updates on their better-known pop stars, but it also was slightly ahead of the curve. For example, the Who's stage show was presented to the readers before their performance at the Monterey Pop Festival or appearance on the Smothers Brothers Comedy Hour.[87] While the Who's music was not entirely new to the US, the Who themselves had not fully broken the US market. The March 1967 "'In' London" column introduces the Who:

> It's getting so you have to wear a gas mask to see some groups perform. They've taken to smokebombs [sic], firework, sparklers—all set off-stage. The Who started it with their Happening . . . dry ice vapour mists about their feet during the act, slowly rising as the finale approaches when the Who destroy everything onstage and amid sparks, explosions and smoke, disappear. This has caught on, and now the Move set off sparklers and fireworks attached to their guitars.[88]

On September 17, 1967, the Who made their first US television debut, and it ended as described above by Gold months earlier, "when the Who ended an already explosive, nationally televised performance of 'My Generation' with a literal bang that singed Pete Townshend's hair, left shrapnel in Keith Moon's arm and momentarily knocked *The Smothers Brothers Comedy Hour* off the

Figure 4.14. Carol Gold and Cream, *TeenSet*, November 1967. Author's collection.

Figure 4.15. Carol Gold and the Jimi Hendrix Experience, *TeenSet*, August 1967. Photograph by Mike James.

air."[89] While this may have been a surprise to the viewers, it was not so to avid *TeenSet* readers who were expecting what Gold depicted.

As with the Hollywood and San Francisco scenes, Gold provided information on who was playing where and when new nightclubs opened, such as the famous Bag O' Nails,[90] or updated readers on the happenings at the popular Marquee.[91] She also introduced groups that were either unknown, remained localized in their fame, or broke later under different circumstances but were popular on the London scene, such as the Move, the Tremeloes, early Pink Floyd (which became more popular with the replacement of Syd Barrett with David Gilmour), Denny Laine and His String Band (known for the Moody Blues, and later Wings), the Small Faces (who became more recognized as the Faces with the addition of Rod Stewart from the Jeff Beck Group), and Liverpool's the Scaffold (with Mike McCartney, who would go on to record under the name Mike McGear). Additionally, Gold had access to the Jimi Hendrix Experience, the Yardbirds, Traffic, Jeff Beck, the Bee Gees, the Spencer Davis Group, Cream, and multiple others who were on the scene and had grown beyond the London scene. As with Hollywood and San Francisco, *TeenSet* and Carol Gold covered the London scene in more depth than any other American publication of the time. Like Sims, Gold was active in popular music scenes and heavily present in her articles about her life and her encounters with the stars.

Ultimately, Gold presented readers with the life of a single, twenty-something American female who moved to London to become part of the pop scene. She shared her experiences of London culture and mundane things such as problems with electricity or possible ghosts in her flat. Yet Gold presented herself as an active, independent woman who had chosen an unorthodox life, including having band members sleep at her flat, staying out all night with artists walking around London's graveyards, and a desire to be a record producer. Like Sims herself, Gold broke the accepted and expected gender norms in rock, not only as a fan but also as a young woman.

CONCLUDING REMARKS

TeenSet provided images of women in popular music fandom that have been forgotten and unacknowledged. As evidenced, the women of *TeenSet* were active in and promoting music scenes during the 1960s, and Judith Sims projected and developed an editorial persona that embodied a voice of authority and command within popular music. Collectively, these women participated in and navigated music scenes that no one else did consistently, presenting their readers with a glimpse into other worlds. Thus, the magazine showed that popular music journalism, written by women, still included the concept of involvement and devotion to aspects of popular music that did not revel in biographical detail, such as Davy Jones's favorite colors and foods. Rather, *TeenSet* considered facets of rock that were (and sometimes still are) considered "male." Christine Feldman-Barrett emphasizes[92] in *A Woman's History of the Beatles* (2021) that one can speak knowledgeably about the Beatles and still be attracted to them. This argument is further evidenced here by *TeenSet*, as it conveys the possibility that a young woman could, for instance, enter a conversation about Buffalo Springfield and have just as much knowledge as her male counterpart but also think Steven Stills is handsome.

Chapter Five

"A NIFTY MUSIC MAGAZINE WITH A MISLEADING NAME"

TeenSet's Duality, Representation of and Interaction with an Evolving Musical and Cultural Landscape

Yesterday, I was down at the store, looking at magazines, and I spotted yours. The thing that captured my interest was the unusual cover.
—Sukey Small[1]

I wish I had adequate words to describe how important I feel Judy was to music history. And how important *TeenSet*'s role was. Yes, the magazine name was horrible. Yes, it was wonderfully LA-centric. But once you latched on to the writing going on at the magazine, *TeenSet* proved to be invaluable. Month by month. Our lives and music were captured in this tiny publication that no one in the outer world paid attention to. All through those crazy, beautiful, horrible, chaotic, unforgettable times.
—Steve Kern[2]

Historically, magazines establish a continuous formula that they rarely veer from. As discussed in chapter 1, the majority of magazines classified as teen fan magazines were cemented within the young preteen and teenage culture. When Sims became editor of *TeenSet*, Capitol Records had not yet established a strong formula for their new venture, as it was originally used as a promotional tool focusing on Capitol artists. However, as Sims immersed

Figure 5.1. Mick Jagger *TeenSet* cover, October 1968. Used by permission of Scholastic Inc.

herself in multiple music scenes and Capitol and Regensteiner Publishing Enterprises paid little attention to the magazine, Sims transformed *TeenSet*. By late 1967, *TeenSet* was transforming and featuring artists and music that were not necessarily charting as the publication began to be associated with countercultural and revolutionary or rock rhetoric; the Top 40 was not necessarily a concern. Therefore, this chapter unpacks the complexities of the transition of *TeenSet* magazine to *AUM*, as well as the evolving musical and cultural landscape of the 1960s that was reflected and constructed throughout the transformation.

TeenSet reflected, constructed, and attempted to navigate an evolving musical and cultural landscape where popular music genres were developing with specific aesthetics attached to the genre of rock. As *TeenSet* evolved, it grew with its readers and attempted to follow them from teenhood to adulthood, not only through a slow transformation of the presentation and focus through its cover designs, featured groups, and musicians but also by the changing of the name of the magazine. Apple Scruff Nancy Furlong advances this by arguing that *TeenSet* grew with its readers:

> The earlier issues were not as reflective of the youth culture—the emerging new political consciousness, global awareness—that the music and artists *TeenSet* reported on, were set or marinating in. Imagine us, their readership, as Jr. High School or High School students becoming College students—*TeenSet* grew with us. Times were changing, awareness was growing, and *TeenSet* captured all of that in their articles.[3]

Carl Ritter's letter to the editor printed in 1969 adds weight to her argument and highlighted his interest in *TeenSet*'s evolution:

> *TeenSet* has suddenly changed again. You see, about a year ago, I was ready, I thought, as a college Freshman, to give up "childish things." [sic] *TeenSet* being one item in the gray area of child-adult, I figured I'd quit buying it. . . . Then, I discovered *Crawdaddy!* and *Eye* and thought, well, *TeenSet* is not where I'm at, so I'll drop it. Then, this fall, you sent my issue to me at college. . . . I thought I'd never see it again and you sent it to me full of the Grateful Dead and Quicksilver and Jorma and I was very very high. . . . Shirley's ["Shirley Poston" was a pen name for Janey Milsted] social commentary. Very good.

> Don't get heavy. *Crawdaddy!* does that. I think you know they can be a little too intellectual at times.[4]

In the same issue, Sims addressed her readers to convey the complexities of *TeenSet* and the changes that were to come:

> Here we are again at the crossroads, perched on the horns of ying and yang, straddling the fence between pillar and post. Sounds comfortable, doesn't it? For the past three years, *TeenSet* had been a magazine; a pop music magazine. It has progressed from a simple reflection of the Top 40 to an almost semi-underground status, and our audience has grown older and more sophisticated, and more demanding. The time has come, the Walrus said, to take heed, make haste, and make changes. Keeping up with our readers is one of the most confusing, hectic, frustrating and rewarding tasks we face and the only one that really matters. Hence, you will notice some changes in this issue. More guts, more speaking out, more articles of general interest and not necessarily related to music. It's only the beginning, and with a little help from our friends, we will continue to change with you, for you, and because of you.[5]

Here, Sims focused on change, not only of the magazine but the growth and interests of the readers. She refers to *TeenSet* not as a fan magazine as she had done in the past but as a "pop music" magazine that was "semi-underground." *TeenSet* could never have been an underground paper as Capitol Records created it to encourage profits—Capitol was focused on their artists and Top 40 artists for the first two volumes. Yet after Capitol relinquished control of the magazine, its identity continued to change under Sims's editorial oversight. As Sims argues above, *TeenSet* was no longer reflecting only the Top 40 (as, say, *16 Magazine* and *Tiger Beat* were).

While *TeenSet* openly struggled with its identity and held a liminal position between the connotations of a teen fan magazine and the underground press (albeit not necessarily intentionally), it attempted to navigate the evolving cultural and musical landscapes. Furthermore, no other magazine of the time went through such a transformation. Thus, through an analysis of the changing cover, selected content, and the name of the magazine, this chapter shows *TeenSet*'s contribution to cultural commentary through its navigation of its position within periodicals of the time and further conveys how it presented popular music beyond the celebrity.

"Covering" a Changing Musical and Cultural Landscape

As *TeenSet* navigated an evolving popular music landscape, it increasingly considered revolutionary and counterculture rhetoric, and this is evident not only in its content but on the covers of the magazine. *TeenSet*'s cover designs changed dramatically over the course of the magazine's existence as the imagery, typeface, artist selection, and overall design reflected this evolution and rhetoric.

The modifications to the cover were not especially striking at first but were visually distinct. The earliest covers featured collages of musicians placed at the center of the magazine. However, by January 1967, with the arrival of a new art director, Nancy Chester, *TeenSet* shifted to publishing a single image of an artist or group (with the exception of the March 1967 issue) on the magazine's cover. While the change to the cover format seen in figure 2.3 was small, it signified a refined focus—no longer was *TeenSet* enticing readers with collages of multiple stars. As readers browse magazine stands, each cover "helps us to distinguish one magazine from another,"[6] thus, by selecting a bold, single image, *TeenSet*'s cover stood out from its competitors, such as *16 Magazine* or *Tiger Beat*, which had similar multi-image, collage-type formats, evident in figures 5.5 and 5.6.

The most notable change occurred to the cover of the October 1967 issue (figure 3.10). Although it still contained a singular image (of Mama Cass in a crowd) with the usual cover lines and a briefing of what can be found inside, the background was wildly different. While previous issues only featured a solid color, this background was a colorful bohemian tapestry-like pattern—a pattern Janis Joplin might wear. In the bottom left corner, there is a banner stating, "Fantastic! *TeenSet* at the Monterey Pop Festival,"[7] signifying to the reader that there is something unique within this issue—*TeenSet*'s coverage of the Monterey Pop Festival. As Selvin argues that "the Monterey International Pop Festival was not only an unprecedented and unmatched collection of talent; the three-day event was also an axis on which the world of rock music turned. Music would never be the same again"[8]—and neither would *TeenSet*. This specific *TeenSet* cover and festival coverage signaled a coming change to the magazine, both aesthetically (in terms of the covers) and in its content. Jack furthers this sentiment by claiming that the coverage of the Monterey Pop Festival itself inspired *TeenSet* and Sims, and the "spirit [of the festival] seemed to inform *TeenSet* thenceforth."[9] However, it was not that

Figure 5.2. *Yellow Submarine* special *TeenSet* cover, November/December 1968. Used by permission of Scholastic Inc.

Figure 5.3. Grace Slick blackface *TeenSet* cover, January 1969. Used by permission of Scholastic Inc.

the magazine's values or objectives changed altogether, but that *TeenSet* was adapting its cover to be more representative of its own developing identity as it was navigating this evolving musical and cultural landscape.

To my knowledge, no other American teen fan magazine[10] featured the festival on its cover or dedicated nearly as much space within. Selvin argues that "over that weekend, the Monterey Pop Festival managed to simultaneously sum up and accelerate the dramatic changes sweeping through pop music."[11] This is captured by *TeenSet*'s dramatic cover change, as well as the content inside. The sixteen-page spread of the Monterey Pop Festival provides an intimate look into the event. Within the issue, the unauthored article titled "The Beatles at Monterey"[12] critically delves into the Beatles' influence on popular music, claiming that Monterey would not have happened without the existence and influence of the Beatles. The Monterey Pop Festival proved to showcase development within popular music, gathering, for the first time, a plethora of popular sounds from London, the American West Coast, and Memphis, and *TeenSet*'s October 1967 issue considered and conveyed this unprecedented gathering of popular musicians. The magazine cover, as well as the content, would never again be quite as uniform or formulaic as it had been before the festival.

The November 1967 Beatles cover also featured a textured background, followed by the December cover that featured an outline of George Harrison (figure 3.12); the uniformity of the previous covers has been replaced by a more eclectic visual aesthetic. While the end of 1967 ushered in a visible change for *TeenSet*, by the beginning of 1968, the magazine transformed in a more radical way. With the developments within popular music and rock culture specifically, Sims was not exclusively concerned with covering the Top 40.

TeenSet's January 1968 issue contains multiple changes to the cover (figure 3.16). The image of the musician Donovan (photographed by Jim Marshall) is not framed or merely cut out and placed on top of a colored background. Rather, the image of Donovan is placed within a flower, and the two images together create a psychedelic effect. The effect of the flower petals is one of smoke and haze and requires closer inspection to realize that it is indeed a flower. A flower in 1968 had become a strong symbol of the counterculture and hippie movement (the Illuminati word for "flower power," "Ewige Blumenkraft," originally appeared in the final issue of *TeenSet*),[13] and this cover not only produces a psychedelic effect but also uses the flower as a symbol. Its use is documented in the 1960s at times of protest as flowers were

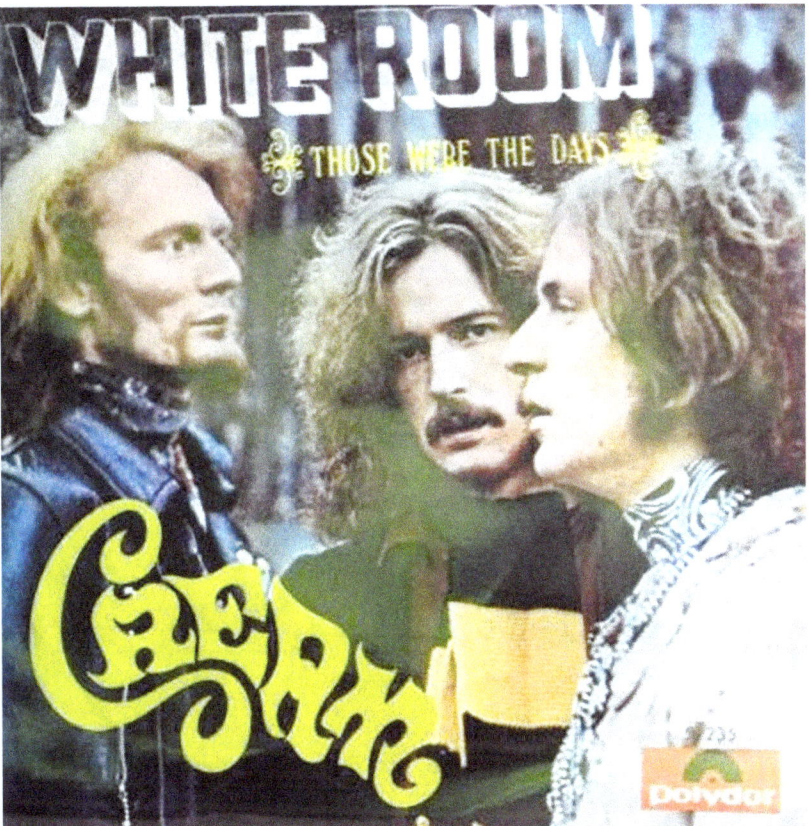

Figure 5.4. Cream's "White Room"/"Those Were the Days" singles, Polydor 1968 release.

offered to US military officers by various protestors. For example, a famous 1967 image of a young woman, now recognized as Jan Rose Kasmir, holding a flower to soldiers in DC titled *The Ultimate Confrontation: The Flower and the Bayonet* "became a defining image of the antiwar era. It remains a fixture of museum exhibitions and appears regularly in print."[14] This image was published over two months before the release date[15] of this cover issue, meaning the cover was conceptualized rather quickly after the events and the photograph was published (if not already planned). Thus, *TeenSet* not only reflected the counterculture but contributed to the construction of it. Additionally, placing Donovan within the flower signifies the concept of a "flower child" and positions him as a representative of the counterculture movement. Donovan himself released the song "Jennifer Juniper" two months

Figures 5.5A, B, and C. *16 Magazine* over ten years. March 1962, June 1966, and October 1972. Author's collection.

after the release of this issue, using flowers to accentuate a young woman: "Jennifer Juniper/ rides a dappled mare/ Jennifer Juniper/ lilacs in her hair."[16] It is evident that Sims and art director Chester were identifying with and "tuned into" what was happening within politics and the counterculture with which popular music was intertwined.

This issue also introduces the third and final typeface *TeenSet* used, although large, two-toned letters changed in color for the last fourteen issues. This typeface contains thick lines that signal a bold, colorful look, which, on a magazine rack, would stand out to a reader, especially if it was not in the front row. From an industry standpoint, a logo is important in the branding and marketing of a product, and the new *TeenSet* logo was used "to convey multiple complicated messages, ideas, and values in the simplest form possible."[17] This new typeface was more modern and became a powerful element of the cover. The title is bold and, again, "tuned into" the evolving musical landscape. While the changing colors of the typeface provided a psychedelic effect, the letters in all capitals connoted rock rhetoric. For example, the typeface is similar to that on rock records such as Cream's "White Room"

Figures 5.5A, B, and C. *16 Magazine* over ten years. March 1962, June 1966, and October 1972. Author's collection.

Belgium single (figure 5.4), which was released six months after *TeenSet*'s typeface change—signaling that *TeenSet* was not only following trends but actively setting them.

The typeface change, along with the redesign of the entire cover, was a clear attempt to rebrand *TeenSet* during a time when its teen fan magazine competitors were continuing forward with their same formula/format, which was evocative of a 1960s children's comic book. Figures 5.5A, B, and C show examples of the cover image of *16 Magazine* from 1962, 1966, and 1972.

The format for *16 Magazine* did not change over the course of the 1960s and early 1970s. However, *TeenSet* (arguably Sims and Chester) was rebranding itself by late 1967. Consider the September 1968 covers of *Tiger Beat* and *TeenSet* (figures 5.6A and B). *16 Magazine* and *Tiger Beat* were continuing with the same format (which was successful in print until the early 2000s).[18] While each magazine continued to update the then-current teen with the then-popular stars, *TeenSet* had radically changed beyond just the content.

The images on the cover began to change as well. *TeenSet*'s February 1968 issue contains a painting (figure 5.7) by art director Nancy Chester depicting John Lennon surrounded by a colorful aura (five subsequent issues that similarly used a painting on the cover followed suit in March, April, May, and July).[19] Along with the aura, the coloring of the image conjures a psychedelic effect, portraying a similar likeness to the popular American West Coast concert posters for, say, Jefferson Airplane or the Doors in the late 1960s. The painting was also a trial for a new, short-lived psychedelic direction for the cover design. In Judith Sims's editorial column "ETC. ETC.," she introduces the new artwork:

> Another *TeenSet* first, she said braggingly—and rightfully so. Our cover, you will note, is a colorful (indeed) portrait of a certain Englishman, not a photograph. Of course, *Life* magazine had an illustration on its cover recently, so we're not really First. We're just the first of the fan mags, which is good enough.... To WIN (yes, win) this once-only offer, just take out a sheet of paper, write your name, address, and age on it, and then tell us, in 25 words or less, just what you think of the cover. You don't have to flatter—be honest. We want to know. Tell us why you like or don't like it. *TeenSet*'s staff will select the winner.... Mail your letter to *TeenSet*, Box 1309, Hollywood, Calif. 90028. And give us a piece of your mind.[20]

Figures 5.6A and B. Covers, *Tiger Beat* and *TeenSet*, September 1968. Author's collection.

The reference to the cover of *Life* is important, as the art featured on the December 1, 1967, cover is a colorful image of a Native American by the artist Milton Glaser. Glaser was known in the popular music world for his commissioned work of Bob Dylan (1966) that was printed as a poster for Dylan's greatest hits album in 1967:

> After suffering serious injuries in a motorcycle accident in 1966, singer-songwriter Bob Dylan was rendered bedridden and rumored to be dead. To generate positive publicity for his forthcoming album, *Bob Dylan's Greatest Hits*, CBS records commissioned Milton Glaser to design a special poster to be packaged with the album. Taking inspiration from a Marcel Duchamp self-portrait, Glaser depicted Dylan in profile, his abundant curly hair rendered in saturated colors that stood out in high contrast from the white ground. The energetic design, with its swirling streams of color, evokes the visual effects of the psychedelic drugs that were gaining popularity among members of the counterculture.[21]

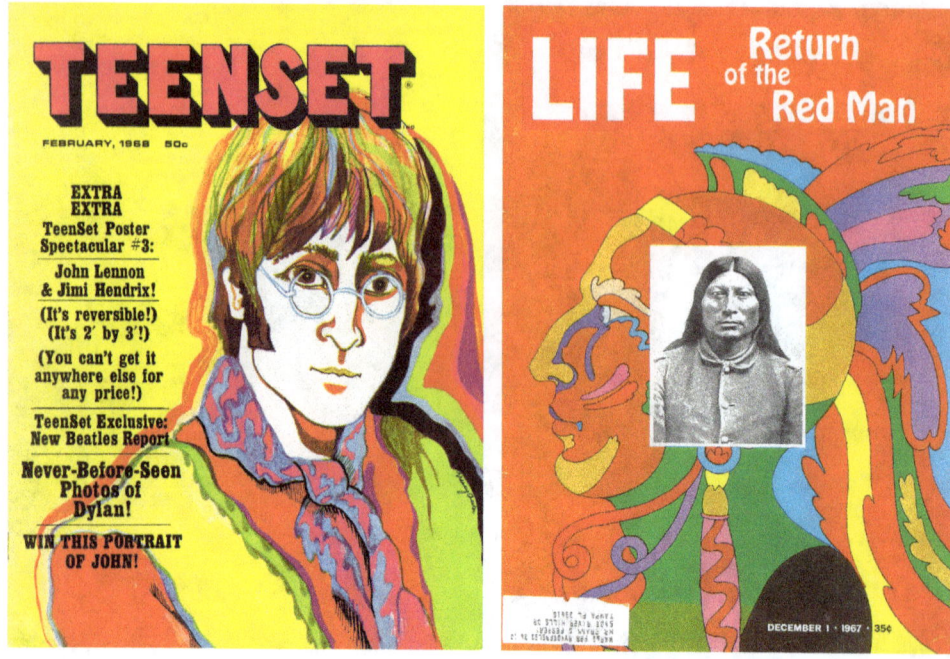

Figures 5.7A and B. The first illustrated issue, *TeenSet*, February 1968 and Milton Glaser cover, *Life*, December 1967. Author's Collection.

The image featured on *TeenSet* is very similar in color, as well as the outlined aura around Lennon, to the image on the cover of *Life*, recognizing a trending style of colorful modern artwork. *TeenSet* tested out a new possible trend seen in *Life* magazine that was directed toward an older audience but also resonated in the popular music scene, as Glaser's work would be relatively recognizable, and *TeenSet* wanted to be first among the teen fan magazines to feature the psychedelic style and trend (which the Donovan cover released a month beforehand was also representative of).

Sims requested that readers send their names, ages, and opinions of the cover, gathering information not only on the age and gender of the readership but also if this new style fit with them, signaling she was genuinely interested in her readers. Chester painted five covers in total (figures 4.1, 4.2, 4.3, 4.8, and 4.11), and the only other artwork featured on the cover was on the November/December 1968 issue, "Yellow Submarine Special!!!!!!," however, this artwork was from the *Yellow Submarine* film (figure 5.2).

The painted covers were short-lived and *TeenSet* transitioned back to photography as the main focus of the cover, and the transition to and from using psychedelic cover art (as *Cheetah* did) instead of photographs signaled yet another change within the magazine. While other teen fan magazines used drawings and *16 Magazine* pasted faces on drawn bodies, this was different. For *TeenSet*, the covers were conveyed as artwork to the fans and were another attempt to redefine and rebrand *TeenSet*. Nevertheless, a painting of Davy Jones would not have reached the individuals who were no longer wearing their Monkees pins. However, Sims asked her readers for feedback, a clear attempt to read her audience. Again, *TeenSet* began producing different types of covers in an attempt to rebrand itself as it was navigating its own identity in the evolving musical and cultural landscape of the late 1960s.

In February 1968, *TeenSet*'s cover featured a slogan for the first time: "THE MAGAZINE FOR TODAY's MUSIC SCENE."[22] The new cover line slogan connoted the need to advertise that *TeenSet* was a music *scene* magazine. *TeenSet* led the field in covering multiple music scenes, and the addition of the subtitle indicates that Sims was aware the title was failing to capture the content. This particular slogan lasted for five issues.

Not only did *TeenSet* echo the sentiment of the counterculture and hippies through stylized psychedelic covers, but it also did so through various angles of photography and its choice of featured musicians. The June 1968 *TeenSet* briefly reverted to a photo, rather than a painting, of Jim Morrison (figure 4.9). In this cover image, Morrison is looking into the camera from a low angle, an angle known to empower the subject. Morrison's reputation as mysterious and rebellious grew, and by the release of the June issue, he was arrested twice in six months: once for inciting a riot during a Doors performance and the other for public drunkenness. The Doors themselves had been banned by *Ed Sullivan* in response to Morrison not censoring his lyrics in 1967. Morrison graced many magazine covers (albeit not many other teen fan magazines), but this cover provides the reader with a different Morrison, a non-rebellious, non-leather-clad or shirtless version, and not an intentional sex symbol version. The story Sims wrote to accompany the image on the cover referred to Morrison putting on an act:

> It wasn't really much of an interview, and I certainly don't know much more about Jim than I did before. He's one of the most naturally sexy people I've ever met, yet he often appears to be playing the role—a calculated portrayal of a modern tormented sex symbol. The disconcerting thing is that I've caught glimpses of him when he isn't playing the role, and he's different then—relaxed, almost talkative.[23]

This photograph of Morrison signifies Sims's "glimpse" of him, showing that *TeenSet* chose this image to consider a part of Morrison's persona that wasn't deeply rooted within the rock rhetoric and mythology that still surrounds Morrison. Additionally, the image of Janis Joplin[24] is a striking example of rock photography (figure 4.13) and as chapter 3 conveyed, a valued piece of rock history photographed by Jim Marshall.

The last four *TeenSet* issues of 1968 further signify a grappling with the evolving musical landscape. The August 1968 cover features Cream (figure 4.12). The photographs, by Jim Marshall and Gino Rossi, are presented in three panes, also known as a triptych. This issue is particularly telling, as it is the first issue with a second new slogan: "THE NIFTY MUSIC MAGAZINE WITH THE MISLEADING NAME."[25] While the slogans will be fully discussed in the next section, it is important to note them here alongside the presentation of the cover images as they are part of the cover lines. The slogan suggests for the first time that the magazine name is misleading, as the title doesn't allude specifically to music, and the images of a critically acclaimed rock band are presented in "window" panes that signify a window into *TeenSet*. The cover image is used to entice an individual to "check out" this "nifty music magazine,"[26] signifying that Cream would not be a choice for the cover of, say, *16 Magazine*, but in the knowledge that Cream was critically considered in *Rolling Stone*.[27] The choice of Cream was a strategic exercise in rock rhetoric to attract readers who would not necessarily read a "teen magazine." Moreover, the choice of Cream signifies a different sound in comparison to what had been featured on the cover in the past; arguably, Cream was the "heaviest" band to be featured on the cover, and a signal that urban and psychedelic blues were on the rise within popular music. It is important to note that the images are of Cream performing, as with the cover featuring Janis Joplin the following month, because no other teen fan magazine featured a performance on the cover (with extremely rare exceptions) or, in the case of Janis, a female rock star. *TeenSet*'s next four covers continued to convey rock rhetoric by featuring Janis Joplin, Mick Jagger, and Grace Slick.

By 1969, the title font was downsized, arguably to allow the cover images to convey the content of the magazine and draw attention away from the title. The decision to place Grace Slick on the January 1969 cover is difficult to ignore. Yet this bold choice to publish a controversial picture of Grace Slick in blackface (figure 5.3) with her left fist up to signal Black Power is a political statement in itself, as the cover choice is as radical as Slick's performance. While Jack points out that Sims, at one point, stated she was not interested in the revolutionary rhetoric, he argues, "The January 1969 issue boasted a provocative cover.... The message was clear: the magazine was aspiring to a more mature audience."[28] In correspondence with Ben Fong-Torres, without being prompted, he noted this particular cover as "adding to its [*TeenSet*'s] credibility"[29] within the rock community. The heading "Grace Slick and Jimi Hendrix on being black"[30] is above her fist in a different color than the rest of the cover lines, suggesting a discussion of race within the magazine.

On November 10, 1968, Jefferson Airplane appeared on the *Smothers Brothers Comedy Hour*. They performed "Crown of Creation," and "Grace Slick appeared covered in dark brown makeup and gave the Black Power salute at the song's end."[31] Within this *TeenSet* issue, Slick is quoted as giving five different reasons for performing in blackface. Yet the act was political, and as scholar Patrick Burke highlighted, less than a month afterward, two American athletes, Tommie Smith and John Carlos, were stripped of their medals for the Black Power salute at the Olympic ceremony. Burke argues in "Tear down the Walls, Jefferson Airplane, Race, and Revolutionary Rhetoric in 1960s rock" that "Slick's gesture was emblematic of a larger tendency in 1960s rock: white musicians casting themselves as political revolutionaries by enacting a romanticized vision of African American identity."[32] As Jerry Hopkins argued in the article accompanying this issue of *TeenSet*, "Grace Slick is an attention-getting device"; "Grace Slick frequently goes out of her way to blow minds, to shock people, to make them notice . . . not necessarily notice her, but what she is doing and what it might represent."[33] Arguably, Jefferson Airplane was not politically active during the mid-1960s but became more political by 1968: "While they did not advance a concrete political platform, Jefferson Airplane nonetheless played a highly visible role in the trend toward radical rhetoric in rock in 1968"[34] with which *TeenSet* was associating itself. Yet featuring Slick's controversial attempt to identify and act as a revolutionary signifies that *TeenSet* identified with a revolutionary ideology or at least acknowledged that revolutionary rhetoric was prevalent within the countercultural and rock canon as the Black Panthers and Yippies[35] were growing in numbers and influence. As considered in chapter 3, Atlas's article on Hendrix conveyed such revolutionary rhetoric from the words of Jimi Hendrix, who was becoming more openly supportive of Black Power or commenting on it out of a response to the criticism he received for not being "Black enough." Sims herself projected revolutionary rhetoric in the following issues in her "ETC. ETC." column, supporting counterculture ideas.

The final *TeenSet* pop art-inspired cover featured Jimi Hendrix's and actress/model Mia Farrow's heads fashioned on Ken[36] and Barbie doll-type bodies (figure 5.9), and behind the figures is a version of pop artist Robert Indiana's "LOVE" image (which became a sculpture the following year). According to Sims, it was a rendition of the Lennon and Yoko *Two Virgins* (1968) album cover.[37] It, like the Slick cover, also contained political overtones, as not only was the *Two Virgins* record covered by a brown sleeve in shops to hide nudity, but here, the "two virgins" are interracial, as were Lennon and Ono. Subscribed readers would have automatically received the magazine, but readers who bought it at the stores would not have recognized *TeenSet* as *TeenSet*. Not only had the design completely changed again, in the fashion of a pop culture magazine, but the name *TeenSet* is not as prominent as it had been, and a question mark followed the title—the final notable change that signified an end to the name "*TeenSet*." The name changed in May 1969 to *AUM* (with no April issue for either publication), which is an alternative spelling of "OM," or (as the slogan of the magazine said) "America's Underthirty Magazine." The magazine lasted for three issues into July and, as previously noted, contained music, astrology, politics, race, fashion, and healthy living (figures 5.11, 12, and 13).

In consideration of *TeenSet* magazine, Armstrong argues that:

> The front cover of a music magazine mediates the content within. It shapes the reader's expectations. A chronological sequence of covers tells the periodical's story during a particular period in popular music history. Changing cover content and style weave a tale with a changing cast of characters and evolving plotline. Underpinning it all, evidence of how a magazine either supported or challenged the mainstream values of its time, musical and social.[38]

As argued, *TeenSet*'s changes are not only significant to *TeenSet* but also represent large cultural and musical changes and developments, such as the growing counterculture, social and political shifts in ideology, and tastes in music. The cover of *TeenSet* conveys these changes, especially from October 1967 onward. Scholar Jay Stein argues in regard to displaying magazines that "the gateway to a magazine's content and purpose is its cover."[39] Scholar Jennifer Scanlon found that "the cover is a magazine's most important advertisement—an advertisement for itself. The cover draws readers in at the newsstand, in the doctor's office, on the supermarket line. It lets readers know what to expect: it provides a connection, a means of identification."[40] Thus, a cover is not only an advertisement for a magazine but also a source of identity for a magazine, which *TeenSet* was attempting to establish. Moreover, as Gabrielle Dean argues in her study of *The Smart Set* magazine:

> Covers are of primary significance within the semiotics of magazine production and reception and play a crucial part in magazine commerce and the print culture economy more generally. Cover design serves the prima facie purpose of marking basic divisions in the periodical taxonomy—helping readers determine whether a given periodical is a general interest magazine, a literary journal, a women's magazine, a professional newsletter, and so forth.[41]

There is no evidence that these changes in *TeenSet* were for economic purposes, as *16 Magazine*, *Tiger Beat*, and *TeenScreen*'s formats did not change, and as noted, *16 Magazine* and *Tiger Beat* were successful into the twenty-first century. This suggests that *TeenSet* was transforming its cover, and eventually its name, for a different reason: "Editors and publishers go to a lot of trouble to make sure that they are creating the kinds of covers that will bring them readers."[42] However, for *TeenSet*, it wasn't only about gaining new readers but also attempting to break away from the connotations it was assumed to have and reach a wider audience altogether, and this most likely would alienate their younger readers. It was clear that Judith Sims and the staff of *TeenSet* were attempting to grapple with an evolving musical landscape and where *TeenSet* fit within it. As the majority of other teen magazines were continuing to cover the Top 40 and younger popular music and film stars such as Sajid Khan, *TeenSet* was attempting to cover material that was no longer seen as appropriate for young teens: rock and the counterculture. For the entire year of 1968 and into 1969, *TeenSet*'s covers and content conveyed a duality in the magazine's identity. It was more representative of the counterculture and rock rhetoric but still considerate of popular music that was not associated with this rhetoric. *TeenSet* was attempting to maintain a balance between their current Monkee-loving fans by continuing to devote pages (albeit fewer) to the band and also attracting a demographic that was identified with urban blues, psychedelic, or the San Francisco sound. That means it was attempting to be in a liminal position

Figure 5.8. John Lennon *TeenSet* cover, February 1969. Used by permission of Scholastic Inc.

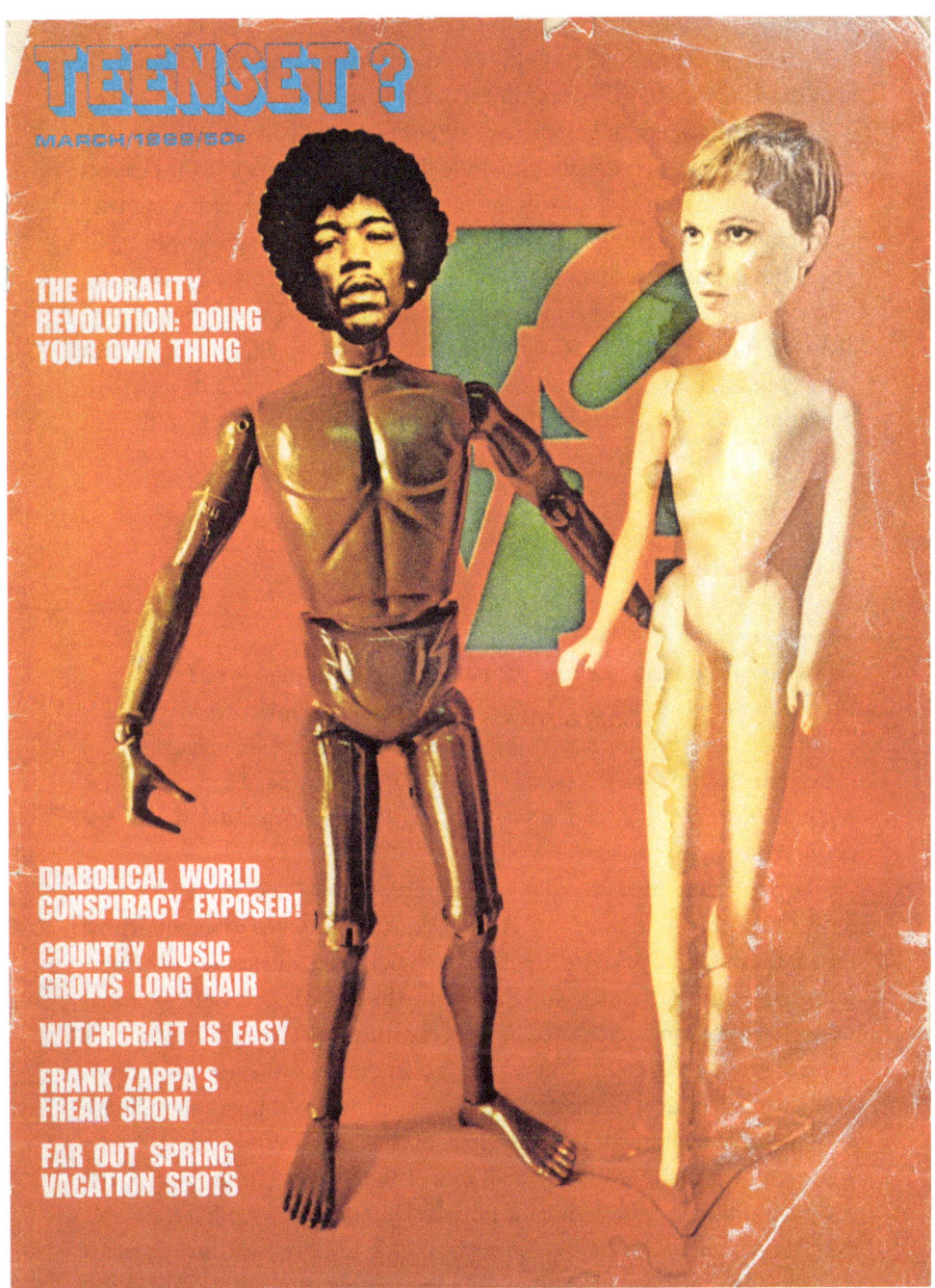

Figure 5.9. Jimi Hendrix and Mia Farrow doll *TeenSet* cover, March 1969. Used by permission of Scholastic Inc.

between teen fan magazines and the underground press. This is not to say that someone cannot like both the Monkees[43] and Cream, but the sounds are different, and they do draw different fan bases.

These changes not only represent all facets discussed here, such as rock and revolutionary rhetoric, the growth of the counterculture and the changes of the sounds and trends within the musical and cultural tableau, but they also represent their fans growing up and *TeenSet* wanting to grow with them. The youth culture was changing, and *TeenSet* recognized this. *Tiger Beat* and *Bop* lost me as a reader because they kept considering the popular "pop" artists in the late 1990s and early 2000s and did not consider the other rock bands that a group like Hanson would lead me to. Those bands were featured in *Rolling Stone* and *Spin*. This is where *TeenSet* differed, as Judith Sims wanted to continue covering the music she liked.

THE RECORD REVIEWS: FROM THE TOP 40 AND OLD STANDARDS TO CONSIDERING ARTISTRY; AN EVOLVING CONSTANT WITHIN

TeenSet began to include record reviews since its separation from full Capitol Record control. The October 1965 issue housed the first review section, which continued into *AUM* magazine. Prior to the claims that teen magazines did not contain record reviews, *TeenSet* had consistently included a record review section. However, this section went through a transformation, as did the cover, articles, and title.

The first unauthored record review within *TeenSet*, titled "Album Review" (and, shortly after, "Albums in Review"), considered seven different artists: the Philharmonia Orchestra, the Beach Boys, Roger Miller, the Lettermen, John Gary, Burt Bacharach, and the Byrds. The records that were reviewed were of artists who had charted or were charting, not specifically what was popular among the youth demographics. The reviews themselves did not provide much critical thought or opinion but provided simple commentary with multiple opening phrases like "one of the hottest things going,"[44] "the wildest,"[45] "without question,"[46] and "one of the biggest hits around."[47] The reviews continued considering the popular "hits" similarly, with few notable exceptions, until 1968. After 1966, *TeenSet* mostly reviewed artists and groups that their fans associated with but still predominantly considered the top artists. The album reviews credited J. Walker Scott as the official reviewer until October 1966, but the "Albums in Review" department did not list any other author until the name of the section changed in 1967.

In October 1966, *TeenSet*'s consideration of Dylan's *Blonde on Blonde* recognized that to consider certain records in depth would require a more lengthy discussion: "A full review of this album would require at least a page, and a fourth of that would be devoted to elements of the packaging."[48] This suggests that full albums were being presented to and received by fans differently and conveys *TeenSet*'s limitations in reviewing albums early on (which is noted in Savage's *1966: The Year the Decade Exploded* [2016]). In March 1967, the section received a new title, "The Groove," with a new writer under the pseudonym "A. J. Phrotus," a nod to the Monkees and Dolenz's slang for marijuana.[49] The writing style and proportion stayed consistent, but more opinions appeared throughout 1967. For example, in December 1967, the reviewer of the *Jimi Hendrix Experience* did not know what to think of the record: "Hendrix is rooted in R&B. The music is strictly overpowering mania of the tune-in type. The profound Soul bit seems at odds with the surrealism of the mental involvement dictated by the tracks (which are sensational): The total thing just doesn't come off for this ear."[50] The review of the record was more critical than usual and was slowly evolving to include an analysis. In-depth changes began to occur by May 1968 as The Groove expanded its critical discussions of changes happening within the record world, but the reviews were similar to what they had been in the past: descriptive. However, the June issue ushered in a more in-depth discussion of changes in the popular music canon in regard to records:

> What's happening with the rock groups today? Suddenly, they're doing more than just singing songs and playing their hearts out to large auditoriums. They're making statements about human condition, about the world and perhaps more importantly about themselves. We can now look at a pop singer's work and evaluate what he has done in much the same manner as we evaluate a novel, a painting, a film. The pop groups are revealing themselves with their music. Top 40 just doesn't really make it with them anymore, not artistically, anyway. The album had become the vehicle for self-expression for creativity.[51]

This review is the beginning of a subsequent theme of considering artistry within popular music and is evidence of a folk political intent (such as meaning and authenticity) deeply rooted within popular music. This is amplified by a consideration of Jefferson Airplane. *TeenSet* states:

> Jefferson Airplane is the first American group to go for continuity on an album. They spent close to six months inside the RCA Victor studios in Los Angeles recording *After Bathing at Baxter's*. The album emerged as a tight expression of the creativity of the Airplane. The album has been called their greatest work and their worst. What it is not is the product of a Top 40 producer; what it is not is the slick corporate offering of the pop industry. What it is is the Airplane . . . for better or worse. It is a total sound, with cut running into cut with voices combining to form one mood. As one reviewer said of their latest single, "'Greasy Heart' may not be Top 40, but it's Grace." Suddenly, that sentiment is where it's at for groups.[52]

Here, *TeenSet* considers authenticity rather than popularity. This signifies that, in 1968, being authentic was more important than making the Top 40.

By mid-1968, "The Groove" was providing readers with more in-depth considerations of albums and artists.[53] Unlike the early days of *TeenSet*, the review section was finding its groove. By this time, the reviews no longer began with phrases such as "biggest hits around."[54] As presented, the musical tableau had evolved beyond focusing on hits, and *TeenSet* contributed to and reflected such changes and considerations. Rather, the reviews attempted to analyze a record. In the final issue of *TeenSet*, in March 1969, "The Groove" received one last makeover and housed the magazine's most critical discussions of albums that, when historically placed, came at the time Lester Bangs and other critics were starting out or gaining name recognition for their record reviews.

While in the beginning, the changes were mostly visual (the cover and typeset), the written content and consideration of the music and culture itself dramatically changed in mid-1968. It is understandable that lengthy record reviews were needed to fully cover an album or a musician. *Crawdaddy!* had produced lengthy record reviews since 1966, and *Rolling Stone* had been in existence for less than a year by mid-1968. It should be noted that these two rock magazines most likely influenced *TeenSet* to provide lengthier record reviews, but writing styles were also developing for rock journalists. Moreover, the concept of what an album was had changed by 1967, "particularly the emergence of the concept album,"[55] signaling a change in how albums would be discussed. *TeenSet* was developing with the albums themselves, and considered this in June 1968 by discussing the Beatles' *Sgt. Pepper's Lonely Hearts Club Band* (1967) within "The Groove":

> Perhaps the trend for continuity in pop music began with the Beatles' super album, *Sgt. Pepper's Lonely Hearts Club Band*. As if by magic, groups throughout the world began to see the potentiality of the album medium as an outlet for totally involved and coordinated sound. Groups and individuals began to view the record album not as a disk for separate entries which do not relate to each other but as a concise vehicle for interrelated sounds.[56]

The record was no longer seen as just a "holder" of an artist's music but an authentic expression of an artist. This is evident in *TeenSet*'s decision to place more emphasis on discussing the record and the artist in more depth rather than what songs will be a hit. The language transitions from descriptions of the records with light commentary, as discussed, to containing more critical thought. "We are into a new phase of pop music: the idol worship days belong only to the past or to the very young. What belongs to today and to the future is the creativity of the new breed of pop groups. They have become musicians, and they are becoming artists."[57]

Fundamentally, what these reviews convey in popular music is of considerable historical interest because they signal a transition within popular music that is deeply rooted in political commentary that had its origins in folk music. This also shows the moment in popular music print media when the genre of rock began to be separated from pop based on rock aesthetics. No longer were the charts the guide to what should be considered; as the evolution of *TeenSet* conveyed, what was starting to matter to many musicians and fans by late 1967 was meaning, authenticity, and artistry, and *TeenSet* was contributing to and identifying with it as well.

"DON'T LET THE NAME FOOL YOU"

Sims recognized that *TeenSet* did have older readers. As she herself candidly admits, she loved what she did. In September 1967, before the open consideration of the name change, *TeenSet* addressed her older audience in an article titled "For the Comfort of Teenagers over Twenty Or . . . How to

Be an Overaged Teenybopper and Like It!" This title signifies that she is also attempting to reach the twenty-somethings who may read *TeenSet*:

> Do you range in age from 20 to 29? Is the shing-a-ling your favorite dance? Do you read all the teen magazines, watch *American Bandstand*, and snap your fingers a lot? Do you attend pop concerts and have Mark Lindsay and the Monkees on your bedroom wall? Is "groovy" your favorite word? . . . Well, folks, if you have answered "yes" to the first and at least four more of the above questions, like it or not—you have succumbed to the malady known as "incurable teenybopper-itis."[58]

The author (most likely Judith Sims) begins the article by claiming that there are more twenty- to twenty-nine-year-old individuals visible at concerts and that loving popular music was no longer a thing for "teens": "Let me tell you a few things about us teenagers in our twenties: first, our number is growing! Letters to teen magazines more often say things like, 'I feel more like a teenager now than when I was one,' more people in their twenties are buying pop records than ever before, and more of us are visible at rock 'n' roll concerts (yeah)!"[59]

Sims was twenty-seven in 1967, and in *TeenSet*'s own words, suffered from "incurable teenybopper-itis." "Believe me, you can be a 22- or 27-year-old teenybopper and STILL have a level head, a true heart, and be a responsible citizen—just ask TeenSet's editor! Being a teenybopper means having fun and enjoying one's youth to the fullest."[60] The word "teenybopper" is not used in a negative way; rather, the overall objective of the article was to encourage and relate to fans of popular music that are beyond "teen years," which popular music was often attached to. Sims herself recognized that youth culture extended beyond ages thirteen to nineteen, and this foreshadowed *TeenSet*'s name change. Shortly after this article appeared, *TeenSet* uniquely began attempting to address the connotations of being connected to a specific age group, and as previously evidenced, a specific gender rather than to youth culture in general.

As noted, in March 1968, *TeenSet* adopted a subtitle cover line phrase that attempted to define *TeenSet*'s purpose. Under the title *TeenSet*, a new phrase positioned it as "THE MAGAZINE FOR TODAY'S MUSIC SCENE" (figure 4.2).[61] The new phrase did not say today's "teen" music scene, but rather "today's," which gestured that *TeenSet* is (or had become) a more broadly conceived music scene magazine,[62] not only a teenage fan magazine. To notice this phrase, one would have to pick up the magazine to read it or be very close to the magazine on the display rack. The typeface is black and smaller than the other typefaces, and it is very difficult to see on the March issue, as the wording is placed over Davy Jones's hair.

Cover lines on a magazine cover "are the phrases or even single words which tell the reader what the magazine has to offer"[63] and "cover lines are seen as points of entry for people browsing at the newsstand."[64] Arguably, the new slogan was created to enhance the understanding of the product. It became apparent by the August 1968 issue that the name did not sufficiently represent the content or message of the magazine. As mentioned in the previous section, the slogan on the cover changed a second time to "THE NIFTY MUSIC MAGAZINE WITH THE MISLEADING NAME,"[65] again signaling to the reader that this magazine's name did not adequately match its content or overall message.

These new phrases, as with the changes discussed in the last section, carry two important connotations. First, the editor felt that *TeenSet* needed to explain what it was to consumers browsing the magazine section or to librarians (if they carried teen fan magazines) and shopkeepers to encourage a specific placement of the magazine, for example, to be placed with *Rolling Stone, Crawdaddy!, Cheetah,* or *Eye,* rather than *16 Magazine* or *Tiger Beat.* Second, the title does not convey the magazine's current intentions, objectives, content, or message. As argued above, just as a typeface or logo conveys a message, so does a name, and the name is a brand that conjures ideas. The phrase appearing on the cover signifies that the staff of *TeenSet* did not feel the name was sending the *correct* message. Teenagers (especially teen girls) were projected as incompetent and "often judged to be less able than they are."[66] Also, by 1968, teen magazines, in general, were classified as read mainly by girls, who were seen as hysterical teenyboppers. While *TeenSet* may have had a positive association for some, the name connoted a set of socially constructed meanings that the magazine did not want to be associated with. The second slogan continued through the October issue, but there is no evidence the slogans helped gain magazine sales. However, since the slogan changed twice and was completely dropped by November 1968, it most likely did not have as much of an impact as the transformation of the cover.

In October 1968, Sims published an editorial asking readers for suggestions for a possible new name.

> So much for our current and continuing hypes. Now I have a request for you: send us any suggestions you might have for a new name for TeenSet. We're considering changing the name (it isn't definite) to something a little less "teeny," so we need a catchy title that will appeal to a wider age group, emphasize the music aspect, and won't be outdated in a short time. Send your suggestions to *TeenSet* Name, Box 1309, Hollywood, Calif. 90028. In return for your help, you get nuttin' except our heartfelt gratitude.... Unless the name you suggest is chosen, in which case we'll think of some extravagant reward (like a bronzed copy of *16 Magazine*?).[67]

Sims was asking for suggestions as she referred to the name as too "teeny" (as noted, *16 Magazine*'s readership included preteens). She was attempting to reach a larger audience, as the title, to her, is outdated, unappealing to non-teens, and not music-oriented. Additionally, in this attempt to reach this larger audience, the November 9, 1968, issue of *Rolling Stone* featured an ad for *TeenSet* magazine (figure 5.10).

In a large, bold typeface is the slogan "Don't Let the Name Fool You."[68] This continues the implications of the slogan "A NIFTY MUSIC MAGAZINE WITH A MISLEADING NAME."[69] Again, the title of the magazine is called into question. Furthermore, *TeenSet* is attempting to gain readers from a magazine that is popular among male, musician, and college-age readers. *Rolling Stone* magazine, in turn, advertised in *TeenSet* in 1969, suggesting that they felt *TeenSet* readers would be interested in *Rolling Stone*.

If both slogans signaled that the name was not a reflection of the content, it is important to consider the makeup of the content. Over the years, the majority of the articles and interviews only discussed popular music and culture, rock stars, fandom, and, at times, other cultural concerns. Additionally, throughout 1968, *TeenSet* mostly concerned itself with what was being referred to as rock music, where "rock" connoted a different meaning than, say, "pop."[70] *TeenSet*'s content was distancing itself, as the readers wanted (which will be discussed in more depth later), from groups such as the Monkees or those that were associated with and labeled as "teenyboppers" whose authenticity was called into question. If the name was misleading, it meant that the name itself was not referring to the content, which was increasingly oriented to rock. As folk's political intent penetrated rock and the revolutionary rhetoric within the counterculture and popular music

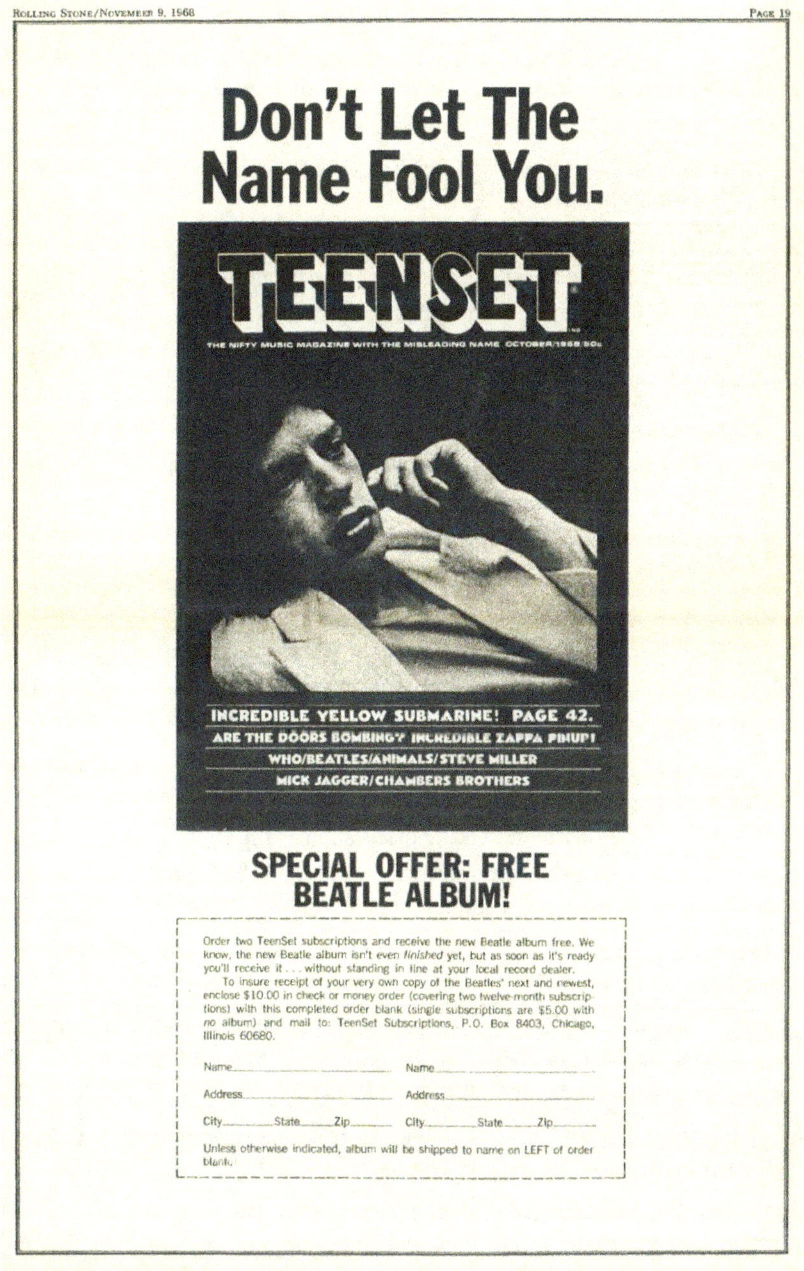
ROLLING STONE/NOVEMBER 9, 1968 PAGE 19

Don't Let The Name Fool You.

SPECIAL OFFER: FREE BEATLE ALBUM!

Order two TeenSet subscriptions and receive the new Beatle album free. We know, the new Beatle album isn't even *finished* yet, but as soon as it's ready you'll receive it . . . without standing in line at your local record dealer.

To insure receipt of your very own copy of the Beatles' next and newest, enclose $10.00 in check or money order (covering two twelve-month subscriptions) with this completed order blank (single subscriptions are $5.00 with *no* album) and mail to: TeenSet Subscriptions, P.O. Box 8403, Chicago, Illinois 60680.

Name________ Name________

Address________ Address________

City____ State____ Zip____ City____ State____ Zip____

Unless otherwise indicated, album will be shipped to name on LEFT of order blank.

Figure 5.10. *TeenSet* advertisement, *Rolling Stone,* November 9, 1968. Author's collection.

asserted itself, the idea that rock or popular music was only to be seen as "teen" music faded. Thus, the word "teen" was no longer a descriptor of rock music fans; rather, rock music no longer connoted "teen."

Sims announced that changes would occur to the content of the magazine, changes which arguably were in motion ever since the October 1967 issue featuring the Monterey Pop Festival:

> The name will change. *TeenSet* has served us well, but the name limits itself. The word "teen" is obsolete because it no longer refers to a well-defined interest or age group; a person in his or her teens certainly does not avoid so-called "adult" topics . . . in fact, there is no longer any real difference between "teenage" interests and "adult" interests, and it's foolish to maintain the illusion that "teenagers live in a different world." As Janey Milstead points out in her article . . . "teenagers" not only live in the same world, they help shape it and influence it . . . in all areas.[71]

She mentioned the name was going to change. However, she provided reasoning that reflected the fact that the word "teenager" denoted something different by this point than it did in the recent past. She argued that the word "teen" was not an appropriate descriptor, not just for the magazine but also for the age group as it had been in the 1950s and early 1960s. As mentioned previously, the 1960s was a very different decade than the 1950s. Many issues were being grappled with and taking place, such as the civil rights movement, the women's liberation movement, and the Vietnam War, and music reflected these events. This context and young people's involvement would challenge the 1950s teenager stereotype. Also, when individuals turned twenty or thirty, their tastes did not automatically turn to jazz or show tunes but rather remained in rock or popular music, often referred to as "teenage" music. It is clear that Sims and her freelance columnists, such as Janey Milstead (a previous editor of *TeenScreen* magazine), felt that the word "teen" was misleading for the magazine as a whole and in the popular music scene. London freelancer Carol Gold told Jack that "for all that its name implied, *TeenSet* was probably the first magazine in the United States to cover pop music properly and include real interviews."[72] Gold underscores the fact that *TeenSet*'s name implied the opposite of a serious view of popular music. Within the same issue, the Mail Scene featured a letter from a fan, only advancing the argument that the name *TeenSet* was limiting and restrictive in reaching older readers:

> I've been racking my brain for days, it seems, trying to come up with a new name for *TeenSet*. I do believe you need a new name. At first, a lot of my friends were reluctant to purchase your magazine because of the name. It sounded teenybopper to them and they aren't even teens anymore. I explained to them that *TeenSet* is really quite an advanced magazine and focused for the older set. I explained the name, I thought, was a big mistake. I also pointed out the statement under the title, and finally, I got one of my friends to purchase a copy. Now they all read it and they all, including me, have subscriptions.[73]

In May 1968, *TeenSet* provided a questionnaire to its readers. It was brief but provided Sims and the *TeenSet* staff with data about the perception of its magazine. Sims had already received returned questionnaires (which were slightly different) from her campus reporters (individuals whom *TeenSet* selected to send in stories and reports that were relevant to music or their experiences). After explaining what the campus reporters' data revealed to the readers, *TeenSet* asked the readers themselves to respond to a similar questionnaire. The article states, "We are printing the questionnaire for the rest of our readers to drown us in opinions. Your opinions. Which are important. Let us know where your head is at."[74]

The questions not only invited responses on whether a cover sells a magazine but also on what kind of music the readers were listening to and what they wanted to read about. The campus reporters' responses were discussed with the presentation of the questionnaire:

> Though it was difficult to compile what people wanted to see more of in teen magazines as there was much variety, there were several things that a good number of readers listed. Among them were the Beatles, San Francisco rock groups, folk music, Donovan, Buffalo Springfield, Paul Revere & the Raiders (Mark Lindsay, mainly),* the Rolling Stones, the Who, the Doors, and up-and-coming groups. Only 170 readers answered the question on what they would like to see less of. 120 of them wanted to see less of the Monkees. Other things mentioned were sensationalized articles, contests, "teenybopper" groups, and stupid letters [referring to printing letters to the editor].[75]

In the August 1968 issue, the new slogan appeared, and by this time, Sims and her staff would have had time to read many of the responses from the questionnaire. This signifies that the new slogan was brought about after reading the responses to the questionnaires, and it acted as an influencer. Sims shared some of the data in the September 1968 issue, stating:

> Our readers are for long hair, beards, and moustaches, and would like to see articles on Viet Nam, the drug problem, generation gap et al. The average age of the reader is 15 or 16. We ought to be patted on the head for this; most fan mags get the 9 to 13 group. . . . It seems that you are turned on by flowers, long hair, Paul McCartney, luv, English accents, music, sex, privacy, Jim Morrison's smile, Oscar Wilde, and meditation. Turn-offs include hate, prejudice, war, and racism (these lead the list of about 200 different items). Others are parents, crew cuts, the *Ted Mack Amateur Hour*, *Ed Sullivan*, sarcasm, suburbia, Lawrence Welk, the fuzz, Twiggy, organized religion, and English leather. . . . The most important word in the English language (to the *TeenSet* reader, at least) is either love, peace, or understanding. Votes were counted for sex, money, cooperation, communication, involvement, equality, and sincerity.[76]

Between both of the surveys overall, the data suggests that *TeenSet* readers desired more rock and cultural coverage and information that may not be suitable for a "teen" audience, encouraging the decision to change the name. This is not to say that teen readers, especially in their late teens, should not have access to coverage of sex or war, as in the case of the baby boomer generation, many of their peers would have been drafted, but according to Sims (and Stavers),[77] many teen fan magazine readers, in general, were estimated to be aged nine to thirteen, yet *TeenSet*'s readers averaged from fifteen to sixteen.[78] This means that a parent or individual might not expect anything of *TeenSet* but to be noncontroversial, especially if compared to *16 Magazine* or teen lifestyle magazines such as *Seventeen*, further suggesting that the word "teen" has specific connotations, and it would not be appropriate to provide such content for them. Again, this evidenced an underestimation of young readers (mostly young women), but more importantly, it conveyed what young readers of *TeenSet* wanted to read about.

By the final issue of *TeenSet* in March 1969, the cover contained a downsized version of the logo with a question mark at the end of the title. Within the magazine, Sims discussed the name change one last time in her "ETC. ETC." column:

By now, you're probably getting a little tired of reading about all our changes. It seems as if I've been cataloging changes in this column for the past year, but it's really been about four months . . . and still no name change. I hate to cop out like this, but you see, the Bavarian Illuminati, as profiled on pages 34–41 of this issue, is behind the plot to keep the TeenSet name . . . perhaps the Illuminati merely want us to look bad because they're secretly financing 16. . . . Keep smiling through your paranoia. And if we're lucky, we'll have a new name next month. Or the month after. Or.[79]

As of the printing of the March issue, there was no name change and thus no ability to announce within the magazine what the new name would be. Although there is evidence that *TeenSet* wrote letters in response to its readers, there is no evidence that a letter may have been sent to its subscribers to inform them of the name change. However, by May 1969, the first issue of *AUM* was released. The new name not only implied meditation, but it was still a magazine for the youth culture as it was for the "underthirty," and as argued by Jack Weinberg, "One can never trust anyone over thirty."[80] Sims is on record as not liking the name, but the staff and management above could not come up with a more fitting one. "We agreed that we had to change the name because it wasn't a fan magazine, it wasn't anything like *16* or *Flip*, but we came up with a shitty name, *AUM* (it's an alternate spelling of 'Om,' the universal mantra. Yuck. We were desperate, all right, but even a good name wouldn't have changed the course)."[81]

As Linda McLoughlin argues, "The title of the magazine plays a large part in shaping the reader's expectations."[82] The nature of the word "teen" can connote many things, but its literal, biological definition denotes people between the ages of thirteen and nineteen, thus the title potentially limits the readership. To further explore the connotation of the title "*TeenSet*," it is pertinent to consider the problems of classification. While there has not yet emerged an academic study delving into the classification of teen fan magazines or teen magazines in general, historically, the typology or genre is assumed, uninterrogated, and generalized. Prior-Miller argues that "the majority of researchers assume that commonly used terms have single-valued, unambiguous meanings, when in fact, the terms carry multiple meanings."[83] For example, teen fan magazines are classified with other things that appeal to teens or have the word "teen" within the title. Sims was aware the name was limiting and changed it with the rock culture in

Figure 5.11. GTO's *AUM* cover, May 1969. Used by permission of Scholastic Inc.

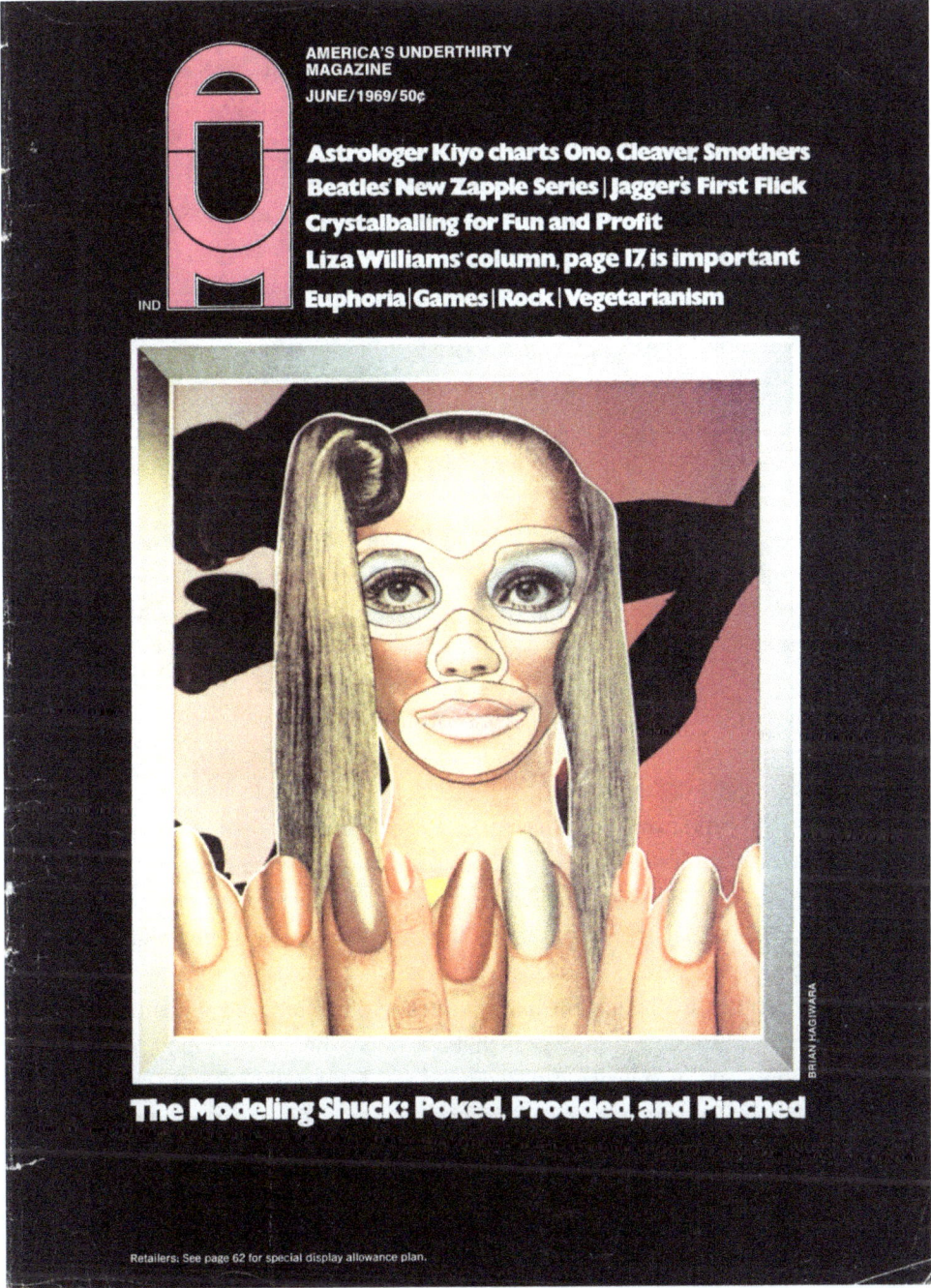

Figure 5.12. Brian Hagiwara Collage *AUM* cover, June 1969. Used by permission of Scholastic Inc.

mind; however, it limited the historical reception of the magazine. As previously argued, the assumed interest of the readership and the assumption that teen fan magazines lacked serious content have led to the historical decay or historical deselection of *TeenSet* within the history of the rock press. For example, Michael Fairchild (in an online introduction to the Hendrix biography *Starting at Zero*) incorrectly refers to *TeenSet* (as well as *Datebook*) as "girly date magazines,"[84] as if *TeenSet* has been placed into a genre or subgenre based on some sort of basic similarity. In addition to Fairchild, Michael Benson's *Why the Grateful Dead Matter* shares the same disposition. Benson claims that:

> On the absolute other side of the coin [previously noting the Monkees' popularity] is the Grateful Dead, one of several San Francisco acts that is musically interpreting the drug movement, mistaken by newsstand-magazine journalists for the next up-and-coming teenybopper band, bound to have a hit single any minute now. Sounds unbelievable? The proof is in the photos of a very well-behaved-looking Grateful Dead posing during their studio shoot for *TeenSet* magazine.[85]

However, if Benson had opened a *TeenSet* or even read the article attached to the photo shoot, considered Jim Marshall's role with *TeenSet*, and Judith Sims's editorial column about the Grateful Dead's lifestyle, he would have retracted this presumptuous and inaccurate statement.

The original name was restrictive not only during the lifespan of the magazine but also historically for consideration in the popular music press canon, as *TeenSet*, among other teen fan magazines, has been assigned a category or subgenre with no critical research or full consideration of the content within. Ultimately, the name limited reaching an older audience and was too easily placed in a category that was not in the same position within the periodical hierarchy as, say, *Rolling Stone*. *TeenSet* did not only change its name and its format to reach a larger audience; rather, the name changed along with cultural and musical ideologies. While the word "teen" has served to limit recognition of *TeenSet*, the changing of the name reflected the publication's developing rock aesthetic and cultural interest. More importantly, a cultural shift occurred in the late 1960s and in popular music (rock specifically). No longer was rock or popular music associated with teen music but rather with youth culture. Like Sims, Hine found the term "teenager" a difficult barrier: "It [teenager] also meant barrier, and "teenage" (with a short *a*) was wood long enough for making a high fence—a meaning with resonance for young people who feel that being categorized as a teenager limits their freedom."[86]

As evidenced in the introduction and chapter 2, the assumed readership of teen fan magazines was young females, typically classified as unserious teenyboppers, and because teenybop is argued to be of the "pop" genre, it is vital to consider the classification of the magazine. As Prior-Miller found, magazines are often loosely categorized by shared characteristics such as titles.[87] The title "*TeenSet*" can be "preread"[88] within the category of other teen magazines. If an observer only browses titles, *TeenSet*'s title does not stand out from *Teen, Teen Life, Seventeen,* or *16 Magazine* (hence the slogans and the name change), and since the title is associated with pop music, it is also preread. This is not to argue that these magazines are exactly alike, but the titles do not suggest anything more than being associated with teens, and these magazines were known to be marketed to young females. However, as shown, the name *TeenSet* was not necessarily representative of the content, and it was (and is still) preread, most likely as not considering rock or countercultural ideas, but rather idols, profiles on their favorite dream dates discussing favorite foods and colors, or female-oriented how-tos.

Feuer suggests that "some genres are accepted by the culture, whereas others are defined by critics."[89] Here, there are two arguments to consider. Firstly, if we again apply genre theory to a magazine, then it is clear that *TeenSet*'s editor and staff felt that being classified with other teen fan magazines was lower in a cultural periodical hierarchy, and Sims herself has commented on other teen fan magazines as a lesser kind of publication.[90] Thus, Sims did not want the magazine or content to be associated with what a teen fan magazine denoted by 1968. Secondly, as *TeenSet* was moving away from the Top 40, the musical content of the magazine began to heavily feature rock; as such, *TeenSet* was associating itself with a specific genre and the revolutionary and countercultural rhetoric associated with it. This signifies that the content did not fit within the confines of the name *TeenSet* and that *TeenSet*'s content would not only be preread by readers, but that rock music or rock rhetoric was not associated with teen fan magazines or teens as it had been. Thus, the implication is that magazines with the word "teen" denoted something else, such as teenybop, something that was *not* rock, did not represent rock aesthetics, and, in some ways, was antithetical to it.[91]

Concluding Remarks

TeenSet illuminated the evolving social construction of teenagers and youth culture and openly acknowledged that the established idea of what a teenager was or should be was not the same in 1965 as it was in 1968. The concept of the teenager evolved from its initial use in the 1940s. Scholars such as Hine and Doherty address this evolution, with Hine suggesting that the category of "teenager" will most likely be obsolete in the near future and replaced with discussions of "youth culture"—a term embraced by scholars such as Andy Bennett, Christine Feldman-Barrett, and many others. As argued in chapter 1, teen fan magazines, specifically *16 Magazine*, did not discuss the evolving social construct of the teenager, and *Rolling Stone* did not single out teenagers as a targeted demographic; thus, *TeenSet*'s usage of the word "teen" provides great insight into the idea of the evolving 1960s teenager and the difficulty of classifying something as "teen."

TeenSet was not only navigating an evolving musical and cultural landscape but attempting to define its own place within it. While magazine covers, in general, "are constantly changing in order to create variety and to keep up to date, they retain sufficient features to mark out their own identity."[92] Yet as shown through this book, the entirety of *TeenSet* changed aesthetically, and the content was elevated to reach college-age readers. The only constant of *TeenSet* from the beginning was Judith Sims's devotion to music. When *TeenSet* transitioned to *AUM*, the magazine no longer adhered to the "teenybopper" per se but to the fading counterculture, rock culture, and anything that was trending within various music scenes. Any strict association with the concept of "teen" beyond 1967 did not accurately describe the direction Judith Sims took the magazine. As this chapter has demonstrated, *TeenSet* was not "teeny" enough to continue to attract the attention of very young teens; the Monkees were no longer the Monkees by 1969, and Janis Joplin and Jimi Hendrix may not have appealed to nine-to-thirteen-year-olds who were buying *16 Magazine* and *Tiger Beat*. Yet the magazine could not fully gain a college-age reading base, as the last thing someone in their early twenties wants to be seen reading is something with "teen" in its title. Flippo argues that the dual identity (or liminal role) that *TeenSet* held was ultimately its downfall, as well as the lack of interest from the publishers:

Figure 5.13. Henry Diltz *AUM* cover, July 1969. Used by permission of Scholastic Inc.

The magazine [*TeenSet*] itself ultimately had little national impact and failed because of its duality: Sims and her writers were eager to write about the musicians who excited them; the publishers were concerned only with profit reports. There was no common ground between ownership and staff and, as a result, the magazine was never able to realize its role—it was determined not to be just another fan sheet, but it wasn't sure just what it was.[93]

While Sims did guide the magazine, she did not have full control of its existence. The folding of the magazine was influenced by many factors, ranging from the lack of interest from the publishers to the inability to gain ad sales, as Sims told Flippo:

> *AUM* lasted three issues; sales didn't pick up, they didn't drop. At that point, it was obvious we had to either fold up or put some money into promotion (not to mention advertising; our ads were pitiful, most of them garnered by a real creep in NY who didn't know his ass from a hole in the ground). So we packed it in.[94]

Even though Flippo notes that the circulation of the magazine, at "200,000 to 250,000 . . . sustained *Rolling Stone* for years,"[95] *AUM* ceased publication. Yet no matter the failure of the magazine, *TeenSet*'s evolution is visible and conveyed throughout the content from its conception to its demise. Arguably, it serves as a visual map of an evolving popular music landscape, specifically among the young counterculture and within the rock canon. *TeenSet* arrived at a time when the music that would be adopted by the counterculture was in the Top 40 and ended publication during a time when artistry and authenticity were valued over chart performance. No other magazine conveys such cultural changes. *Rolling Stone* did not convey such cultural and musical shifts in the mid to late 1960s and historically could not have done so.

CONCLUSION

"ETC, ETC,"

RECONSIDERING THE POPULAR MUSIC JOURNALISM HISTORICAL DISCOURSE

TeenSet's depiction of rock, at times, may not have fit within rock aesthetics that rock journalists were slowly defining as the way one must act as an artist, consider as a journalist, or understand as a reader, and not every page was used to attempt to elevate rock music or musicians to a high art status. Nonetheless, it did take popular music "seriously" and critically considered what was presented. *TeenSet* not only questions the male-dominated rock journalism history, but it also advances the argument that female participation in rock has not been accurately documented and has been mythologized as dominated by men. Women *were* present in rock culture, and as this book has shown, in regard to writing about popular music. Ellen Willis and Lillian Roxon were not the first, nor were they alone. As mentioned in the introduction and chapter 2, the stories of women popular music journalists are not at the forefront of the rock journalism discourse. Although Weinstein has since positioned Jane Scott as the grandmother of rock, Scott is still lacking from the majority of popular music journalism narratives (as well as Gloria Stavers). Many of the women freelancers (as well as Sims and Chester) of *TeenSet* went on to work for other music publications. Sims herself had already simultaneously written for the UK's *Disc and Music Echo* (also known as *Disc*) and then went on to write for *Rolling Stone* (as a rock journalist). Art director Nancy Chester designed many album covers, including the Byrds (*Untitled*, 1970), and later became an art director for CBS; Jacoba Atlas went on to have an accomplished career in journalism and television. *TeenSet* was an apparent springboard for many, but more importantly, it concretely shows us that women were participants in music scenes, were actively interested in music, and wrote about popular music—further challenging Frith and McRobbie's original statement that women were passive in rock.

Although *TeenSet* is unique and unlike any other popular music publication at the time, it was not unusual for women to write about popular music, as evidenced in *The Women Who Wrote Rock, Meow, Rock She Wrote*, and other texts presented in the introduction. This book, at the very least, challenges this limited history of rock journalism and shows that the historical discourse around it needs to continue to be reconsidered. It is evident that it is a matter existing beyond only reexamining the general history of popular music journalism, but that we also reconsider and redirect how women are discussed (fans, journalists, performers, etc.) in relation to rock or popular music.

Considering Teen Fan Magazines in History

This book has shown that *all* teen fan magazines have been generalized in the same manner in most popular music texts, resulting in a systematic dismissal of the magazines and the readers. However, very little scholarly research has been conducted in regard to teen fan magazines and popular music. The overall aim of this book has been to reassess *TeenSet*'s role and perception in popular music history. In doing so, it has become evident that the generalization of what a 1960s teen fan magazine is (and was) has led to a long-term misconception about what *TeenSet* represents. In arguing that *TeenSet* has been overlooked as a result of the dismissal of teen fan magazines, this book becomes the first extended piece of scholarship to consider how 1960s teen fan magazines have been depicted, underrepresented, and overlooked within popular music and cultural history. These magazines allowed for a community to grow and provided proof that if the print media focused on popular music, there was a market for it. Thus, this consideration of *TeenSet* is the beginning of what I hope will be a broader reconsideration of the contributions of teen fan magazines such as *16 Magazine* and *Tiger Beat*.

In placing *TeenSet* within a unique liminal role between the rock press and teen fan magazines, I have claimed that, in general, the other teen fan magazines did not consider rock or culture in the same way, but that is not to denigrate them or to imply that the way that they covered popular music and stars was or is not of value or that they lacked seriousness. As this book has shown, these magazines were in publication before the underground or rock press arrived, and while they were the first to show that popular music was of interest to readers, they were serving a different purpose by the late 1960s; consequently, they should be examined more closely to consider shifts in culture, popular music, and genre. It is evident that *TeenSet* itself conveyed these changes, but by the late 1960s, teen fan magazines, in general, were covering younger musicians and stars, thus signaling that they, too, are evidence of an evolving cultural and musical landscape, even if they continued to cover pop as rock became more politically charged. Instead of dismissing teen fan magazines within the genre of rock, a greater examination of the way they presented popular music and culture, the impact they had on record sales and readers, and their long-term success is required.

It is difficult to discuss teen fan magazines of the 1960s (or of any era) and not consider genre. In analyzing the rock press' historical discourse, it is evident that teen fan magazines have been generalized as unserious, and their association with the genre of pop has contributed to such claim. However, as this book shows, this is an extremely complex matter, as teen fan magazines are dismissed within the music genre of rock, suggesting that these magazines are not only classified as general "teen magazines" or "teen books" as periodicals but as pop—inauthentic and meaningless. As argued, by the late 1960s, the juxtaposition of rock and pop in the press separated not only the style of journalism in popular music magazines but also the coverage. The majority of teen fan magazines covered chart-topping pop in low depth in the late 1960s, whereas the rock and underground press covered rock and associated cultural issues in depth (which also was evident in the music charts). By arguing that *TeenSet* holds a liminal position, this book presents a complex and evolving concept of genre and *TeenSet*'s reaction to it. As Brennan suggests, genre definitions have been negotiated throughout their existence and are still evolving.[1] The consideration of *TeenSet* builds on prior considerations of music and magazine genres, such as Brennan's *When Genres Collide*, because it conveys the evolution of rock and pop in the mid to late 1960s throughout its pages. However, additional analysis of the usage of the words "rock" and "pop" in the popular music press of the late 1960s and into the early 1970s would advance the understanding of the evolution and social commentary of the genres of rock and pop and how the press shaped them, as well as the role teen fan magazines played.

While this book began by considering teen fan magazines and their readers as active and a connected community, greater attention needs to be paid to fandom and reception as the continued generalization of these magazines has, in turn, generalized the readership. *16 Magazine* and other teen fan magazines have often been dismissed for being overly "safe" or not providing "serious journalism," but this prejudice serves to devalue the interests and consumption practices of fans. As a topic of scholarly inquiry, teenage girl fandom has not always received its due. Teen girls are recognized as the main consumers of teen fan magazines. A study of the impact of teen fan magazines would, therefore, serve to reappraise how deeply the sense of community was rooted, especially through the pen pal sections, and how they encouraged fandom and participatory culture. Many fans like Debbie Gendler not only still possess their original 1960s purchased teen fan magazines (including *TeenSet*) but also cherish and protect them from damage. In the case of the 1960s, such research is time-sensitive, as it will soon begin to move beyond living memory. As I noted in chapter 5, I read several teen magazines in the late 1990s. We did not have the internet in my home, and no other magazines were covering Hanson and the Spice Girls; thus, I devoured any bit of information I could obtain. I took my magazines with me to school to hold well-informed discussions of my obsession with peers with the same interests, and we bonded (and fought) over our fandom of the then-trending popular music.

Teen fan magazines were (and historically are) meaningful toward the beginning of their ending in the early 2000s. As Tyler and Gendler found, their mid-1960s Beatles experiences, which included reading and sharing teen fan magazines, gave them hope for a bigger future than they imagined. I remember my wall of Hanson posters (provided by teen fan magazines) and going to their concert feeling like I was free from judgment when I wanted to scream and geek out. One of my favorite teen-marketed posters that I purchased at a book fair (around the age of ten) was a large fold-out that said, "Girls who rock" and featured only women—Gwen Stefani, the Spice Girls, Celine Dion (*Titanic* was very popular), Jewel, and Alanis. Teen fan magazines also provided me with this message, with their excellent coverage and posters of the Spice Girls specifically. At the time, the Spice Girls were promoting girl power, and it was a message that I welcomed and embraced (and still do) in a patriarchal home.[2] I wanted to rock, and for me, this meant singing and learning to play an instrument, like many of the women (and Hanson) on my posters. Musically, by no means have I played beyond open mics (which I love), but this book would not have been possible without having teen fan magazines early on to feed my love of all things popular music. However, these types of memories and meanings are not often shared or examined in popular music history, as young female fans have been routinely dismissed.

In history, teen fan magazines have been generalized to the point that I did not *expect TeenSet* because, as chapter 2 shows, a strong hierarchy exists between teen fan magazines and the rock press, and the magazine was *unexpected* in the rock press's historical narrative—which has taught us that something written, read, and valued by women is often of little worth. Everything I thought I knew about teen fan magazines, in general, was lacking in truth or disregarded readers' experiences. I was guilty of assuming that teen fan magazines did not cover rock and, worse, that they were not as valuable to popular music journalism history, even though I knew how impactful they were in my life. As Norma Coates admits, I, too, found at a young age that "rock critic aesthetics had already entered my thinking."[3]

Miles Parks Grier's exploration of rockism suggests that such dismissal is ingrained in our history and attempting to stretch "rock to include forgotten women, dismissed genres, or even non-musical fields of culture is no guarantee of a way out of rockism,"[4] as allowing some to fit within the established narrative still leads to othering and exclusion. For example, when asked if *TeenSet* belonged in rock journalism history and if Sims should be credited with this, Ben Fong-Torres responded, "Yes, because it was there at the start, along with *Hit Parader, Creem, Crawdaddy!* And something called *Rolling Stone*. *TeenSet* gave a number of writers and photogs their start and published its share of thoughtful articles about social changes."[5] However, when asked if it was surprising teen fan magazines (in general) were left out of the discussion of 1960s popular journalism history, Fong-Torres responded, "No. They are admittedly two different worlds, and many of the fanzines were devoid of journalism. But they were a major part of the evolution of young people reading about stars and, ultimately, about the music they made and the things they were saying."[6] Although Fong-Torres acknowledges that teen fan magazines are valuable in popular music history, he does not qualify or consider many teen fan magazines to contain the same *type* of journalism as *Rolling Stone*. Yes, *TeenSet* is no doubt a contributor to rock journalism, but as I have found, if it is only argued that *TeenSet* is worthy of being part of the strong rock journalism narrative, this allows for a continued marginalization of other teen fan magazines and belittles *TeenSet*'s uniqueness. Essentially, it would open the door for *TeenSet* to join the ranks in rock journalism history but close the door for *16 Magazine* and others.

Considering mythologies in rock, Daphne Brooks suggests in her article "The Write to Rock: Racial Mythologies, Feminist Theory, and the Pleasures of Rock Music Criticism" "that we think really hard about how to forge new methodologies, newly uncovered genealogies and legacies, and new ways of writing."[7] In the case of teen fan magazines, as scholarship moves forward, we must carefully consider the way we discuss teen fan magazines and young female fans—redirecting the conversation from the ways in which teen fan magazines are antithetical to rock and refocus on ways teen fan magazines were meaningful to the development of the popular music press and to the readers (such as Gendler, Furlong, and many more), the meaning that has been made of them, and the impact they have had on society, possibly as a "way out" of rockism. This book, hopefully, will contribute to a refocus and a reevaluation of *all* teen fan magazines and encourage scholarship to look at how teen fan magazines discussed and presented popular music of all kinds.

CONCLUDING THOUGHTS

In the spring of 2022, first-generation *TeenSet* reader Steve Kern reached out to me when he found my name in connection with the magazine. He wanted to share the enormous impact *TeenSet* and Sims had on him as a teenager and into adulthood and that approximately fifty-five years later, he still reflects on *TeenSet*'s role in his life, why the magazine (and the staff) meant so much to him, and his correspondence with Judith Sims. "*TeenSet* certainly mattered to me. . . . There was vital information there and a sense of fun that could brighten anyone's day. I related to the underlying vibe of the magazine. The *TeenSet* staff was of our generation, lovers of the music they covered." When asked if and why he kept the letters between himself and Sims all these years, he states:

> I kept her letters because everything she said to me was the truth. The magazine jumped out at me at that first newsstand. Each issue of the magazine was directed to me. The articles called to me. The music that *TeenSet* covered was calling to me. LA was calling to me. Judy wrote that I needed to get out

of Iowa [a place Sims herself lived when she attended Coe College]. It was the truth. I needed to be in LA. Via *TeenSet* and direct letters to me, Judy was reminding me to let in the truth.[8]

Because of *TeenSet* and Sims, Kern relocated from Des Moines, IA, to Los Angeles in the mid-1970s and has never looked back. *TeenSet* impacted him in a profound way, and that matters.

Around the same time, I found personal items of Judith Sims (pertaining to her time with *TeenSet*) for sale online. The large collection of *TeenSet* items Sims held onto certainly shows that her time as editor was important to her, and I wanted to know how these items were obtained. I reached out to the collector, Jeff Hoganson, a Beatles and popular music memorabilia collector who began collecting in the 1970s, to better understand how he obtained the items. He explained that he came across her items through Christie's New York-based auction house in 2007, where they advertised Sims's items listed as "Miscellaneous Photo and Ephemera Archive." In the beginning, the attraction to the auction was the Beatles items, but he ended up bidding on Sims's collection:

> The *TeenSet* lots from Judy Sims's estate caught my eye due to the diversity of 1960s bands and photographers represented. There were about twenty lots of photos categorized by band, but the one that interested me most was what they called the "Magical Mystery Box" of roughly 300 photos, press releases, vintage magazines, etc., and that was the lot I won. When the box was delivered, I didn't open it until two close friends came over and we made an evening of it . . . that was a great night![9]

Hoganson was intrigued by these photographs, *TeenSet* and Judith Sims, and he began collecting *TeenSet* to catalog which photos were used and which issue they were published in.

> Getting almost all of the past issues of *TeenSet* was great to see how the magazine developed over the years and sort of sadly ended with *AUM*. I loved how Judy immersed herself in the music scene at the time. Even though she was based in LA, there are Fillmore West concert advertising postcards addressed to her as well as pictures of her at the Monterey Pop Festival and in San Francisco, so she was completely switched on to the entire California music scene and beyond!

It was so cool to vicariously travel back to the sixties music scene through Judy's archive. I wish I had a chance to meet her.[10]

He also went on to collect items from the press officer of the Association (the band) and *TeenSet* freelancer Marilyn Doerfler's estate but argues, "I probably would not have had as much interest in [Doerfler's items] if I hadn't started with the *TeenSet* items. I also hadn't realized how many of the teen magazines from the time ... were led by women."[11]

As mentioned, when I first read about *TeenSet*, I was surprised that it existed, and I was curious if Jeff, as a collector of Beatles and popular music memorabilia, was surprised, too. He knew it existed due to Capitol's 1964/65 record sleeve ads, but stated, "What did surprise me was the progressive hipness that the magazine displayed once I started digging into the photos I bought and matching them up with the various issues."[12] Some past contributors of the rock press may not take the time to understand the importance *TeenSet* has to a fan like Kern or analyze the magazine as Hoganson has; when I asked one late 1960s *Creem* critic (in passing) if he would be interested in looking through *TeenSet*, he replied that he wasn't interested in "picture" magazines. This response suggests that, just by the name alone, he (like many others) misconstrued the entire publication and displayed no interest in examining *TeenSet* in the future. Yet as argued in chapter 5, it is not just *TeenSet* or 1960s teen fan magazines that are dismissed. For example, in 2016, when *Teen Vogue* published an article titled "Donald Trump is Gaslighting America," NPR reporter David Folkenflik, on Twitter, openly questioned *Teen Vogue*'s possibility of considering serious issues.[13] He tweeted, "Did not expect this exegesis of gaslighting in relation to current politics in Teen Vogue."[14] He was met with a response accusing him of being sexist; however, Folkenflik responded, "No, my surprise was that it came from a publication titled 'teen.'"[15] Folkenflik, like many others, preread the word "teen" to be lacking in journalistic value. In regard to *TeenSet* and teen fan magazines (or teen-related magazines in general), the nature of the word "teen," especially in relation to teen girls, still carries pejorative associations of adolescence and simplicity, describing individuals who are not capable of understanding complex concepts.

Although this book focuses on *TeenSet* and argues that it is its own entity while also fitting within the rock journalism historical narrative, this does not remove it from its role as a teen fan magazine; it occupies a uniquely liminal position. Ultimately, I would argue that *TeenSet* should be considered a youth music and culture magazine (with an older teen and young adult readership) because the editor and freelance staff heavily participated in and considered music scenes and little-known musicians throughout its existence and addressed broader issues such as race and culture. This is not to dismiss the value of teen fan magazines but rather to allow for a better understanding of what *TeenSet* was and is in the history of US popular culture. However, while considering *TeenSet*'s liminality, this book suggests throughout that teen and young adult females are of value as active fans, regardless of whether or not they are reading *16 Magazine* or *Rolling Stone*. As such, the consideration of *TeenSet* is only the beginning of what must be a larger exploration of teen fan magazines' readers and teen music fans as worthy of study, especially young female fans.

Considering the entirety of any magazine, even a short-lived one, is a monumental task; this is especially true of a magazine like *TeenSet*, which evolved into another category of magazine. Thus, there is more to consider in the future, and I fully intend to continue exploring *TeenSet*, teen fan magazines, and their readers. This book establishes many of *TeenSet*'s contributions to cultural commentary and its rightful position within the popular music press, but it is only the beginning of a long-overdue, serious reappraisal of *TeenSet*, which requires continued research in regard to fandom, its readers, and a deeper consideration of the impact of its coverage of specific groups and musicians. While *TeenSet*'s publishing run was brief, lasting for only approximately five years under the leadership of Judith Sims, its impact is far from ephemeral. *TeenSet*'s impact is momentous, and it is still shaping the way we understand mid- to late-1960s popular music and culture. As considered in the introduction, due to the inaccessibility (and lack of archiving) of *TeenSet*, the publication has been underutilized as a primary source, with some issues being rare and very expensive through resale platforms. The need to preserve texts on popular culture and the value in doing so are as important as ever. It is difficult to speculate how *TeenSet* may be utilized in future years, but it is hoped that *TeenSet*'s content will continue to inform future scholarship in the areas of popular music and cultural history.

APPENDICES

Appendix 1

An account of *TeenSet*'s Buffalo Springfield coverage.

Issue	Author/Article/Interview/Mention/Title	Pages
December 1966	"'In' Hollywood" (An introduction to the band before they go national)	26
January 1967	Pam Fourzon, "Have You Heard of (a) Buffalo (Springfield?)"	50–51, 59
February 1967	Judith Sims, "The First Annual *TeenSet* Grudge Croquet Match and Free-For-All"	32–39
	"Albums in Review–Buffalo Springfield"	56
March 1967	Karalynne and Laurayne, "Hollywood Underground"	24
	"'In' San Francisco"	47
April 1967	Karalynne and Laurayne, "Hollywood Underground"	21
	"*TeenSet*'s First Ever All-Star Scavenger Hunt and Escapade"	34–40
	Buffalo Pin-Up: "The Buffalo Springfield, for What They're Worth . . . Which Is a Lot"[1]	63
May 1967	"Quiz Number Two: Who's Where?"	7
	Karalynne and Laurayne, "Hollywood Underground"	18–19
June 1967	Karalynne and Laurayne, "Hollywood Underground"	18–19
	"*TeenSet* Tests Your Knowledge of Other People"	37
	Steven Stills, as told to Ginni Ganahl: "Peter Tork Way Back When: Old Friend Steven Stills Reminisces about the Good Old Days."	40–41
July 1967	"Who's Been Buffaloed?"	14–15, 57
	Karalynne and Laurayne, "Hollywood Underground"	18–19
August 1967	Dolly Glenney, "Mail Scene—Buffaloed"	6–7
	Karalynne and Laurayne, "Hollywood Underground"	18–19

Issue	Author/Article/Interview/Mention/Title	Pages
September 1967	"Roaming with the Buffalo (On the Plains of San Francisco, No Less)!"	14–17
	Karalynne and Laurayne, "Hollywood Underground"	18–19
October 1967	"The New Buffalo Springfield"	12–13
	Karalynne and Laurayne, "Hollywood Underground"	21
	Buffalo Fan, "Mail Scene—BUFFALO GUNS"	55
November 1967	Leslie Milleson, "A Conversation with Steven Stills"	18–19
December 1967	Karalynne and Laurayne, "Hollywood Underground"	24–25
	"*TeenSet*'s First Annual Christmas Party and Ice-Skating Debacle"	32–39
January 1968	"Image of Buffalo"	45
	Kassy Gerrick, "Buffalo Richie: First in a Series of Buffalo Lifetimes"	46, 52–54
February 1968	Kassy Gerrick, "Buffalo Dewey Martin"	11–13, 48
	"*TeenSet*'s First Annual Christmas Party and Ice-Skating Debacle"	32–39
	"The Groove—Buffalo Springfield Again"	47
March 1968	I Know, "Mail Scene—BUFFALO!"	8
	Ginni Ganahl, "Hollywood Underground"	26
	Kassy Gerrick, "Buffalo Bruce Palmer/The Quiet One Speaks"	52–54
April 1968	Judith Sims, "Buffalo Neil Young/His Past, Present, and Future"	11–13
	Myrtle Athome, "Mail Scene—We're Not Alone (After All)"	19
	Poster Spectacular Pull-out	N/A
	Ginni Ganahl, "Hollywood Underground"	24–25
	"A Buffalo Wedding/Dewey Martin Takes the Step!"	52–53
May 1968	"Go Fly a Kite/TeenSet's party—and Your Very Own Kite!"	8–13
	Amy Jones, "Mail Scene—Water Buffalo"	18
	The Great Ethnarch, "Hollywood Underground"	26–27
	Judith Sims, "Steven Stills: Fifth in Our Buffalo Series"	49–51, 54
June 1968	The Great Ethnarch, "Hollywood Underground"	18–19
July 1968	Judith Sims, "ETC. ETC." (Judith Sims Says Goodbye to the Buffalo)	6
	Allison Krohn, "Mail Scene—Another Buffalo Stampede!"	18
August 1968	Janie Morrison, "Mail Scene—Buffalo Again"	11
September 1968	Old Faithful, "Mail Scene—Buffalo"	10

Issue	Author/Article/Interview/Mention/Title	Pages
	The Great Ethnarch, "Hollywood Underground"	19
November/ December 1968	Collage by Eve Babitz, "Buffalo Springfield, Alive and Well but Not Together"	52–53

APPENDIX 2

Jim Marshall's photographs within *TeenSet*.

Issue	Number of Photos	Topic	*Shared Credit(s)	Page(s)
Special Sears "Back-to-Cool" Issue Summer 1967	5 2	Jefferson Airplane The Monkees*	Shared credit with Gene Trindl	40 44
July 1967	12 8	San Francisco groups such as Jefferson Airplane, Moby Grape, and the Grateful Dead The Monkees	N/A	21–23 44–45
August 1967	2	Jefferson Airplane	N/A	44–45
September 1967	15 3*	Moby Grape and Buffalo Springfield Mama Cass*	Shared credit with Chuck Boyd	12–13 14–17 52–53
October 1967	4 56*	Gangbusters The Monterey Pop Festival*	Shared credit with Bruce McBroom	24 32–47
November 1967	3 2*	Stephen Stills Jim Morrison*	Shared credit with Gene Trindl	18–19 50–58
January 1968	1 2	Donovan (cover) Donovan	N/A	1 12–13
February 1968	9 8*	Bob Dylan Jefferson Airplane*	Shared credit with Chuck Boyd	14–17 24–27
April 1968	5	Quicksilver Messenger Service	N/A	58–59
May 1968	22	*Positively San Francisco*: Multiple San Francisco groups from the Dead to Big Brother	N/A	31–39

Issue	Number of Photos	Topic	*Shared Credit(s)	Page(s)
June 1968	3 5	The Who Cream	N/A	14–17, 46 52–54
July 1968	9 8 2 3 1	Marty Balin Quicksilver Messenger Service Grateful Dead Richie Havens Cream (center spread)	N/A	10–13 48–51 52–53 60, 54 30–31
August 1968	3* 2 4*	Cream (cover)* Jim Morrison Steve Miller*	Shared credit with Gino Rossi Shared credit with Elaine Mayes	1 12–13 48–50
September 1968	1 4* 7 4	Janis Joplin (cover) Jim Morrison and the Doors* Big Brother and the Holding Company Jack Cassidy	Shared credit with Paula Ferra and Jim Morrison. Solo shot is Jim Marshall's.	1 28–31 32–37 52–55
October 1968	4 1	Jorma Kaukonen Janis Joplin (poster for sale)	N/A	8–11 61
November and December 1968	23 3	Newport Pop Festival Spencer Dryden	N/A	11–19 54–56
January 1969	3 3 7	Jimi Hendrix Grace Slick Considering a Second Wave in San Francisco: Creedence Clearwater Revival	N/A	23 34–35, 50–52 59
February 1969	1 7	Jefferson Airplane "Hippies"	N/A	32–33 39–43

NOTES

INTRODUCTION

1. Van Dyke Parks, email questionnaire with author, May 17, 2020.

2. In this study, teen lifestyle magazines are not necessarily of concern and to be separated from the focused teen fan magazines but are of note as they are the first to reach the teen market. These magazines were presented as guiding tales and interests that would further one into adulthood. The creators of *Seventeen* were among the first to breach the lucrative teenage magazine market in 1944 (see Massoni or Helgren), which gave traction to the creation of more lifestyle and teen-type magazines. Other studies consider more modern texts such as *Sassy* from a sociological perspective. See McRobbie and Frazer.

3. *Seventeen* began production in 1944 as the first teen magazine marketed to girls. It eventually developed into a teen-type magazine, and as of 2024, has been reformatted from a magazine to a website. This particular magazine was a first of its kind, modeled after women's lifestyle magazines but written for young teenage women preparing for their adult lives.

4. *Photoplay* was a Hollywood fan magazine that existed from 1911 to 1980.

5. Simon Frith and Angela McRobbie, "Rock and Sexuality," in *On Record: Rock, Pop and the Written Word*, edited by Simon Frith and Andrew Goodwin (London: Routledge, 1990), 317–32.

6. Frith and McRobbie, 317–32.

7. Frith and McRobbie, 321.

8. Marion Leonard, *Gender in the Music Industry: Rock, Discourse and Girl Power* (Aldershot, England: Ashgate, 2007), 25.

9. Christopher R. Martin, "The Naturalized Gender Order of Rock and Roll," *Journal of Communication Inquiry* 19, no. 1 (April 1995): 54.

10. Christine Feldman-Barrett, *A Women's History of the Beatles* (London: Bloomsbury Academic & Professional, 2021), 6.

11. Norma Coates, "Teenyboppers, Groupies, and Other Grotesques: Girls and Women and Rock Culture in the 1960s and early 1970s," *Journal of Popular Music Studies* 15, no. 1 (2003): 68.

12. Daniel Cavicchi, *Tramps Like Us: Music and Meaning Among Springsteen Fans* (New York: Oxford University Press, 1998), 6.

13. Feldman-Barrett, 145.

14. Debbie Gendler, in "I Was a Teenaged Screamer with Debbie Gendler and Carol Tyler." Moderated by Allison Bumsted, Fab4ConJam, hosted online through InLive, February 23, 2021.

15. Carol Tyler, in "I Was a Teenaged Screamer with Debbie Gendler and Carol Tyler." Moderated by Allison Bumsted, Fab4ConJam, hosted online through InLive, February 23, 2021.

16. Gendler.

17. Diane Pecknold, "The Politics of Voice in Tween Girls' Music Criticism," *Jeunesse, Young People, Texts, Cultures* 9, no. 2 (2017): 69.

18. Coates, 65–94.

19. Sheila Whiteley, *Too Much Too Young: Popular Music, Age and Gender* (New York: Routledge, 2005).

20. Helen Davies, "All Rock and Roll Is Homosocial: The Representation of Women in the British Rock Music Press," *Popular Music* 20, no. 3 (2001): 311.

21. Elizabeth M. Weinstein, "Married to Rock and Roll: Jane Scott, Grandmother of Rock Journalism," *Journalism History* 32, no. 3 (2006): 147–55.

22. Matt Brennan, *When Genres Collide: DownBeat, Rolling Stone, and the Struggle between Jazz and Rock* (New York: Bloomsbury Academic, 2017), 143.

23. Here, fans are defined as individuals who convey enthusiasm toward a group, television series, movie franchise, artist, sports team, author, book series, fashion designer, and so on. Levels of fandom are not easily classified, and there are degrees of fandom (see Cavicchi and Lewis). One may be a professional and a fan, but in this book, the defining difference is that the professional is in a paid career or a paid freelancer. It is also possible to be a biased fan and a professional.

24. John Burks and Jerry Hopkins, *Groupies and Other Girls*, edited by Jann Wenner (New York: Bantam, 1970), 6.

25. Burks and Hopkins, back cover.

26. Cheryl Cline, "Essays from Bitch: The Women's Rock Newsletter with Bite," in *The Adoring Audience: Fan Culture and Popular Media*, edited by Lisa Lewis (London: Routledge, 1992), 73.

27. Coates, 85.

28. Coates, 68.

29. Sheryl Garratt, "Teenage Dreams," in *On Record: Rock, Pop and the Written Word*, edited by Simon Frith and Andrew Goodwin (Florence: Taylor & Francis Group, 2000), 342.

30. Coates, 68.

31. Evelyn McDonell and Ann Powers, "Preface," in *Rock She Wrote: Women Write About Rock, Pop, and Rap*, edited by Evelyn McDonnell and Ann Powers (London: Plexus Publishing, 1995), 1.

32. McDonell and Powers, 2.

33. McDonell and Powers, 4.

34. Daphne A. Brooks, "The Write to Rock: Racial Mythologies, Feminist Theory, and the Pleasures of Rock Music Criticism," *Women and Music* 12, 2008: 58.

35. André Doehring, "Male Journalists as 'Artists': The Ideological Production of Recent Popular Music Journalism," In M. Buscatt, M. Leontsini, and D. Naudier, eds., *Du Genre dans La Critique/Gender in Art Criticism*, English ed. Paris: Éditions des archives contemporaines, (2017): 5.

36. Kate Mossman, "Women Who Wrote Rock," written by Kate Mossman, aired March 22 and 26, 2016, on BBC Radio 4, https://www.bbc.co.uk/programmes/b07428bt.

37. Mossman.

38. Mossman.

39. Mossman.

40. Suzanne Franks, *Women and Journalism* (London: I. B. Tauris, 2013), 3.

41. John Mendelsohn, interview with the author, July 23, 2023.

42. Diana L. Belscamper, "'Your Ticket to Dreamsville': The Functions of *16 Magazine* in American Girl Culture of the 1960s" (unpublished diss., University of Wisconsin-Milwaukee, 2014), 189.

43. Franco Fabbri, "A Theory of Musical Genres: Two Applications," in *Popular Music: Critical Concepts in Media and Cultural Studies* vol. 3 (2004): 7.

44. Fabian Holt, *Genre in Popular Music* (Chicago: University of Chicago Press, 2007), 2.

45. Holt, 8–9.

46. Jane Feuer, "Genre Study and Television," in *Channels of Discourse, Reassembled*, edited by Robert C. Allen (Chapel Hill: University of North Carolina Press, 1992), 144.

47. Feuer, 139.

48. Rick Altman, in Feuer, Jane, "Genre Study and Television," in *Channels of Discourse, Reassembled*, edited by Robert C. Allen (Chapel Hill: University of North Carolina Press 1992), 144.

49. Marcia R. Prior-Miller, "Research Review: Issues in Magazine Typology," in *The American Magazine*, edited by David Abrahamson (Ames, IA: Iowa State University Press, 1995), 3.

50. Prior-Miller, 3.

51. Keir Keightley, "Reconsidering Rock," in *The Cambridge Companion to Pop and Rock*, edited by Simon Frith, Will Straw, and John Street, (Cambridge: Cambridge University Press, 2001), 109.

52. Miles Parks Grier, "Said the Hooker to the Thief: Some Way out of Rockism," *Journal of Popular Music Studies* 25, no. 1 (2013), 36.

53. Jody Rosen, "The Perils of Poptimism: Does Hating Rock Make You a Music Critic?" *Slate*, May 9, 2006. Accessed May 1, 2021. https://slate.com/culture/2006/05/does-hating-rock-make-you-a-music-critic.html.

54. Rock aesthetics, values, and principles within the argued ideology of rock will be considered and defined in chapter 2.

55. Allison Bumsted, "Which Side Is This Ex-Beatle On? A Reassessment of the 1970s Rock Press' Framing, Interpretation, and Consideration of Paul McCartney and Wings," in *Words, Music, and the Popular: Global Perspective on Intermedial Relations*," edited by Thomas Gurke and Susan Winnett, (Cham, Switzerland: Palgrave Macmillan 2021).

56. Keightley, 110.

57. For more on the consideration of "good" journalism and practices, see Harcup.

58. Keightley, 110.

59. *Tiger Beat* no longer exists as a magazine in any format. At the time of writing, the website was no longer updated.

60. *Rolling Stone* includes past (reformatted) articles on its current site. However, the design of the website requires a detailed and specific search to find older articles.

61. *Rock's Backpages*, edited by Barney Hoskyns, is available for subscription to institutions or individuals and can be found at https://www.rocksbackpages.com/.

62. Sunshine Factory, https://monkees.coolcherrycream.com/games/dress-up.

63. Anthony Slide, *Inside the Hollywood Fan Magazine: A History of Star Makers, Fabricators, and Gossip Mongers* (Jackson: University of Mississippi Press, 2010), 16.

64. For more on popular music and musicology, see Middleton, Longhurst, Tagg, Fink, Shuker, and Negus.

65. B. Lee Cooper, Frank Hoffman, and Wayne S. Haney, *Rock Music in American Popular Culture: Rock 'n' Roll Resources* (New York: Harrington Park Press, 1995), 7.

66. The term "Apple Scruff" (originated by George Harrison in 1970) refers to the Beatles fans (men and women) who waited daily outside of EMI's Abbey Road studios and various Beatles houses in the late 1960s, notably Paul McCartney's home, as it was close to EMI. Furlong and others, such as Lizzie Bravo, refer to themselves as Apple Scruffs, wearing the term as a badge of honor.

67. Ulf Lindberg, Gestur Gudmundsson, Morten Michelsen, and Hans Weisethaunet, *Rock Criticism from the Beginning: Amusers, Bruisers, and Cool-Headed Cruisers* (New York: Peter Lang, 2005), 131.

68. For more on revolutionary rhetoric in 1960s rock, see Burke.

Chapter One: A *Capitol* Idea! The Origins of Teen Fan Magazines and *Teenset*

1. Nancy Furlong, email questionnaire with author, July 9, 2020.

2. Charles H. Brown, "Self-Portrait: The Teen-Type Magazine," The Annals of the American Academy of Political and Social Science 338 (1961): 13–21.

3. Thomas Doherty, *Teenagers and Teenpics: The Juvenilization of American Movies* (Philadelphia: Temple University Press, 2010), 46.

4. Doherty, 47.

5. *DIG*, cover, November 1965.

6. Dixie Dean Harris, also known as Dixie Dean Trainer, was a Hollywood fan magazine writer. She is featured in Canadian reporter Pierre Burton's out-of-print *Voices of the Sixties* as an important voice that shaped the 1960s. Her interview is among twenty-two others, including Malcolm X and Ray Bradbury.

7. Dixie Dean Harris, "And This, Dear God, Is What They Read," *Esquire*, July 1, 1965, 106.

8. In regard to Hollywood fan magazines, Canadian reporter Pierre Burton felt that they had such an impact on society that he included fan magazine writer and editor Dixie Dean (Harris) Trainer's interview within the book is among twenty-two other impactful voices of the 1960s in his text titled *Voices from the Sixties: Twenty-Two Views of a Revolutionary Decade*. She was featured as "The Queen of Fan Magazines" among Ray Bradbury, Malcolm X, and a Catholic choosing to take birth control. Historically, all of these individuals are/were seen as impactful (and, to some, controversial) and as representing change. The majority of high school students across America read Bradbury and X. Although Burton questions the sensationalism of Trainer's work, he nonetheless recognizes the impact it had.

9. Mary Desjardins, "'Fan Magazine Trouble': The AMPP, Studio Publicity Directors, and the Hollywood Press, 1945–1952," *Film History* 26, no. 3 (2014): 49.

10. Erin Torkelson Weber, *The Beatles and the Historians: An Analysis of Writings About the Fab Four* (Jefferson: McFarland & Company Inc., 2016), 17.

11. This is not to say that music magazines were not printing sheet music of music that was popular, but rather that magazines that considered music did not critically discuss popular music and culture.

12. Jazz, like rock, was dismissed or ignored by critics of other music genres. This dismissal was rooted in racism and classism. In the early 1920s, jazz was legally deemed to corrupt the minds of unborn children (see Johnson).

13. David Abrahamson, *Magazine-Made America: The Cultural Transformation of the Post War Periodical* (Cresskill, Hampton Press Inc., 1996), 2.

14. Abrahamson, 25.

15. Abrahamson, 25.

16. Victor Brooks, *Last Season of Innocence* (Plymouth: Rowman & Littlefield Publishers Inc. 2012), 136.

17. Harris, 106.

18. *Time*, "The Press: Aiming at the Hip," June 2, 1967, 36.

19. *Time*, 36.

20. Gloria Stavers, in John Burks and Jerry Hopkins, *Groupies and Other Girls*, edited by Jann Wenner (New York, Bantam, 1970), 94.

21. David Galassie, "Gloria Stavers and *16 Magazine*." Internet Archive: Wayback Machine, last modified October 16, 2006. Accessed June 20, 2020. https://web.archive.org/web/20061016014724/http://www.loti.com/sixties_history/Gloria_Stavers_and_16_Magazine.htm.

22. *16 Magazine*, cover, May 1957.

23. Danny Fields and Randi Reisfeld, *Who's Your Fave Rave?: Teen Idols as You Knew Them . . . AND as They Really Were!* (New York: Boulevard Books, 1997), Kindle edition.

24. Fields and Reisfeld.

25. Diana L. Belscamper, "'Your Ticket to Dreamsville'": The Functions of *16 Magazine* in American Girl Culture of the 1960s" (unpublished diss., University of Wisconsin-Milwaukee, 2014), 220.

26. Belscamper, 220.

27. Belscamper, 214.

28. Fields and Reisfeld.

29. Nicolette Rohr, "Yeah Yeah Yeah: The Sixties Screamscape of Beatlemania." *Journal of Popular Music Studies* 29, no. 2 (June 2017): 2.

30. Harris, 106.

31. Harris, 106.

32. Ann Moses and Ann Wicker, *Meow! My Groovy Life with Tiger Beat's Teen Idols* (self-published, 2017), 34.

33. Harris, 106.

34. Lloyd Thaxton was the host of a pop variety hour from 1961 to 1968. He was a sponsor of *Tiger Beat* magazine and wrote a column in the early start of *Tiger Beat*. Northwestern University hosts the physical Lloyd Thaxton archives that include the *Tiger Beat*s his name was associated with.

35. *16 Magazine*, cover, October 1968.

36. Ann Moses, email questionnaire with author, June 11, 2020.

37. *Soul Teen* was a Black teen magazine created by George Leviathan, a white man from Good Publishing Company, Fort Worth, Texas. There is no evidence of an academic analysis of this magazine. Both *Soul Teen* and *Right On!* are very rare. See Elkind for more information on *Soul Teen*.

38. Ann Moses and Ann Wicker, *Meow! My Groovy Life with Tiger Beat's Teen Idols* (self-published, 2017), 24.

39. Devon Powers, *Writing the Record: The Village Voice and the Birth of Rock Criticism* (Amherst, MA: University of Massachusetts Press, 2013), 13.

40. Ann Moses, email questionnaire with author, June 11, 2020.

41. Moses.

42. Belscamper, 138.

43. Moses.

44. Richie Furay, email questionnaire with author, May 21, 2020.

45. *16 Magazine*. "Marc-David Glam-Rock!" October 1972, 10–11.

46. Debbie Gendler is well known in the Beatles world of fandom as a guest of Brian Epstein on the February 9, 1964, *Ed Sullivan Show*. Gendler can be seen as the first audience close-up during the Beatles' performance of "All My Loving." She was a *Datebook* stringer through high school and is known for her fandom participation in popular music. See Gendler.

47. Debbie Gendler, email questionnaire with author, May 28–29, 2020.

48. Carolyn Kitch, "Theory of Methods of Analysis: Modes for Understanding Magazines," in *The Routledge Handbook of Magazine Research: The Future of the Magazine Form*, edited by David Abrahamson and Marcia R. Prior-Miller (New York: Routledge, 2015), 12.

49. Moses.

50. The *Las Vegas Voice* was a Black newspaper. See "*Las Vegas Sentinel-Voice*."

51. The *Capitol News* and *Music News* are digitally archived. At the time of writing, open access to both magazines was granted through the Johnny Mercer Foundation and Georgia State University.

52. Dave Dexter Jr., "Let's Go for Another 25!," *Billboard*, September 16, 1967, C8.

53. Trade papers like *Billboard* mostly considered the music industry.

54. Ken Mansfield, email questionnaire with author, May 12, 2020.

55. *Cashbox*, "The *Teen Set* Advertisement," October 24, 1964, 13.

56. *Cashbox*, like *Billboard*, was a popular music industry magazine that existed from 1942 to 1996.

57. *Cashbox*, 13.

58. Allan Kozinn, "Brown Meggs, 66, a Recording Executive Who Signed the Beatles," *New York Times*, October 10, 1966. Accessed June 1, 2020. https://www.nytimes.com/1997/10/16/arts/brown-meggs-66-a-recording-executive-who-signed-the-beatles.html.

59. Joan Ormrod, "Endless Summer (1964): Consuming Waves and Surfing the Frontier," *Film and History: An Interdisciplinary Journal of Film and Television Studies* 35, no. 1 (2001): 39.

60. *Cashbox*, "Capitol *TeenSet* Magazine Is Building Up to a Bantom Bonanza," January 1, 1966, 8. Bantom is most likely an alternative or misspelling spelling to Bantam, which refers to small fowl; this reference only furthers the argument of this book that young female voices are often dismissed.

61. *Cashbox*, "Capitol *TeenSet* Promo Seek Close Teen Ties," October 24, 1964, 40.

62. *Teen Set*, "Capitol Records *TeenSet* Membership," advertisement, 1965, 37.

63. Brown Meggs, in unlisted "Capitol *TeenSet* Promo Seek Close Teen Ties," *Cashbox*, October 24, 1964, 40.

64. Bruce Spizer, *The Beatles' Story on Capitol Records, Part Two: The Albums* (New Orleans: 498 Productions LLC, 2001), 196.

65. Spizer, 196.

66. *Billboard Magazine*, "Capitol Diversifies; Enters Teen Fan Magazine Market," August 28, 1965, 6.

67. See Belscamper for a detailed account of *DIG*.

68. By Sims's senior year of college, she married Jack Canon. Both were English majors, and at least Sims was positioned to become a secondary English teacher. She and Canon parted ways shortly after they moved to LA. Evidence suggests that at the time, the Canons moved to LA to pursue careers. Jack Canon pursued acting and was a lead in the 1974 horror film *Axe*. In correspondence with Sims's friend and colleague, Ben Fong-Torres, who was

unaware of the name "Canon" or that Sims had been married in the first place, suggested it was not something she shared with others.

69. For *16 Magazine*, Stavers was an unusual choice as well, as she had no experience, but she was known for modeling and knew some of the business.

70. Chester Flippo, "Rock Journalism and *Rolling Stone*" (master's thesis, University of Texas at Austin, 1974), 23.

71. *Billboard*.

72. Milstead also edited *TeenScreen* for a period in the late 1960s. She wrote under multiple pseudonyms in *TeenSet* magazine; one of note was "Shirley Poston." Milstead was known in the popular music world until her death in the mid-2010s. Before her passing, she collaborated with Ben Fong-Torres on an unpublished collection.

73. Richard Morton Jack, "*TeenSet*: The story behind this pioneering 1960s American rock magazine," *Flashback Magazine*, Winter 2014, 18.

74. *TeenSet*, "Features—A Go Go Teenage Magazine," November 1965, 2.

75. Jack, 15.

76. Judith Sims, "ETC. ETC.," *TeenSet*, May 1968, 5.

77. Frank Zappa first appeared in *Teen Set* in November 1966 and was featured throughout *TeenSet*'s existence.

78. The fashion covered was often in connection to pop stars and music scenes like London or San Francisco.

79. *16 Magazine*, cover, May 1968.

80. *Cheetah* was a short-lived popular music and culture magazine from 1967 to 1968.

81. *EYE* was a short-lived, Hearst-published, youth culture-focused magazine published from 1968 to 1969.

82. Judith Sims, *AUM*, June 1969, 4.

83. Shortly after the completion of his master's degree, Chester Flippo would go on to work as an editor of *Rolling Stone*. Judith Sims was already employed by *Rolling Stone*.

84. Flippo.

85. Flippo, 2.

86. Flippo, 9.

87. Flippo, 122.

88. "Cultist," Merriam-Webster, https://www.merriam-webster.com/dictionary/cultist.

89. "Cultist," The Free Dictionary, https://www.thefreedictionary.com/cultist.

90. Chester Flippo, 37.

91. Jon Landau, *It's Too Late to Stop Now: A Rock and Roll Journal* (San Francisco: Straight Arrow Books, 1972).

92. Andrew Sarris, *Confessions of a Cultist: On the Cinema, 1955/1969* (New York: Simon and Schuster, 1971), 13.

93. Roger Ebert, "Andrew Sarris, 1928–2012: In Memoriam," RogerEbert.com, last modified June 20, 2012. Accessed May 2, 2021. https://www.rogerebert.com/interviews/andrew-sarris-1928-2012-in-memoriam.

94. Ebert.

95. *Fortune*, August 1933.

96. *Billboard Magazine*, "Rózsa—Music from Madame Bovary—Album Reviews," August 20, 1949, 94.

97. Jon Landau, *It's Too Late to Stop Now: A Rock and Roll Journal* (San Francisco: Straight Arrow Books, 1972), 219.

98. Sarris.

99. Brian Longhurst, *Popular Music & Society* (Cambridge: Polity Press, 2007), 262.

100. Chester Flippo, "Rock Journalism and *Rolling Stone*" (master's thesis, University of Texas at Austin, 1974), 37.

101. Flippo's text has been used to advance the understanding of *Rolling Stone*'s contribution to rock criticism in recent scholarship, such as Lindberg et al.'s *Rock Criticism from the Beginning* and Devon Powers's *Writing on the Record*. It has also been used to consider aspects of the record industry in R. Serge Denisoff's 1975 *Solid Gold: The Popular Record Industry*.

102. Beatles.Net, "The Beatles' Story on Capitol Records, Part 2: The Albums" (digital edition). Accessed July 11, 2020. https://www.beatle.net/product/the-beatles-story-on-capitol-records-part-2-the-albums/.

103. Spizer, 198.

104. Richard Morton Jack, 15.

105. Jack, 17.

106. Don Armstrong, "*TeenSet* Magazine Part 1," Music Journalism History, last modified October 21, 2019. Accessed November 29, 2019. https://www.music-journalism-history.com/2019/10/21/teenset-magazine-part-1/.

107. Don Armstrong, "TeenSet Magazine Part 2," Music Journalism History, last modified October 23, 2019. Accessed November 29, 2019. https://www.music-journalism-history.com/2019/10/223/teenset-magazine-part-1/.

108. Armstrong, "TeenSet Magazine Part 2."

109. Grace Slick (@graceslickoffcial), "Drawn and on the cover of *TeenSet* magazine, 1968," Instagram photo, July 3, 2017, Instagram.com.

110. Future Ex-Mrs. Malcolm, "Let's Read *TeenSet*, September 1967!," The Avocado, last modified February 23, 2018. Accessed October 10, 2018. https://the-avocado.org/2018/02/23/lets-read-teen-set-september-1967/.

111. Van Dyke Parks (@parksvandyke), "Do I dare?" Instagram photo, May 17, 2020, Instagram.com.

112. Benmont Tench (@benmonttench), in response to Van Dyke Parks (@parksvandyke), "Do I dare?" Instagram photo, May 17, 2020, Instagram.com.

113. Peter Jackson, *The Beatles: Get Back—A Sneak Peak from Peter Jackson*, Disney Plus (December 20, 2020).

114. See chapter 5, figure 5.8.

CHAPTER TWO: IT'S ONLY ROCK 'N' ROLL JOURNALISM: THE ABSENCE OF *TeenSet* WITHIN A HISTORY SHAPED BY CRITICS

1. *TeenSet*, "The Unimportance of Being Earnest: A Letter from an Editor." January 1968, 9. Although the article does not cite Janey Milstead as the author, she admits to writing this letter in another article discussed later in this book.

2. See Belscamper, Moser, Moses, or chapter 1.

3. Margaret Moser, "Dreamsville: Gloria Stavers, *16 Magazine*, and the Roots of Rock Journalism," *The Austin Chronicle*, November 30, 2007. Accessed April 10, 2020. https://www.austinchronicle.com/music/2007-11-30/565815/.

4. Jim DeRogatis, *Let it Blurt: The Life and Times of Lester Bangs, America's Greatest Rock Critic* (New York: Crown, 2000), 48–49.

5. Devon Powers, *Writing the Record: The Village Voice and the Birth of Rock Criticism* (Amherst, MA: University of Massachusetts Press, 2013), 13.

6. Maureen Cleave, "How Does a Beatles Live? John Lennon Lives Like This," *London Evening Standard*, March 4, 1966, 10.

7. Fields has openly discussed the reprinting of two of Cleave's articles in the documentary *Danny Says*. In regard to the controversy caused by the reprinting of the two articles, Fields claims he was not attempting to hurt the Beatles. See Toller.

8. Brian Ward, "'The "C" is for Christ': Arthur Unger, *Datebook* Magazine and the Beatles." *Popular Music and Society* 35, no. 4 (2012): 542.

9. Ward, 542.

10. Ward does not make an argument for the importance of all teen fan magazines; he focuses solely on *Datebook*.

11. Ward, 541.

12. Ward, 551.

13. Robert Rodriguez, *Revolver: How the Beatles Reimagined Rock 'n' Roll* (Milwaukee, WI: Backbeat Books, 2012), 169.

14. Simon Frith, *Sound Effects: Youth, Leisure, and the Politics of Rock 'n' Roll* (New York: Pantheon Books, 1981), 168.

15. Simon Frith and Angela McRobbie, "Rock and Sexuality," in *On Record: Rock, Pop and the Written Word*, edited by Simon Frith and Andrew Goodwin, (London: Routledge, 1990), 323.

16. Matt Brennan, *When Genres Collide: DownBeat, Rolling Stone, and the Struggle between Jazz and Rock* (New York: Bloomsbury Academic, 2017), 121.

17. David Fricke, "The First Rock Critic," *Rolling Stone*, April 25, 2013, 28.

18. Fricke, 28.

19. In online communication with Furay, he suggested the comment came from Einarson's perspective of the business side of music. He personally had nothing but positive things to say about *TeenSet*. However, Furay's name is on the text, so it is included here as part of the discussion.

20. John Einarson and Richie Furay, *For What It's Worth; The Story of Buffalo Springfield* (New York: Cooper Square Press, 1997, 2004).

21. Einarson and Furay, 107.

22. Einarson and Furay, 107–8.

23. "Rockism" refers to an elitist attitude that rock is not only better, but to be rock, one must adhere to specific rock aesthetics. The term is often accredited to Pete Wylie in a 2001 interview with Paul Dunoyer (see Gorman), but this is a misconception. Wylie appears to have coined the concept of "race against rockism," not rockism as a general concept. The earliest source I have found of the term appears in Christgau's *Robert Christgau's Record Guide: Rock Albums of the '80s*. However, Brennan notes in *When Genres Collide* that the term has UK origins beginning in the 1980s. It has appeared in multiple texts.

24. "Teenybopper," Merriam-Webster. https://www.merriam-webster.com/dictionary/teenybopper.

25. However, *TeenSet* itself recognized and considered up-and-coming rock writers and rock criticism in early 1969 in an article titled "The Rogue Gallery of Rock Writers." See chapter 4.

26. Ralph J. Gleason, *The Jefferson Airplane and the San Francisco Sound*, (New York: Ballantine Books, 1969), 1.

27. Richard Goldstein, *The Poetry of Rock* (New York: Bantam Books Inc., 1969), xii.

28. Greil Marcus, introduction to "The Aesthetics of Rock" (1968), last modified July 5, 2014. https://greilmarcus.net/2014/07/05/introduction-to-the-aesthetics-of-rock-1986/.

29. Jon Landau, *It's Too Late to Stop Now: A Rock and Roll Journal* (San Francisco: Straight Arrow Books, 1972), 13.

30. Christgau is also known as the "dean" of rock criticism, claiming to have given himself this name in 1970. *TeenSet* first referred to Ralph J. Gleason as the "dean" in March 1969. See Swaney.

31. Robert Christgau, *Any Old Way You Choose It: Rock and Other Pop Music, 1967–1973* (New York: Penguin Books, 1973).

32. Andrew Milner, *Literature, Culture and Society*, 2nd ed. (London: Routledge, 2005), 7.

33. Since 2011, multiple UK websites have referred to Gambaccini as the "Professor of Pop."

34. Paul Gambaccini, *Rock Critic's Choice: The Top 200 Albums* (New York: Omnibus Press, 1978), 3–4.

35. Motti Regev, "Producing Artistic Value: The Case of Rock Music," *The Sociological Quarterly* 35, no. 1 (February 1994): 90.

36. Malcolm Doney, *Summer in the City: Rock Music and Way of Life* (Berkhamsted, England: Lion Publishing, 1978), 102.

37. Erin Torkelson Weber, *The Beatles and the Historians: An Analysis of Writings about the Fab Four* (Jefferson: McFarland & Company Inc., 2016), 15.

38. Jim DeRogatis, in *Ticket to Write: A Golden Age of Rock Music Journalism* (2016), directed by Raul Sandelin, Amazon Digital UK.

39. Dean Biron, "Towards a Popular Music Criticism of Replenishment," *Popular Music and Society* 34, no. 5 (December 2011): 666.

40. Ben Fong-Torres's documentary *Like a Rolling Stone: The Life and Times of Ben Fong-Torres* is streaming on Netflix as of May 2022. It focuses on Fong-Torres's time as a rock critic and also his life and involvement in his community. It lacks the same rockist elements as *Ticket to Write* and *Almost Famous*. This documentary is particularly important, as not many writers of color or Asian descent are discussed in rock journalism history. However, his role with *TeenSet/AUM* is not highlighted within this; the focus is mainly on his tenure with *Rolling Stone*.

41. Raul Sandelin, dir., *Ticket to Write: A Golden Age in Rock Journalism* (2016), Amazon Digital UK.

42. Carrie Kahn, "Noise Pop Film Review: *Ticket to Write: The Golden Age of Rock Music Journalism*," SpinningPlatters.com, last modified February 26, 2017. Accessed January 2020. http://spinningplatters.com /2017/02/26/noise-pop-film-review-ticket-to-write-the-golden-age-of-rock-music-journalism/.

43. DeRogatis.

44. Bill Holdship, in *Ticket to Write: A Golden Age of Rock Music Journalism* (2016), directed by Raul Sandelin, Amazon Digital UK.

45. Sandelin.

46. Patricia Aufderheide, Peter Jaszi, and Mridu Chandra, "Honest Truths: Documentary Filmmakers on Ethical Challenges in Their Work," Center for Media and Social Impact, last modified September 2009. Accessed March 1, 2020. https://cmsimpact.org/resource/honest-truths-documentary-filmmakers-on-ethical-challenges-in-their-work/.

47. Michael Chanan, *The Politics of Documentary* (London: British Film Institute, 2007), 4.

48. Richard M. Blumenberg, "Documentary Films and the Problem of 'Truth,'" *Journal of the University Film Association* 29, no. 4 (1977): 19.

49. E. H. Carr, *What Is History?* (Middlesex: Pelican Books, 1961), 23.

50. Box Office Mojo, "Almost Famous." https://www.boxofficemojo.com/title/tt0181875/?ref_=bo_se_r_1.

51. Lester Bangs, *Almost Famous*, performed by Phillip Seymour Hoffman, dir. by Cameron Crowe (Universal City, CA: DreamWorks Home Entertainment, 2001), DVD.

52. Bangs.

53. Bangs.

54. Bangs.

55. Bangs.

56. Bangs.

57. "Archetype," Merriam-Webster, https://www.merriam-webster.com/dictionary/archetype.

58. "Sage," Merriam-Webster, https://www.merriam-webster.com/dictionary/sage.

59. "Sage."

60. Mark A. Lewis and Ian P. Renga, "Wisdom, Mystery, and Dangerous Knowledge: Exploring Depictions of the Archetypal Sage in Young Adult Literature," *Study and Scrutiny: Research in Young Adult Literature* 3, no. 1 (May 25, 2018): 26.

61. Bangs.

62. Lewis and Renga, 44.

63. Michael Stanford, *A Companion to the Study of History* (Hoboken: Wiley, 1994), 276.

64. Anthony Brundage, *Going to the Sources*, 5th ed. (Chichester, England: John Wiley & Sons Ltd., 2012), 65.

65. Roger Ebert, "Reviews: *Almost Famous*," RogerEbert.com, last modified September 15, 2000. Accessed November 10, 2019. https://www.rogerebert.com/reviews/almost-famous-2000.

66. Brundage, 64.

67. Ben Fong-Torres, "Ben Fong-Torres." Accessed June 10, 2020. http://benfongtorres.com/.

68. Fong-Torres.

69. Jennifer Otter Bickerdike, *Fandom, Image and Authenticity: Joy Devotion and the Second Lives of Kurt Cobain and Ian Curtis* (Basingstoke, England: Palgrave Macmillan, 2014), 48.

70. Bickerdike, 49.

71. Bickerdike, 65.

72. A fanzine is defined as a magazine created by fans who are enthusiastic about the chosen subject matter but who are not necessarily professional publishers or writers. An example in popular music is Greg Shaw's 1970s *Who Put the Bomp!* rock fanzine.

73. Motti Regev, "Producing Artistic Value: The Case of Rock Music," *The Sociological Quarterly* 35, no. 1 (February 1994): 90.

74. Simon Frith, *Sound Effects: Youth, Leisure, and the Politics of Rock 'n' Roll* (New York: Pantheon Books, 1981), 168.

75. A nonfictional, subjective, and unconventional writing style developed in the late 1960s. New Journalism also had subgenres within it, such as gonzo journalism, popularized by Hunter S. Thompson.

76. Also referred to as the aesthetic (or "aesthetics") of rock.

77. Frith, 169.

78. Regev, 86.

79. Frith, 165.

80. Kembrew McLeod, "★: A Critique of Rock Criticism in North America," *Popular Music* 20, no. 1 (January 2001): 47.

81. This is highlighted in "Which Side Is This Ex-Beatle On? A Reassessment of the 1970s Rock Press' Framing, Interpretation, and Consideration of Paul McCartney and Wings," in *Words, Music, and the Popular: Global Perspective on Intermedial Relations*, edited by Thomas Gurke and Susan Winnett (Cham, Switzerland: Palgrave Macmillan 2021). See Bumsted.

82. Biron, "Towards," 675.

83. Steve Jones and Kevin Feathery, "Re-Viewing Rock Writing: Narrative of Popular Music Criticism," in *Pop Music and the Press*, edited by Steve Jones (Philadelphia: Temple University, 2002), 31.

84. For more on rock aesthetics, see Keightley, McLeod, Brennan, Jones, Regev, Atton, and Bumsted.

85. Ulf Lindberg, Gestur Gudmundsson, Morten Michelsen, and Hans Weisethaunet, *Rock Criticism from the Beginning: Amusers, Bruisers, and Cool-Headed Cruisers* (New York: Peter Lang, 2005), 8.

86. Regev, 98.

87. Lindberg, 131.

88. Lindberg, 133.

89. Biron, 661.

90. Biron, 662.

91. Brennan, *When Genres Collide*, 187.

92. See Powers, Brooks, Atton, Davies, and Brennan.

Chapter Three: Show Me *TeenSet*! *TeenSet* as a Valuable Source in Popular Music

1. This analysis does not explore unlicensed uses or repostings of *TeenSet*'s content on web pages or texts that may exist but were not found.

2. Laura Nyro was a popular musician and songwriter from the late 1960s until her death in 1997. Her songs have been covered by artists such as Blood, Sweat & Tears, the Fifth Dimension, Barbra Streisand, Three Dog Night, Alison Krauss, and others. She has since been inducted into the Songwriters and Rock 'n' Roll Hall of Fame for her songwriting and musical achievements.

3. Michele Kort, *Soul Picnic: The Music and Passion of Laura Nyro* (New York: Thomas Dunne Books, 2002), 43.

4. At the time of writing, no other discussions of Nyro's performance were found in the 1960s print media.

5. Patricia S. Rudden, "Stacking the Wax: The Structure of Laura Nyro's Studio Albums," in *Singing for Themselves: Essays on Women in Popular Music*, edited by Patricia S. Rudden (Cambridge: Cambridge Scholars Publishing, 2007), 29.

6. Sharry Wilson, *Young Neil: The Sugar Mountain Years* (Toronto: ECW Press, 2014), 110.

7. Wilson, 396.

8. Jimmy McDonough, *Shakey: Neil Young's Biography* (New York: Random House, 2002), 182.

9. At the time of writing, I have been approached by a Neil Young biographer for information on *TeenSet*, only furthering the importance of *TeenSet*.

10. Jacoba Atlas, "Jimi Hendrix, Black Power, and Money," *TeenSet*, January 1969, 21–25, 58–59.

11. Atlas, 22.

12. Daryl Hale, "Quicker than a Wink of an Eye," in *Jimi Hendrix and Philosophy: Experience Required*, edited by Ammon G. Theodore (Chicago: Open Court Publishing, 2017), 81–82.

13. Hale, 82.

14. Mick Wall, *Two Riders Were Approaching: The Life & Death of Jimi Hendrix* (London: Orion Publishing, 2017), 262.

15. Harry Shapiro, and Caesar Glebbeek, *Jimi Hendrix: Electric Gypsy* (New York: Macmillan, 1995), 369.

16. Steven Roby ed., *Hendrix on Hendrix: Interview and Encounters with Jimi Hendrix* (Chicago: Chicago Press, 2012), xi.

17. Roby, xi.

18. The Epstein family's record store and music corporation. Most notably run and expanded by Beatles manager Brian Epstein.

19. Mr. Rossi did not respond to three attempts to include his voice in this book.

20. Chuck Boyd's photography collection is captured in his book *Forever Young*.

21. The full count is 267. However, due to shared credits, the number is lower, around 250 photographs, before it became *AUM*. Sims introduced Marshall as the lead photographer for *AUM* in June 1969 (see Sims).

22. The images within the Monterey Pop spread are credited to Jim Marshall and Bruce McBroom, and while the photographs are not individually attributed to either photographer, Marshall's multiple compilation books contain many of the same photographs as well as other photographs from the same photo shoot.

23. Michelle Margetts, "The Monterey Pop Festival," in *Jim Marshall: Show Me the Picture*, edited by Amelia Davis (San Francisco: Chronicle Books, 2019), 194.

24. This nomination is contested as to whether or not Joplin did it as a joke, but the current consensus is that she did not, and this nomination was painful for her.

25. Robert Draper, "O Janis," *Texas Monthly*, October 1992, 182.

26. Sheila Whiteley, *Women and Popular Music* (New York: Routledge, 2005), 131–34.

27. Robert Courtney, "Positively San Francisco," *TeenSet*, May 1968, 39.

28. Jim Marshall, in Michelle Margetts's "The Monterey Pop Festival," in *Jim Marshall: Show Me the Picture*, edited by Amelia Davis (San Francisco: Chronicle Books, 2019), 206.

29. When Dylan went electric, folk musicians and fans boycotted him for a time as it was seen as moving away from his folk roots.

30. *TeenSet*, "Look Back," February 1968, 14–17.

31. *TeenSet*, 14–17.

32. Access to the *Saturday Evening Post* was unattainable at the time of writing, but I found no evidence that this particular photo was published within.

33. Michelle Margetts, "Dylan with the Tire," in *Jim Marshall: Show Me the Picture*, edited by Amelia Davis (San Francisco: Chronicle Books, 2019), 64.

34. Margetts, 64.

35. This photograph and the outing with Bob Dylan have gained a fan following in popular music tourism. The website PopSpotsNYC features an in-depth discussion of the day with full maps so one can retrace Dylan and Marshall's steps.

36. *TeenSet*, cover, February 1968.

37. Paul Williams, "How Rock Communicates," in *The Penguin Book of Rock & Roll Writing*, edited by Clinton Heylin (New York: Viking, 1992), 75–80.

38. Joel Selvin, in *Jim Marshall: Show Me the Picture*, edited by Amelia Davis (San Francisco: Chronicle Books, 2019), 107.

39. Joshua Brown, "Historians and Photography," *American Art* 21, no. 3 (2007): 9.

40. Brown, 9.

41. Selvin, 107.

42. *Show Me the Picture: The Story of Jim Marshall*, directed by Alfred G. Bailey, 2019 (London: Modern Films, 2020), DVD.

43. Joel Selvin, email questionnaire with author, March 15, 2022.

44. Jim Marshall, *Trust* (London: Omnibus Press, 2009), 8.

45. Marshall, 60.

46. Marshall, 8.

47. Amelia Davis was a longtime friend and colleague and is currently the sole controller of Jim Marshall's estate.

48. Amelia Davis, email questionnaire with author, June 11, 2020.

49. Ben Fong-Torres, "Like A Rolling Stone, The Mean, Mean Month of March," *Gavin*, April 5, 1996, 6.

50. Joel Selvin, email questionnaire with author, March 15, 2022.

51. Amelia Davis, email questionnaire with author, June 11, 2020.

52. John Louis Lucaites and Robert Hariman, "Visual Rhetoric, Photojournalism, and Democratic Public Culture," *Rhetoric Review* 20, no. 1/2 (2001): 37.

53. Robert Hariman and John L. Lucaites, "Icons, Iconicity, and Cultural Critique," *Sociologica* 9, no. 1 (January 2015): 4.

54. Joel Selvin, in *Show Me the Picture: The Story of Jim Marshall*, directed by Alfred G. Bailey, 2019; (London: Modern Films, 2020), DVD.

55. Hariman and Lucaites, 4.

56. While I have obtained an original poster, it was separate from *TeenSet* and very costly. It does not state anywhere that it was Marshall's image or housed within *TeenSet*.

57. Joel Selvin, "Shooting Stars/Jim Marshall's Photographs of Rock 'n' Roll Icons Helped Define the Artists," *SFGate*, November 2, 1997. Accessed February 2, 2020. https://www.sfgate.com/entertainment/article/Shooting-Stars-Jim-Marshall-s-photographs-of-2823806.php.

58. Miriam Coleman, "Rare Beatles Shea Stadium Photos Auctioned for Nearly $47,000," *Today*, March 25, 2013. Accessed March 6, 2020. https://www.today.com/news/rare-beatles-shea-stadium-photos-auctioned-nearly-47-000-1B9048122.

59. Marc Weinstein, in "Marc Weinstein at Shea Stadium," The Daily Beatle, February 14, 2010. Accessed February 10, 2020. http://webgrafikk.com/blog/uncategorized/marc-weinstein-at-shea-stadium/.

60. Coleman.

61. Judith Sims, "Beatlemania, 1966! Or, Life Aboard the Yellow Submarine," *TeenSet*, December 1966, 62.

62. The Bob Bonis Archive. Accessed February 29, 2020. https://bobbonis.com/.

63. Beatles Bible, "The Lost Beatles Photographs: The Bob Bonis Archive 1964–1966." Accessed February 26, 2020. https://www.beatlesbible.com/books/lost-beatles-photographs-bob-bonis-archive-1964-1966/.

64. *TeenSet*, "As Time Goes By . . . The Rolling Stones," March 1967, 32–40.

65. *TeenSet*, 35.

66. Larry Marion, *The Lost Rolling Stones Photographs: The Bob Bonis Archive, 1964–1966* (New York: Harper Collins, 2010), book jacket.

67. Marion, xi.

68. Marion, xx.

69. Beatles Bible, "The Lost Beatles Photographs: The Bob Bonis Archive 1964–1966." Accessed February 26, 2020. https://www.beatlesbible.com/books/lost-beatles-photographs-bob-bonis-archive-1964-1966/.

70. Larry Marion, email correspondence with author, March 14, 2022.

71. Marion.

72. In correspondence with Larry Marion, he stated he found evidence that other fan magazines used Bonis's photos but not likely with permission.

73. Morrison Hotel Gallery: Fine Art Music Photography. Accessed March 6, 2020. https://morrisonhotelgallery.com/products/jim-morrison-the-doors-new-york-city-1967-qdlzfn.

74. Magazine Photographer, *The Doors*, performed by Mimi Rogers, directed by Oliver Stone (1991; USA: Lionsgate, 2006), DVD.

75. *TeenBeat* and *Datebook* both featured Morrison on their covers but were not included here.

76. Magazine Photographer.

Chapter Four: Taking Popular Music Seriously: Judith Sims and the Women on the Scene

1. Judith Sims in Chester Flippo, "Rock Journalism and *Rolling Stone*" (master's thesis, University of Texas at Austin, 1974), 38.

2. David Abrahamson, *Magazine-Made America; The Cultural Transformation of the Postwar Periodical* (Cresskill, NJ: Hampton Press Inc., 1996), 56.

3. Abrahamson, 56.

4. Abrahamson, 57.

5. It would be negligent to say that Gloria Stavers, editor of *16 Magazine*, did not have a crucial role in guiding the publication but catered to a younger age than *TeenSet*. Stavers, while present in her magazine, was not as young as Sims or reflective of the counterculture herself.

6. Assistant editor Ginni Ganahl wrote the editorial for the July 1967 issue as Judith Sims was in London to attend a Beatles studio session when the issue was compiled.

7. Abrahamson, 56.

8. Judith Sims, "ETC. ETC.," *TeenSet*, December 1966, 4.

9. Maureen Cleeve, "How Does a Beatle Live? John Lennon Lives Like This," in *Datebook*, September 1966.

10. Judith Sims, "Mail Scene," *TeenSet*, December 1966, 5.

11. Many comments in the "ETC. ETC." section conveyed that she and Chester responded to fans who wrote directly to them, and not only through the editorial section.

12. Sims, "Mail Scene," 5.

13. Capitol Records is still connected to this publication and it would be in their best interest to quash the controversy and support the Beatles, but it is evident Sims's response reflected her personal opinion based on her history of fandom in the magazine.

14. *TeenSet*, "The Unimportance of Being Earnest: A Letter from an Editor," January 1968, 8–9.

15. Judith Sims, "Beatlemania, 1966! Or, Life Aboard the Yellow Submarine," *TeenSet*, December 1966, 35.

16. Carol Tyler, in "Fab 4 Mania with Carol Tyler," in *Something about the Beatles* (podcast), hosted by Robert Rodriguez, October 9, 2018. Accessed October 10, 2020. https://somethingaboutthebeatles.com/146-fab-4-mania-carol-tyler/.

17. Judith Sims, "ETC. ETC.," *TeenSet*, June 1967, 6.

18. *TeenSet*, "Truth or Fiction?" June 1967, 26.

19. Janey Milstead, "The Necessity of Being Involved," *TeenSet*, August 1968, 38.

20. See Weber for more information on Epstein's presentation of the Beatles.

21. However, Sims argues that the misinformation was information she was given, not information she created. See Sims.

22. Sims, March 1968, 5.

23. Sims, February 1969, 6.

24. Nancy Furlong, email questionnaire with author, July 9, 2020.

25. Richard Morton Jack, "*TeenSet*: The Story behind This Pioneering 1960s American Rock Magazine," *Flashback Magazine*, Winter 2014, 15–16.

26. Fashion is often dismissed, but pop stars such as David Bowie used fashion to help develop their personas.

27. Judith Sims in Chester Flippo, "Rock Journalism and *Rolling Stone*" (master's thesis, University of Texas Austin, 1974), 38.

28. *TeenSet*, "All-Star Scavenger Hunt," *TeenSet*, April 1967, 34–40.

29. *TeenSet*, "Go Fly a Kite," May 1968, 8–10.

30. *TeenSet*, "All-Star Croquet Match," February 1967, 32–39.

31. *TeenSet*, "*TeenSet*'s First Annual Christmas Party and Ice Skating Debacle," December 1967, 32–39.

32. Derek Taylor, a Liverpudlian, was a close friend and confidant of the Beatles and Brian Epstein. Taylor began working for the Beatles as a press officer in 1964, and by 1965, he moved to California to become a publicist to many musicians, such as Van Dyke Parks, the Beach Boys, and the Mamas & the Papas. He helped organize the Monterey Pop Festival (which may have been attributed to Sims's attendance). By 1968, Taylor became the Apple Records press officer. In my correspondence with Van Dyke Parks, he suggested that Sims and Taylor had a very close relationship.

33. *TeenSet*, "All-Star Croquet Match," 36.

34. Richie Furay, email questionnaire with author, May 21, 2020.

35. Van Dyke Parks, email questionnaire with author, May 17, 2020.

36. Abrahamson, 57.

37. Nancy Furlong, email questionnaire with author, July 9, 2020.

38. Debbie Gendler, email questionnaire with author, May 27, 2020.

39. While Ann Moses was a peer and an editor, she did not have the editorial control or influence Judith Sims did, as *Tiger Beat* founder Chuck Laufer had a specific vision for *Tiger Beat*.

40. Steve Kern, email questionnaire with author, April 15, 2022

41. Furay.

42. Furlong.

43. Kern.

44. Carolyn Kitch, "Anniversary Journalism, Collective Memory, and the Cultural Authority to Tell the Story of the American Past," *Journal of Popular Culture* 36, no. 1 (2002), 45.

45. Photographs by Jim Marshall.
46. Judith Sims, "Janis Joplin and the Boys in the Band," *TeenSet*, September 1968, 35.
47. Sims, 36.
48. Sims, 37.
49. Paul Nelson. "Janis: The Judy Garland of Rock and Roll?" *Rolling Stone*, March 15, 1969, 6.
50. Sims refers to her approach to considering popular music in *TeenSet* as a reflection of "feminine appreciation" in response to why she was not "heavy" (or analytical) enough in comparison to other male-led music magazines. However, feminine appreciation suggests that her presentation and consideration of *TeenSet*'s content came from a perspective that is unique to being female. While one cannot deny that she is female and her experiences as a woman in a male-dominated field informed her and her writing, it is impossible to completely decipher what is and is not unique to a female in the 1960s within her writings. Sims also did not argue that her presentation or appreciation was the same as, say, editor Gloria Stavers or Ann Moses. Rather, Sims steered *TeenSet* away from being connected to teen fan magazines, which were mostly written by females. She also employed male writers and photographers within her magazine. However, it is understandable that she would identify her consideration and presentation of popular music and culture as "feminine appreciation" as a female in a predominantly male field. What she was doing, how she was presenting musicians, was different from the way prominent male rock writers were writing about popular music; *TeenSet*, specifically Sims, presented musicians, culture, and groups with no attempt to explain to the reader what made music "good" or "bad" or what should be avoided.
51. Judith Sims, "ETC. ETC.," *TeenSet*, September 1968, 6.
52. Dave Swaney, "The Rogue Gallery of Rock Writers," *TeenSet*, March 1969, 50.
53. Jet-setting was where critics were flown to concerts, received complimentary hotel rooms, food, and drinks, and were invited to exclusive parties, all sponsored by the record companies.
54. *TeenSet*, "Table of Contents," March 1969, 3.
55. Dave Swaney, "The Rogue's Gallery of Rock Writers," *TeenSet*, March 1969, 51
56. Ben Fong-Torres, email questionnaire with author, March 16, 2022.
57. Judith Sims, "ETC. ETC.," *TeenSet*, May 1968, 5.
58. Judith Sims in Chester Flippo, "Rock Journalism and *Rolling Stone*" (master's thesis, University of Texas at Austin, 1974), 24.
59. Lee O'Dill, "Color It Blues," *TeenSet*, December 1966, 24.
60. For more reading on the blues and racial politics, see Adelt.
61. Lee O'Dill, "Color It Rhythm and Blues," *TeenSet*, January 1967, 27.
62. O'Dill, "Color It Blues," December 1966, 25.
63. See Brennan for a further discussion of Ruth Cage.
64. Judith Sims, "1967, the Summer of Love: There Was a Brief Moment When the Sun Really Shone," *Los Angeles Times*, 1987.
65. David Bruenger, *New Models for Understanding Music Business* (Berkeley: University of California Press, 2019), 145.
66. Richard Weissman, *Understanding the Music Business* (New York: Routledge, 2016), 129.
67. *TeenSet*, "'In' Hollywood," June 1966, 26.
68. This is additional proof of how far-removed Capitol Records was from *TeenSet*, as Capitol rejected the Nitty Gritty Dirt Band in 1966.

69. Former KHJ radio host in LA, whose fame grew due to his playing of pop/rock and continued even after a 1971 guilty plea to killing his wife.

70. *TeenSet*, October 1966, 17.

71. *TeenSet* was the first to consider Buffalo Springfield and the Monkees. For a short time, Buffalo Springfield was presented as "The" Buffalo Springfield.

72. Sue Cameron, "Hollywood Group Scene," *TeenSet*, November 1966, 42–43.

73. *TeenSet*, December 1966, 26.

74. *TeenSet*, "'In' San Francisco," January 1967, 28.

75. *TeenSet*, May 1967, 46.

76. Around the same time as Sims's report, Jon Landau provided a scathing report of the Boston bands and the alleged Boston sound in a *Rolling Stone* article titled "The Sound of Boston: Kerplop." See Landau.

77. Judith Sims, "Boston: Hype of Happening," *TeenSet*, May 1968, 44.

78. Sims, 47.

79. David Bruenger, *New Models for Understanding Music Business* (Berkeley: University of California Press, 2019), 143.

80. Jeff Hoganson, email questionnaire with author, March 16, 2022.

81. Richard Morton Jack, "*TeenSet*: The Story behind This Pioneering 1960s American Rock Magazine," *Flashback Magazine*, Winter 2014, 16.

82. Carol Gold, "How to Swing in London without Even Trying," *TeenSet*, November 1966, 19.

83. Gold. If it had been 1969, the regular individuals waiting would have been referred to as "Apple Scruffs."

84. Gold.

85. Carol Gold, "Another Chapter in Carol's Crisis," *TeenSet*, March 1967, 22.

86. Nancy Furlong, email questionnaire with author, July 9, 2020.

87. *The Smothers Brothers Comedy Hour* (1967–1969) featured comedy skits and musical acts from musicians ranging from Pete Seeger to Buffalo Springfield. The Smothers Brothers often encountered censorship and pushback from the selected content, specifically Peter Seeger's first 1967 performance.

88. *TeenSet*, "'In' London," March 1967, 46.

89. History.com, "The Who Literally Spark an Explosion on National Television," *This Day in History*, last modified September 16, 2019. Accessed May 15, 2020. https://www.history.com/this-day-in-history/the-who-spark-an-explosion-on-national-television.

90. Bag O'Nails was a popular nightclub in the London scene in the late 1960s that featured rock acts such as the Who. This club is particularly well known in Beatles history as the club where Paul McCartney and Linda Eastman met.

91. The Marquee was a London club known for its many rock performances throughout the 1960s. Famous bands/artists such as Led Zeppelin, the Rolling Stones, and David Bowie performed there.

92. Christine Feldman-Barrett, *A Women's History of the Beatles* (London: Bloomsbury Academic & Professional, 2021), 59, 66.

Chapter Five: "a Nifty Music Magazine with a Misleading Name": *TeenSet*'s Duality, Representation of, and Interaction with an Evolving Musical and Cultural Landscape

1. Sukey Small, "Mail Scene," *TeenSet*, July 1968, 6.
2. Steve Kern, email questionnaire with author, April 15, 2022.
3. Nancy Furlong, email questionnaire with author, September 26, 2020.
4. Carl Ritter, "Mail Scene—Changes," *TeenSet*, February 1969, 7.
5. Judith Sims, "ETC. ETC.," *TeenSet*, January 1969, 4.
6. Linda McLoughlin, *The Language of Magazines* (London: Taylor & Francis Routledge, 2000), 5.
7. *TeenSet*, cover, October 1967.
8. Joel Selvin and Jim Marshall, *Monterey Pop* (San Francisco: Chronicle Books, 1992), 5.
9. Richard Morton Jack, "*TeenSet*: The Story Behind This Pioneering 1960s American Rock Magazine," *Flashback Magazine*, Winter 2014, 18.
10. *Tiger Beat* ran a two-page feature of the Monterey Pop Festival in the September 1967 issue.
11. Joel Selvin and Jim Marshall, *Monterey Pop* (San Francisco: Chronicle Books, 1992), 5.
12. *TeenSet*, "The Beatles at Monterey," October 1967, 52, 60.
13. Sandra Glass, "The Most Sinister, Evil, Subversive Conspiracy in the World," *TeenSet*, April 1969, 37.
14. Andrew Curry, "Flower Child: A Vietnam War Protester Recalls a Seminal '60s Image, Part of a New Book Celebrating French Photographer Marc Riboud's 50-Year Career," *Smithsonian Magazine*, last modified April 2004. Accessed April 2, 2020. https://www.smithsonianmag.com/history/flower-child-102514360/.
15. Magazines were and are often released a month before their issue date.
16. Donovan Leitch, "Jennifer Juniper," 1967, track 8 on *Hurdy Gurdy Man*, Epic Records, 1968, vinyl record.
17. Stephen Peate, "Finding Your 'Type': Font Psychology and Typography Inspiration in Logo Design," Fabrik, last modified February 9, 2018. https://fabrikbrands.com/font-psychology-and-typography-inspiration-in-logo-design/.
18. At the time of writing, *Tiger Beat* is presented in an online format, but the website was last updated in 2020.
19. June featured a photograph rather than a painting.
20. Sims, February 1968, 3.
21. MoMA, "Milton Glaser, Dylan 1966," last modified 2016. Accessed May 20, 2020. https://www.moma.org/collection/works/8108.
22. *TeenSet*, cover, February 1968.
23. Judith Sims, "An Afternoon with Jim Morrison," *TeenSet*, June 1968, 36.
24. This photograph of Janis Joplin by Jim Marshall was also offered as a poster for purchase within *TeenSet*.
25. *TeenSet*, cover, August 1968.
26. *TeenSet*.
27. Carol Gold discussed Cream in *TeenSet* before the existence of *Rolling Stone*.
28. Richard Morton Jack, "*TeenSet*," *Flashback Magazine*, Winter 2014, 18.
29. Ben Fong-Torres, email correspondence with author, March 16, 2022.
30. *TeenSet*, cover, January 1969.

31. Patrick Burke, "Tear Down the Walls: Jefferson Airplane, Race, and Revolutionary Rhetoric in 1960s Rock," *Popular Music* 29, no. 1 (2010): 61.

32. Burke, 63.

33. Jerry Hopkins, "Grace Slick Is an Attention-Getting Device," *TeenSet*, January 1969, 35.

34. Burke, 67–68.

35. The Yippies were members of the YIP Party (Youth International Party) of the late 1960s. This group demonstrated through street performances, protested the Vietnam War, and encouraged free speech. They also vocalized at music festivals (such as Woodstock). Two of the most famous members are Abbie Hoffman and Jerry Rubin.

36. In 1969, Mattel released a Black male Barbie named Brad, but this is not his body in the image. A Black Ken doll was not introduced until 1982.

37. Judith Sims, "ETC. ETC.," *TeenSet*, January 1969, 4.

38. Don Armstrong, "Gallery: *TeenSet/AUM*," Music Journalism History, last modified October 30, 2019. Accessed November 29, 2019. https://www.music-journalism-history.com/2019/10/30/gallery-teen-set-aum/.

39. Jay W. Stein, "Magazine Covers on the Library Display Shelves," *Reference & User Services Quarterly* 37, no. 1 (1997): 29.

40. Jennifer Scanlon, "Not Just a Pretty Face," *The Women's Review of Books* 19, no. 6 (2002): 18.

41. Gabrielle Dean, "Cover Story: The Smart Set's Clever Packaging, 1908–1923," *The Journal of Modern Periodical Studies* 4, no. 1 (2013): 3.

42. Jenny McKay, *The Magazines Handbook* (London: Routledge, 2000), 164.

43. The Monkees' place in history is also extremely complicated in popular music. Their legacy is evolving and changing.

44. *TeenSet*, "Albums in Review," October 1965, 8.

45. *TeenSet*, February 1966, 6.

46. *TeenSet*.

47. *TeenSet*, September 1966, 20.

48. *TeenSet*, October 1966, 56.

49. Phrotus was an alternative spelling for frodis, which was a slang word for marijuana attributed to Monkee Micky Dolenz. It appeared as a reference to the *Monkees'* episode "The Monkee's Paw," where, when attempting to teach Micky to speak again, they write the word "frodis" on a chalkboard as well as an alternative spelling of "phrotus." The word also appears on a 1968 *Monkees* episode titled "The Frodis Caper."

50. A. J. Phrotus, "The Groove," *TeenSet*, December 1967, 47.

51. *TeenSet*, "The Groove," June 1968, 48.

52. *TeenSet*.

53. At that time, "The Groove" did not list an author.

54. J. Walker Scott, "Albums in Review," *TeenSet*, September 1966, 20.

55. Alan Durant, *Conditions of Music* (New York: SUNY Press, 1984), 212.

56. *TeenSet*.

57. *TeenSet*.

58. *TeenSet*, "For the Comfort of Teenagers over Twenty or . . . How to Be an Overaged Teenybopper and Like It!" September 1967, 38.

59. *TeenSet*.

60. *TeenSet*.

61. *TeenSet*, cover, March 1968.

62. As discussed in chapter 4, *TeenSet* included regular updates from various music scenes, such as San Francisco and London, while considering other developing or possible scenes.

63. Jenny McKay, *The Magazines Handbook* (London: Routledge, 2000), 139.

64. Dylan Stableford, "Minimalism Is In: When It Comes to Magazine Covers These Days, Less Is Definitely More," *Folio*, November 24, 2008. Accessed April 18, 2020.

65. *TeenSet*, cover, August 1968.

66. Thomas Hine, *The Rise and Fall of the American Teenager* (New York: Perennial, 2000), 7.

67. Judith Sims, "ETC. ETC.," *TeenSet*, October 1968, 3.

68. *Rolling Stone*, *TeenSet* Advertisement, November 9, 1968, 19.

69. *TeenSet*, cover, August 1968.

70. See introduction for the definition of rock and pop. Also, that is not to say that *TeenSet* discussed or presented rock in the same way as other rock publications.

71. Sims, January 1969, 4.

72. Carol Gold, in Richard Morton Jack, "*TeenSet*: The Story behind This Pioneering 1960s American Rock Magazine," *Flashback Magazine*, Winter 2014, 19.

73. Pamn Mestler, "Mail Scene—Names Anyone?" *TeenSet*, January 1969, 6.

74. *TeenSet*, "Let Us Know Questionnaire," May 1968, 40.

75. *TeenSet*.

76. *TeenSet*, "*TeenSet* Questionnaire: Some Surprising Results," September 1968, 48.

77. Stavers claimed her average reader age was between thirteen and fourteen, but she noted even younger girls read *16 Magazine*. See page 17.

78. Later, in the interview with Chester Flippo, Sims claims the average reader's age to be older than fifteen to sixteen. See Flippo.

79. Judith Sims, "ETC. ETC.," *TeenSet*, March 1969, 3.

80. Dennis Dalrymple, "Opinion: Before Jerry Rubin," *New York Times*, last modified August 10, 1988. https://www.nytimes.com/1988/08/10/opinion/l-before-jerry-rubin-603488.html.

81. Judith Sims, in Chester Flippo, "Rock Journalism and *Rolling Stone*" (master's thesis, University of Texas at Austin, 1974), 24.

82. Linda McLoughlin, *The Language of Magazines* (London: Taylor & Francis Routledge, 2000), 6.

83. Marcia R. Prior-Miller, "Research Review: Issues in Magazine Typology," in *The American Magazine*, edited by David Abrahamson (Ames, IA: Iowa State University Press, 1995), 19.

84. Michael Fairchild, *Jimi Hendrix Starting at Zero*, Gravity Limited, 2013. Accessed October 20, 2018. starting-at-zero.com/book/sources/.

85. Michael Benson, *Why the Grateful Dead Matter* (New England: University Press, 2016), 71.

86. Hine, 9.

87. Marcia R. Prior-Miller, "Research Review: Issues in Magazine Typology," in *The American Magazine*, edited by David Abrahamson (Ames, IA: Iowa State University Press, 1995), 3.

88. Rick Altman, in Feuer, Jane, "Genre Study and Television," in *Channels of Discourse, Reassembled*, edited by Robert C. Allen (Chapel Hill: University of North Carolina Press 1992), 144.

89. Altman, 140.

90. Sims occasionally insults *16 Magazine* and general teen fan magazines throughout the existence of *TeenSet*.

91. However, the magazine was always representative of females who "dug" rock, and the feminine connotation of the word "teen" was not what Sims was trying to distance from, as discussed in chapter 4.

92. McLoughlin, 5.

93. Judith Sims, in Chester Flippo, "Rock Journalism and *Rolling Stone*" (master's thesis, University of Texas at Austin, 1974), 10.

94. Sims, 11.

95. Sims, 11.

CONCLUSION: "ETC. ETC.": RECONSIDERING THE POPULAR MUSIC JOURNALISM HISTORICAL DISCOURSE

1. Matt Brennan, *When Genres Collide: DownBeat, Rolling Stone, and the Struggle between Jazz and Rock* (New York, NY: Bloomsbury Academic, 2017), 193.

2. I am not alone; in 2014, actress Emma Stone unapologetically discussed her love of the Spice Girls and their representation of girl power on the *Graham Norton Show*. See Stone for her statement.

3. Norma Coates, "Teenyboppers, Groupies, and Other Grotesques: Girls and Women and Rock Culture in the 1960s and early 1970s," *Journal of Popular Music Studies* 15, no. 1 (2003), 65.

4. Miles Parks Grier, "Said the Hooker to the Thief: Some Way Out of Rockism," *Journal of Popular Music Studies* 25, no. 1 (2013), 46, 48.

5. Ben Fong-Torres, email questionnaire with author, March 16, 2022.

6. Fong-Torres.

7. Daphne A. Brooks, "The Write to Rock: Racial Mythologies, Feminist Theory, and the Pleasures of Rock Music Criticism," *Women and Music* 12, (2008), 62.

8. Steve Kern, email questionnaire with author, April 15, 2022.

9. Jeff Hoganson, email questionnaire with author, March 15, 2022.

10. Hoganson.

11. Hoganson.

12. Hoganson.

13. See Carpenter for a consideration of David Folkenflik's dismissive comment to the readership of *Teen Vogue*.

14. David Folkenflik. Twitter, December 10, 2016. Google. Accessed December 15, 2018. twitter.com/davidfolkenflik/status/807684025892634624.

15. Folkenflik.

APPENDIX I

1. *TeenSet*, "Buffalo Springfield Pin-Up," April 1967, 63.

BIBLIOGRAPHY

16 Magazine (cover). May 1957.

16 Magazine (cover). May 1968.

16 Magazine (cover). October 1968.

16 Magazine. "Marc-David Glam-Rock!" October 1972, 10–11.

Abrahamson, David. *Magazine-Made America: The Cultural Transformation of the Postwar Periodical.* Cresskill, NJ: Hampton Press Inc., 1996.

Adelt, Ulrich. "Black, White and Blue: Racial Politics of Blues Music in the 1960s." PhD diss. University of Iowa, 2007. Accessed April 15, 2020. https://iro.uiowa.edu/esploro/outputs/doctoral/Black-white-and-blue-racial-politics/9983777108802771.

Altman, Rick. In Feuer, Jane, "Genre Study and Television." In *Channels of Discourse Reassembled*, edited by Robert C. Allen, 144. Chapel Hill: University of North Carolina Press, 1992.

Anolik, Lili. *Hollywood's Eve: Eve Babitz and the Secret History of L.A.* New York: Scribner, 2019.

Armstrong, Don. "Gallery: *Teen Set/AUM*." Music Journalism History. Last modified October 30, 2019. Accessed November 29, 2019. https://www.music-journalism-history.com/2019/10/30/gallery-teen-set-aum/.

Armstrong, Don. "*TeenSet* Magazine Part 1." Music Journalism History. Last modified October 21, 2019. Accessed November 29, 2019. https://www.music-journalism-history.com /2019/10/21/teenset-magazine-part-1/.

Armstrong, Don. "TeenSet Magazine Part 2." Music Journalism History. Last modified October 23, 2019. Accessed November 29, 2019. https://www.music-journalism-history.com /2019/10/223/teenset-magazine-part-1/.

Atlas, Jacoba. "Jimi Hendrix, Black Power, and Money." *TeenSet*, January 1969.

Atton, Chris. "Writing about Listening: Alternative Discourses in Rock Journalism." *Popular Music* 28, no. 1 (2009): 53–67.

Aufderheide, Pat, Peter Jaszi, and Mridu Chandra. "Honest Truths: Documentary Filmmakers on Ethical Challenges in Their Work." Center for Media & Social Impact. Last modified September 2009. Accessed March 1, 2020. https://cmsimpact. org/resource /honest-truths-documentary-filmmakers-on-ethical-challenges-in-their-work/.

Bailey, G. Alfred, dir. *Show Me the Picture: The Story of Jim Marshall.* 2019; London: Modern Films, Amazon Prime Video, 2020.

Bangs, Lester. "Album Reviews—Kick Out the Jams." *Rolling Stone*, April 5, 1969, 16–17.

Barker, Hugh, and Yuval Taylor. *Faking It: The Quest for Authenticity in Popular Music.* London: W. W. Norton & Company, 2007.

Barrett, Thomas M. "The Unidentified Agent: Illya Kuryakin: Making the Russian (In)Visible in *The Man from U.N.C.L.E.*" In *James Bond and Popular Culture: Essays on the Influence of the Fictional Superspy*, edited by Michele Brittany, 103–20. Jefferson, NC: McFarland & Company Inc., 2014.

Bayton, Mavis. "Women and the Electric Guitar." In *The Gender and Media Reader*, edited by Mary C. Kearny, 265–72. New York: Routledge, 2012.

Beatles Bible. "The Lost Beatles Photographs: The Bob Bonis Archive 1964–1966." Accessed February 26, 2020. https://www.beatlesbible.com/books/lost-beatles-photographs-bob-bonis-archive-1964-1966/.

Beatles.Net. "The Beatles' Story on Capitol Records—Part 2: The Albums" (digital edition). Accessed July 11, 2020. https://www.beatle.net/product/the-beatles-story-on-capitol-records-part-2-the-albums/.

Belscamper, Diana L. "'Your Ticket to Dreamsville': The Functions of *16 Magazine* in American Girl Culture of the 1960s." PhD diss. University of Wisconsin-Milwaukee, 2014.

Belsey, Catherine. "Textual Analysis as a Research Method." In *Research Methods for English Studies*, edited by Gabriele Griffin, 160–78. Edinburgh: Edinburgh University Press, 2013.

Benaron, Joe. "Twang, Thump, and Plunk: The Guitar." *TeenSet*, December 1966, 18–19.

Benmont Tench (@benmonttench). In response to Van Dyke Parks (@parksvandyke). "Do I Dare?" Instagram photo. May 17, 2020. Instagram.com.

Benson, Michael. *Why the Grateful Dead Matter*. New England: University Press, 2016.

Berton, Pierre. *Voices From the Sixties: Twenty-Two Views from a Revolutionary Decade*. New York: Doubleday & Company Inc., 1967.

Billboard Magazine. "Capitol Diversifies; Enters Teen Fan Magazine Market." August 28, 1965, 6.

Billboard Magazine, "Rozsa—Music from *Madame Bovary*—Album Reviews," August 20, 1949, 94.

Biron, Dean. "Towards a Popular Music Criticism of Replenishment." *Popular Music and Society* 34, no. 5 (December 2011): 661–82.

Blumenberg, Richard M. "Documentary Films and the Problem of 'Truth.'" *Journal of the University Film Association* 29, no. 4 (October 1977): 19–22.

Bob Bonis Archive. Accessed February 29, 2020. https://www.bobbonis.com.

Borst, William A. *The Scorpion and the Frog: A Natural Conspiracy*. Bloomington, IN: Xlibris, 2004.

Box Office Mojo. "Almost Famous." https://www.boxofficemojo.com/release/rl256083457/weekend/.

Brennan, Matt. *When Genres Collide: DownBeat, Rolling Stone, and the Struggle between Jazz and Rock*. New York, NY: Bloomsbury Academic, 2017.

Brooks, Daphne A. "The Write to Rock: Racial Mythologies, Feminist Theory, and the Pleasures of Rock Music Criticism." *Women and Music* 12 (2008): 54–62.

Brooks, Victor. *Last Season of Innocence*. Plymouth: Rowman & Littlefield Publishers Inc., 2012.

Brown, Charles H. "Self-Portrait: The Teen-Type Magazine." *The Annals of the American Academy of Political and Social Science* 338, 1961: 13–21.

Brown, Joshua. "Historians and Photography." *American Art* 21, no. 3 (2007): 9–13.

Brown, Stacy and Dennis Love. *Blind Faith: The Miraculous Journey of Lula Hardaway, Stevie Wonder's Mother*. New York: Simon & Schuster, 2002.

Bruenger, David. *Create, Produce, Consume: New Models for Understanding Music Business*. Berkeley: University of California Press, 2019.

Brundage, Anthony. *Going to the Sources*. 5th ed. Chichester, England: John Wiley & Sons Ltd., 2012.

Bumsted, Allison. "Which Side Is This Ex-Beatle On? A Reassessment of the 1970s Rock Press' Framing, Interpretation, and Consideration of Paul McCartney and Wings." In *The Popularity of Words and Music*. Edited by Thomas Gurke and Susan Winnett. Cham, Switzerland: Palgrave Macmillan, 2021.

Burke, Patrick. "Tear Down the Walls: Jefferson Airplane, Race, and Revolutionary Rhetoric in 1960s Rock." *Popular Music* 29, no. 1 (2010): 61–79.

Burks, John and Jerry Hopkins. *Groupies and Other Girls*. Edited by Jann Wenner. New York: Bantam, 1970.

Cameron, Sue. "Hollywood Group Scene." *TeenSet*, November 1966, 42–43.

Carpenter, Julia. "Teen Magazines Have Always Covered More than Fashion. You Just Didn't Notice." The *Washington Post*, May 12, 2007. Accessed December 14, 2018. https://www.washingtonpost.com/lifestyle/style/teen-magazines-have-always-covered-more-than-fashion-you-just-didnt-notice/2017/05/12/2ba8cb04-1964-11e7-9887-1a5314b56a08_story.html?noredirect=on&utm_t,.

Carr, E. H. *What is History?* Middlesex: Pelican Books, 1961.

Cashbox. "Capitol *TeenSet* Magazine Is Building Up to a Bantom Bonanza." January 1, 1966, 8.

Cashbox. "Capitol *TeenSet* Promo Seek Closer Teen Ties." October 24, 1964, 7, 40.

Cashbox. "The *TeenSet* Advertisement." October 24, 1964, 13.

Cavicchi, Daniel. *Tramps Like Us: Music and Meaning Among Springsteen Fans*. New York: Oxford University Press, 1998.

Chanan, Michael. *The Politics of Documentary*. London: British Film Institute, 2007.

Chambers, Deborah, Linda Steiner, and Carole Fleming, *Women and Journalism*. London: Routledge, 2004.

Christgau, Robert. *Any Old Way You Choose It: Rock and Other Pop Music, 1967–1973*. New York: Penguin Books, 1973.

Christgau, Robert. *Going into the City: Portrait of a Critic as a Young Man*. New York: Harper Collins, 2015.

Christgau, Robert. "Rock Critics." *Harper's Magazine*, September 1969. Accessed July 10, 2019. https://www.robertchristgau.com/xg/bkrev/rockcrit-69.php.

Clarke, Paul, dir. *Mother of Rock: Lillian Roxon*. 2010; Saint Kilda, East Victoria, AUS: Lowlands Media Pty. Ltd.

Cleeve, Maureen. "How Does a Beatle Live? John Lennon Lives Like This." *Datebook*, September 1966.

Cline, Cheryl. "Essays from Bitch: The Women's Rock Newsletter with Bite." In *The Adoring Audience: Fan Culture and Popular Media*, edited by Lisa Lewis, 69–83. London: Routledge, 1992.

Coates, Norma. "Teenyboppers, Groupies, and Other Grotesques: Girls and Women and Rock Culture in the 1960s and early 1970s." *Journal of Popular Music Studies* 15, no. 1 (2003): 65–94.

Cohen, Sara. "Popular Music, Gender and Sexuality." Chapter. In *The Cambridge Companion to Pop and Rock*, edited by Simon Frith, Will Straw, and John Street, 226–42. Cambridge Companions to Music. Cambridge: Cambridge University Press, 2001.

Cohn, Nik. *Rock from the Beginning*. New York: Stein & Day, 1969.
Coleman, Miriam. "Rare Beatles Shea Stadium Photos Auctioned for Nearly $47,000." *Today*, March 25, 2013. Accessed March 6, 2020. https://www.today.com/news/rare-be atles-shea-stadium-photos-auctioned-nearly-47-0-0-1B9048122.
Constantine, Alex. *The Covert War Against Rock: What You Don't Know About the Deaths of Jim Morrison, Tupac Shakur, Michael Hutchence, Brian Jones, Jimi Hendrix, Phil Ochs, Bob Marley, Peter Tosh, John Lennon, The Notorious B.I.G.* London: Feral House, 2000.
Cooper, B. Lee, Frank Hoffman, and Wayne S. Haney. *Rock Music in American Popular Culture: Rock 'n' Roll Resources*. New York: Harrington Park Press, 1995.
Courtney, Robert. "Positively San Francisco." *TeenSet*, May 1968, 34–39.
Crawford, Anwen. "The World Needs Female Rock Critics." *The New Yorker*, May 26, 2015. Accessed June 16, 2019. https://www.newyorker.com/culture/cultural-comment/the-world-needs-female-rock-critics.
Crowe, Cameron, dir. *Almost Famous*. 2000; Universal City, CA: DreamWorks Home Entertainment, Video, 2001. DVD.
Curley, Mallory. *Beatle Pete, Time Traveller: Annotated Instructions for a Cartoon Book*. N.p.: Randy Press, 2005.
Curry, Andrew. "Flower Child: A Vietnam War Protester Recalls a Seminal '60s Image, Part of a New Book Celebrating French Photographer Marc Riboud's 50-Year Career." *Smithsonian Magazine*. Last modified April 2004. Accessed April 2, 2020. https://www.smithsoni anmag.com/history/flower-child-102514360/.
Daily Beatle. "Marc Weinstein at Shea Stadium." February 14, 2010. Accessed February 10, 2020. http://webgrafikk.com/blog/uncategorized/marc-weinstein-at-shea-stadium/.
Dalrymple, Dennis. "Before Jerry Rubin." *New York Times*, August 10, 1988. *Gale Academic OneFile Select*. link.gale.com/apps/doc/A175928575/EAIM?u=anon~de614a6&sid=sitemap&xid=5e88fa35. Accessed January 8, 2024.
Davies, Helen. "All Rock and Roll is Homosocial: The Representation of Women in the British Rock Music Press." *Popular Music* 20, no. 3 (2001): 301–09.
Davis, Amelia. Email questionnaire with author. June 11, 2020.
Davis, Amelia, ed. *Jim Marshall: Show Me the Picture*. San Francisco: Chronicle Books, 2019.
De Bruin, Marjan. "Gender and Newsroom Cultures." In *Media and Gender: A Scholarly Agenda for the Global Alliance on Media and Gender*, edited by Aimée Vega Montiel, 50. N.p.: UNESCO, 2014.
Dean, Gabrielle. "Cover Story: The Smart Set's Clever Packaging, 1908–1923." *The Journal of Modern Periodical Studies* 4, no. 1 (2013): 1–29.
Denisoff, R. Serge. *Solid Gold: Popular Record Industry*. Oxfordshire, UK: Transaction Publishers, 1975.
Derogatis, Jim. *Let it Blurt: The Life and Times of Lester Bangs, America's Greatest Rock Critic*. New York: Crown, 2000.
Des Barres, Pamela. *I'm With the Band: Confessions of a Groupie*. Sag Harbor, NY: BeechTree Books, 1987.
Desjardins, Mary. "'Fan Magazine Trouble': The AMPP, Studio Publicity Directors, and the Hollywood Press, 1945–1952." *Film History* 26, no. 3 (2014): 29–56.
Dexter, Dave Jr. "Let's Go for Another 25!" *Billboard*, September 16, 1967, C8-C10.
DIG (cover). November 1965.
Doehring, André. "Male Journalists as 'Artists': The Ideological Production of Recent Popular Music Journalism." In M. Buscatt, M. Leontsini and D. Naudier, eds., *Du Genre*

dans la Critique/Gender in Art Criticism. English ed. Paris: Éditions des archives contemporaines, (2017): 3–16.
Doherty, Thomas. *Teenagers and Teenpics: The Juvenilization of American Movies in the 1950s*. Philadelphia: Temple University Press, 2010.
Doney, Malcolm. *Summer in the City: Rock Music and Way of Life*. Berkhamsted, England: Lion Publishing, 1978.
Draper, Robert. "O Janis." *Texas Monthly*, October 1992, 120–26, 179–84.
Duca, Lauren. "Donald Trump Is Gaslighting America." *Teen Vogue*. December 10, 2016. https://www.teenvogue.com/story/donald-trump-is-gaslighting-america.
Durant, Alan. *Conditions of Music*. New York: SUNY Press, 1985.
Ebert, Roger. "Andrew Sarris, 1928–2012: In Memoriam." RogerEbert.com. Last modified June 20, 2012. https://www.rogerebert.com/interviews/andrew-sarris-1928-2012-in-memoriam.
Ebert, Roger. "Reviews: Almost Famous." Roger Ebert.com. Last modified September 15, 2000. Accessed November 10, 2019. https://www.rogerebert.com/reviews/almost-famous-2000.
Egan, Bob. "Dylan and Friends, Greenwich Village 1963 by Jim Marshall." Pop Spots. Accessed March 1, 2020. www.popspotsnyc.com/dylanwalk/.
Einarson, John and Richie Furay. *For What It's Worth: The Story of Buffalo Springfield*. New York: Cooper Square Press, 1997, 2004.
Eldridge, Ying-Bei. "Between Feminism and Femininity: Shifting Cultural Representations of Girlhood in the 1960s." PhD. diss., Bowling Green State University, 2017.
Elkind, Peter. "Soul on Ink." The Reporter. *Texas Monthly*, October 1983, 114–18.
Evans, Liz, ed. *Girls Will Be Boys: Women Report on Rock*. London: Pandora Press, 1997.
Fabbri, Franco. "A Theory of Musical Genres: Two Applications." In *Popular Music: Critical Concepts in Media and Cultural Studies* 3 (2004): 7–35.
Fab4ConJam. "I Was a Teenage Screamer with Debbie Gendler and Carol Tyler." Moderated by Allison Bumsted. Hosted online through InLive.com. February 23, 2021.
Fairchild, Michael. *Jimi Hendrix Starting at Zero: His Own Story*. Gravity Limited, 2013. Accessed October 20, 2018. www.starting-at-zero.com/book/sources/.
Feldman-Barrett, Christine. *A Women's History of the Beatles*. London: Bloomsbury Academic, 2021.
Feuer, Jane. "Genre Study and Television." In *Channels of Discourse Reassembled*, edited by Robert C. Allen, 138–60. Chapel Hill: University of North Carolina Press, 1992.
Fields, Danny, and Randi Reisfeld. *Who's Your Fave Rave?: Teen Idols as You Knew Them . . . AND as They Really Were!* New York: Boulevard Books, 1997. Kindle edition.
Flippo, Chester. "Rock Journalism and *Rolling Stone*." Master's thesis. University of Texas Austin, 1974.
Fong-Torres, Ben. "Ben Fong-Torres." Accessed June 10, 2020. http://benfongtorres.com.
Fong-Torres, Ben. *Becoming Almost Famous*. London: Backbeat Books, 2006.
Fong-Torres, Ben. Email and phone interview with author. March 16, 2022.
Fong-Torres, Ben. "Like A Rolling Stone: The Mean, Mean Month of March." *Gavin*, April 5, 1996, 6.
Fortune, August 1933.
Free Dictionary. "Cultist." https://www.thefreedictionary.com/cultist.
Franks, Suzanne. *Women in Journalism*. London: I. B. Tauris, 2013.
Frazer, Elizabeth. "Teenage Girls Reading Jackie." *Media, Culture, and Society* 9, no. 4 (1987) 407–25.

Fricke, David. "The First Rock Critic." *Rolling Stone*, April 25, 2013.
Friedlander, Emilie. "The World Doesn't Need More Female Music Critics." *Fader*, June 3, 2015. Accessed June 16, 2019. https://www.thefader.com/2015/06/03/the-world-doesnt-need-more-female-music-critics.
Frith, Simon. "Rock and Sexuality." In *Taking Popular Music Seriously: Selected Essays*, edited by Simon Frith, 41–58. Hampshire: Ashgate, 2007.
Frith, Simon. *Sound Effects: Youth, Leisure, and the Politics of Rock 'n' Roll*. New York: Pantheon Books, 1981.
Furay, Richie. Email questionnaire with author. May 21, 2020.
Furlong, Nancy. Email questionnaire with author. July 9, 2020.
Galassie, David. "Gloria Stavers and *16 Magazine*." Internet Archive: Wayback Machine. Last modified October 16, 2006. Accessed June 20, 2020. https://web.archive.org/web/20061016014724/http://www.loti.com/sixties_history/Gloria_Stavers_and_16_Magazine.htm.
Gambaccini, Paul. *Rock Critics' Choice: The Top 200 Albums*. New York: Omnibus Press, 1978.
Garratt, Sheryl. "Teenage Dreams." In *On Record: Rock, Pop, and the Written Word*, edited by Simon Frith and Andrew Goodwin, 341–50. Florence: Taylor & Francis Group, 2000.
Gendler, Debbie. Accessed May 15, 2020. https://debbiegendler.com/.
Gendler, Debbie. Email questionnaire with author. May 27, 2020.
George-Warren, Holly. *Janis: Her Life and Music*. New York: Simon & Schuster, 2019.
Glass, Sandra. "The Most Sinister, Evil, Subversive Conspiracy in the World." *TeenSet*, April 1969, 34–38.
Gleason, Ralph J. *The Jefferson Airplane and the San Francisco Sound*. New York: Ballantine Books, 1969.
Gold, Carol. "Another Chapter in Carol's Crisis." *TeenSet*, March 1967, 22–23.
Gold, Carol. "How to Swing in London without Even Trying." *TeenSet*, November 1966, 18–19.
Goldstein, Richard. *The Poetry of Rock*. 7th ed. New York: Bantam Books Inc., 1969.
Gorman, Paul. *In Their Own Write: Adventures in the Music Press*. London: Sanctuary Press, 2001.
Grace Slick (@graceslickofficial). "Drawn and on the Cover of *TeenSet* Magazine, 1968." Instagram photo, July 3, 2017. Instagram.com.
Grier, Miles Parks. "Said the Hooker to the Thief: Some Way Out of Rockism." *Journal of Popular Music Studies* 25, no. 1 (2013): 31–55.
Hale, Daryl. "Quicker than a Wink of an Eye." In *Jimi Hendrix and Philosophy: Experience Required*, edited by Ammon G. Theodore, 71–84. Chicago: Open Court Publishing, 2017.
Harcup, Tony. *Journalism: Principles and Practice*. 3rd ed. London: SAGE Publications, 2015.
Hariman, Robert and John L. Lucaites. "Icons, Iconicity, and Cultural Critique." *Sociologica* 9, no. 1 (January 2015): 1–31.
Harris, Dixie Dean. "And This, Dear God, Is What They Read." *Esquire*. July 1, 1965, 55–51, 105–6.
Harry, Bill. *Paperback Writers: The History of the Beatles in Print*. London: Virgin Books, 1984.
Hefner, Brooks E. and Edward Timke. "Beyond Little and Big: Circulation, Data, and American Magazine History." *The Journal of Modern Periodical Studies* 11, no. 1 (2020): 25–51.

Helgren, Jennifer. *American Girls and Global Responsibility: A New Relation to the World during the Early Cold War*. New Brunswick, NJ: Rutgers University Press, 2017.
Heylin, Clinton. *The Act You've Known for All These Years: The Life, and Afterlife, of Sgt. Pepper*. Edinburgh: Canongate Ltd., 2007.
Hine, Thomas. *The Rise and Fall of the American Teenager*. New York: Perennial, 2000.
History.com. "The Who Literally Spark an Explosion on National Television." *This Day in History*. Last modified September 16, 2019. Accessed May 15, 2020. https://www.history.com/this-day-in-history/the-who-spark-an-explosion-on-national-television.
Hoganson, Jeff. Email questionnaire with author. March 15, 2022.
Holt, Fabian. *Genre in Popular Music*. Chicago: University of Chicago Press, 2007.
Hopkins, Jerry. "Grace Slick Is an Attention-Getting Device." *TeenSet*, January 1969, 35, 67–68.
Jack, Richard Morton. "*TeenSet*: The Story behind This Pioneering 1960s American Rock Magazine." *Flashback Magazine*, Winter 2014, 15–18.
Jackson, Peter. *The Beatles: Get Back—A Sneak Peak from Peter Jackson*. Disney Plus, December 20, 2020.
Johnny Mercer Foundation. "The Capitol News Magazine." Accessed October 9, 2019. https://www.johnnymercerfoundation.org/capitol-records/.
Johnson, Pete. "Purple, Tuna, and Laura Nyro." *TeenSet*, February 1969, 50–51, 60.
Johnson, Russell L. "'Disease Is Unrhythmical': Jazz, Health, and Disability in 1920s America." *Health and History* 13, no. 2 (2011): 13–42.
Jones, Steve, ed. *Pop Music and the Press*. Philadelphia: Temple University, 2002.
Jones, Steve and Kevin Feathery. "Re-Viewing Rock Writing: Narrative of Popular Music Criticism." In *Pop Music and the Press*, edited by Steve Jones, 19–40. Philadelphia: Temple University, 2002.
Kane, John. *The Last Seat in the House: The Story of Hanley Sound*. Jackson: University of Mississippi Press, 2020.
Keightley, Keir. "Reconsidering Rock." In *The Cambridge Companion to Pop and Rock*. Edited by Simon Frith, Will Straw, and John Street, 109–42. Cambridge: Cambridge University Press, 2001.
Kern, Steve. Email questionnaire with author. April 15, 2022.
Khan, Carrie. "Noise Pop Film Review: *Ticket to Write: The Golden Age of Rock Music Journalism*." SpinningPlatters.com. Last modified February 26, 2017. Accessed January 21, 2020. http://spinningplatters.com/2017/02/26/noise-pop-film-review-ticket-to-write-the-golden-age-of-rock-music-journalism/.
Kitch, Carolyn. "Anniversary Journalism, Collective Memory, and the Cultural Authority to Tell the Story of the American Past." *Journal of Popular Culture* 36, no. 1 (2002): 44–67.
Kitch, Carolyn. "Theory of Methods of Analysis: Modes for Understanding Magazines." In *The Routledge Handbook of Magazine Research: The Future of the Magazine Form*, edited by David Abrahamson and Marcia R. Prior-Miller, 9–21. New York: Routledge, 2015.
Kort, Michele. *Soul Picnic: The Music and Passion of Laura Nyro*. New York: Thomas Dunne Books, 2002.
Kozinn, Allan. "Brown Meggs, 66, a Recording Executive Who Signed the Beatles." *New York Times*. October 10, 1966. Accessed June 1, 2020. https://www.nytimes.com/1997/10/16/arts/brown-meggs-66-a-recording-executive-who-signed-the-beatles.html.
Kubernik, Harvey. *Canyon of Dreams: The Magic and the Music of Laurel Canyon*. New York: Sterling, 2009.

Landau, Jon. *It's Too Late to Stop Now: A Rock and Roll Journal*. San Francisco: Straight Arrow Books, 1972.

Landau, Jon. "The Sound of Boston: 'Kerplop.'" *Rolling Stone*, April 6, 1968, 1, 8, 22.

Larsen, Gretchen. "'It's a Man's Man's Man's World': Music Groupies and the Othering of Women in the World of Rock." *Organization* 24, no. 3 (2017): 397–417.

"Las Vegas Sentinel-Voice." UNLV: University Archives Special Collection and Archives. https://special.library.unlv.edu/collections/newspapers/sn86076451.

Leitch, Donovan. "Jennifer Jupiter." 1967. Track 8 on *Hurdy Gurdy Man*. Epic Records, 1968. Vinyl record.

Leonard, Marion. *Gender in the Music Industry: Rock, Discourse and Girl Power*. Aldershot, England: Ashgate, 2007.

Lewis, Mark A., and Ian P. Renga. "Wisdom, Mystery, and Dangerous Knowledge: Exploring Depictions of the Archetypal Sage in Young Adult Literature." *Study and Scrutiny: Research in Young Adult Literature* 3, no. 1 (May 25, 2018): 25–50.

Lindberg, Ulf, Gestur Gudmundsson, Morten Michelsen, and Hans Weisethaunet. *Rock Criticism from the Beginning: Amusers, Bruisers, and Cool-Headed Cruisers*. New York: Peter Lang, 2005.

Linenthal, Peter, and Abigail Johnston. *San Francisco's Potrero Hill*. Mount Pleasant, SC: Arcadia Publishing, 2005.

Lucaites, John Louis, and Robert Hariman. "Visual Rhetoric, Photojournalism, and Democratic Public Culture." *Rhetoric Review* 20, no. 1/2 (2001): 37–42.

Lyons, John F. *Joy and Fear: The Beatles, Chicago and the 1960s*. New York: Permuted Press, 2021.

Malcolm, Future Ex-Mrs. "Let's Read *TeenSet*, September 1967!" The Avocado. Last modified February 23, 2018. Accessed October 10, 2018. https://the-avocado.org/2018/02/23/lets-read-teen-set-september-1967/.

Mansfield, Ken. Email questionnaire with author. May 12, 2020.

Marcus, Greil. *History of Rock 'n' Roll in Ten Songs*. London: Yale University Press, 2014.

Marcus, Greil. Introduction to *The Aesthetics of Rock* (1968). July 5, 2014. https://greilmarcus.net/2014/07/05/introduction-to-the-aesthetics-of-rock-1986/.

Marcus, Greil. *Mystery Train: Images of America in Rock 'n' Roll Music*. Boston: E. P. Dutton, 1975.

Marcus, Greil, ed. *Psychotic Reactions and Carburetor Dung—The Work of a Legendary Critic: Rock 'n' Roll as Literature and Literature as Rock 'n' Roll*. New York: Anchor Books/Random House, 2003.

Margetts, Michelle. "Dylan with Tire." In *Jim Marshall: Show Me the Picture*. Edited by Amelia Davis. San Francisco: Chronicle Books, 2019, 64–69.

Margetts, Michelle. "The Monterey Pop Festival." In *Jim Marshall: Show Me the Picture*. Edited by Amelia Davis. San Francisco: Chronicle Books, 2019, 194–203.

Marion, Larry. Email questionnaire with author. March 14, 2022.

Marion, Larry. *The Lost Rolling Stones Photographs: The Bob Bonis Archive, 1964–1966*. New York: Harper Collins, 2010.

Marsh, Dave. *Fortunate Son: The Best of Dave Marsh; Criticism and Journalism by America's Best-Known Rock Writer*. New York: Random House, 1985.

Marshall, Jim. "Look Back." *TeenSet*, February 1968, 14–17.

Marshall, Jim. *Not Fade Away*. New York: Little Brown, 2000.

Marshall, Jim. *Trust*. London: Omnibus Press, 2009.

Martin, Christopher R. "The Naturalized Gender Order of Rock and Roll." *Journal of Communication Inquiry* 19, no. 1 (April 1995): 53–74.
Massoni, Kelley. "'Teena Goes to Market': *Seventeen Magazine* and the Early Construction of the Teen Girl (As) Consumer." *Journal of American Culture* (Malden, MA) 29, no. 1 (March 2006): 31–42.
McDonell, Evelyn, and Ann Powers, eds. *Rock She Wrote: Women Write About Rock, Pop, and Rap*. London: Plexus Publishing, 1995.
McDonough, Jimmy. *Shakey: Neil Young's Biography*. New York: Random House, 2002.
McKay, Jenny. *The Magazines Handbook*. London: Routledge, 2000.
McKee, Alan. *Textual Analysis: A Beginner's Guide*. Washington, DC: Sage Publications, 2003.
McLeod, Kembrew. "★: A Critique of Rock Criticism in North America." *Popular Music* 20, no. 1 (January 2001): 47–60.
McLeod, Kembrew. "Between Rock and a Hard Place: Gender and Rock Criticism." In *Pop Music and the Press*, edited by Steve Jones, 93–113. Philadelphia Temple University, 2002.
McLoughlin, Linda. *The Language of Magazines*. London: Taylor & Francis Routledge, 2000.
Meggs, Brown. "Capitol 'Teen Set' Promo Seek Close Teen Ties." *Cash Box*, October 24, 1964, 7, 40
Mestler, Pamn. "Mail Scene–Names Anyone?" *TeenSet*, January 1969, 6.
Meltzer, Richard. *Aesthetics of Rock*. Boston: De Capo Press, 1970.
Mendelsohn, John. Interview with the author. July 23, 2023.
Merriam-Webster. "Archetype." https://www.merriam-webster.com/dictionary/archetype.
Merriam-Webster. "Cultist." https://www.merriam-webster.com/dictionary/cultist.
Merriam-Webster. "Sage." https://www.merriam-webster.com/dictionary/sage.
Merriam-Webster. "Teenybopper." https://www.merriam-webster.com/dictionary/teenybopper.
Middleton, Richard. *Studying Popular Music*. Milton Keynes: Open University Press, 1990.
Miles, Barry. *Frank Zappa*. London: Atlantic Books Ltd., 2005.
Millican, Robert. *Lillian Roxon: Mother of Rock*. Melbourne, Black Inc., 2002.
Milner, Andrew. *Literature, Culture and Society*. London: Taylor and Francis, 2016.
Milstead, Janey. "The Necessity of Being Involved." *TeenSet*, August 1968, 38–39.
MoMA. "Milton Glaser, Dylan 1966." Last modified 2016. Accessed May 20, 2020. https://www.moma.org/collection/works/8108.
Morrison Hotel Gallery: Fine Art Music Photography. Accessed March 6, 2020. https://morrisonhotelgallery.com/products/jim-morrison-the-doors-new-york-city-1967-qdlzfn.
Morthland, John, ed. *Mainlines, Blood Feasts, and Bad Taste: A Lester Bangs Reader*. New York: Anchor Books/Random House, 2003.
Moser, Margaret. "Dreamsville: Gloria Stavers, *16 Magazine*, and the Roots of Rock Journalism." *Austin Chronicle*, November 30, 2007. Accessed April 10, 2020. https://www.austinchronicle.com/music/2007-11-30/565815/.
Moser, Margaret. "The Singer Not the Song." *Austin Chronicle*. Last modified June 14, 1999. Accessed April 10, 2020. https://www.austinchronicle.com/music/1999-06-11/522176/.
Moses, Ann. Email questionnaire with author. June 11, 2020.
Moses, Ann, and Ann Wicker. *Meow! My Groovy Life with Tiger Beat's Teen Idols*. Self-published, 2017.
Mossman, Kate. "Women Who Wrote Rock." Aired March 22 and 26, 2016, on BBC Radio 4. https://www.bbc.co.uk/programmes/b07428bt.

Mouse Studios. "About Stanley Mouse." Accessed December 1, 2020. https://mousestudios.com/about/.

Nelson, Paul. "Janis: The Judy Garland of Rock and Roll?" *Rolling Stone*, March 15, 1969, 6.

Newman, Jason. "10 Things We Learned from the Godfather-of-Punk-Rock Doc 'Danny Says.'" *Rolling Stone*. October 7, 2016. Accessed July 1, 2020. https://www.rollingstone.com/tv-movies/tv-movie-news/10-things-we-learned-from-godfather-of-punk-rock-doc-danny-says-2-186956/.

O'Brien, Lucy. *She Bop: The Definitive History of Women in Popular Music*, 3rd ed. London: Jawbone, 2013.

O'Dill, Lee. "Color It Blues." *TeenSet*, December 1966, 24–25, 57.

O'Dill, Lee. "Color It Rhythm and Blues." *TeenSet*, January 1967, 26–27, 57.

Ogden, Russel. "Bias." In *The SAGE Encyclopedia of Qualitative Research Methods*. Edited by Lisa Given, 60–61. Thousand Oaks, CA: SAGE, 2008.

Ormrod, Joan. "Endless Summer (1964): Consuming Waves and Surfing the Frontier." *Film and History: An Interdisciplinary Journal of Film and Television Studies* 35, no.1 (2001): 39–51.

Otter Bickerdike, Jennifer. *Fandom, Image and Authenticity: Joy Devotion and the Second Lives of Kurt Cobain and Ian Curtis*. Basingstoke, England: Palgrave Macmillan, 2014.

Parks, Van Dyke. Email questionnaire with author. May 17, 2020.

Peate, Stephen. "Finding your 'type': Font Psychology and Typography Inspiration in Logo Design." Fabrik. Last modified February 9, 2018. Accessed May 1, 2020. https://fabrikbrands.com/font-psychology-and-typography-inspiration-in-logo-design/.

Pecknold, Diane. "The Politics of Voice in Tween Girls' Music Criticism." *Jeunesse: Young People, Texts, Cultures* 9, no. 2 (2017): 69–90.

Peterson, Richard A. "Why 1955? Explaining the Advent of Rock Music." *Popular Music* 9, no. 1 (1990): 113–114.

Phrotus, A. J. "The Groove." *TeenSet*, December 1967, 47.

Potash, John L. *Drugs as Weapons Against Us: The CIA's Murderous Targeting of SDS, Panthers, Hendrix, Lennon, Cobain, Tupac, and Other Activists*. Waterfield, OR: Trine Day, 2015.

Povich, Lynn. *The Good Girls Revolt: How the Women of Newsweek Sued Their Bosses and Changed the Workplace*. New York: Public Affairs, 2012.

Powers, Devon. *Writing the Record: The Village Voice and the Birth of Rock Criticism*. Amherst, MA: University of Massachusetts Press, 2013.

Prior-Miller, Marcia R. "Research Review: Issues in Magazine Typology." In *The American Magazine*, edited by David Abrahamson. Ames, IA: Iowa State University Press, 1995, 3–23.

Regev, Motti. "Producing Artistic Value: The Case of Rock Music." *The Sociological Quarterly* 35, no. 1 (February 1994): 85–102.

Riordan, James, and Jerry Prochnicky. *Break on Through: The Life and Death of Jim Morrison*. New York: William Morrow, 1991.

Ritter, Carl. "Mail Scene—Changes." *TeenSet*, February 1969, 7.

Rizzo, Mary. *Consuming Class, Buying Identity: Middle-Class Youth Culture, "Lower-Class" Style and Consumer Culture, 1945–2000*. PhD diss. University of Minnesota, 2005.

Robert Rodriguez, host. "Fab 4 Mania with Carol Tyler." *Something About the Beatles* (podcast). October 9, 2018. Accessed October 10, 2020. https://somethingaboutthebeatles.com/146-fab-4-mania-carol-tyler/.

Robinson, Nan. *The Girls in the Balcony: Women, Men, and the New York Times.* New York: Random House, 1992.

Roby, Steven, ed. *Hendrix on Hendrix: Interview and Encounters with Jimi Hendrix.* Chicago: Chicago Press, 2012.

Rock's Back Pages. Last modified January 2021. https://www.rocksbackpages.com/.

Rodriguez, Robert. *Revolver: How the Beatles Reimagined Rock 'n' Roll.* Milwaukee, WI: Backbeat Books, 2012.

Rohr, Nicolette. "Yeah Yeah Yeah: The Sixties Screamscape of Beatlemania." *Journal of Popular Music Studies* 29, no. 2 (June 2017): 1–13.

Rolling Stone. "*TeenSet* Advertisement." November 9, 1968.

Rosen, Jody. "The Perils of Poptimism: Does Hating Rock Make You a Music Critic?" *Slate.* May 9, 2006. Accessed May 1, 2021. https://slate.com/culture/2006/05/does-hating-rock-make-you-a-music-critic.html.

Roxon, Lillian. *Lillian Roxon's Rock Encyclopedia.* Grosset & Dunlap: New York, 1969.

Rudden, Patricia S. "Stacking the Wax: The Structure of Laura Nyro's Studio Albums." In *Singing for Themselves: Essays on Women in Popular Music,* edited by Patricia S. Rudden, 25–38. Cambridge: Cambridge Scholars Publishing, 2007.

Sandelin, Raul, dir. *Ticket to Write: A Golden Age in Rock Journalism.* Amazon Digital UK, 2016.

Sarris, Andrew. *Confessions of a Cultist: On the Cinema, 1955/1969.* New York: Simon and Schuster, 1971.

Savage, John. *1966: The Year the Decade Exploded.* London: Faber & Faber, 2015.

Scanlon, Jennifer. "Not Just a Pretty Face." *The Women's Review of Books* 19, no. 6 (2002): 18–19.

Scott, J. Walker. "Albums in Review." *TeenSet*, September 1966, 20.

Searles, Malcolm C. *The Association "Cherish": The Story of America's First Folk-Rock Band.* Leicester: Troubador Publishing Ltd., 2018.

Selvin, Joel. Email questionnaire with author. March 15, 2022.

Selvin, Joel. "Shooting Stars/Jim Marshall's Photographs of Rock 'n' Roll Icons Helped Define the Artists." *SFGate.* November 2, 1997. Accessed February 2, 2020. https://www.sfgate.com/entertainment/article/Shooting-Stars-Jim-Marshall-s-photographs-of-2823806.php.

Selvin, Joel, and Jim Marshall. *Monterey Pop.* San Francisco: Chronicle Books, 1992.

Shapiro, Harry, and Caesar Glebbeek. *Jimi Hendrix: Electric Gypsy.* New York: Macmillan, 1995.

Shipton, Alyn. *Nilsson: The Life of a Singer-Songwriter.* Oxford: Oxford Press, 2013.

Sims, Judith. "An Afternoon with Jim Morrison." *TeenSet*, June 1968, 34–37.

Sims, Judith. *AUM*, June 1969, 4.

Sims, Judith. "Beatles Mania 1966: Or, Life Aboard the Yellow Submarine." *TeenSet*, December 1966, 34 39, 60 62.

Sims, Judith. "Boston: Hype of Happening." *TeenSet*, May 1968, 44–47.

Sims, Judith. "ETC. ETC." *TeenSet*, December 1966, 4.

Sims, Judith. "ETC. ETC." *TeenSet*, June 1967, 6.

Sims, Judith. "ETC, ETC." *TeenSet*, February 1968, 3.

Sims, Judith. "ETC. ETC." *TeenSet*, March 1968, 5.

Sims, Judith. "ETC. ETC." *TeenSet*, May 1968, 5.

Sims, Judith. "ETC. ETC." *TeenSet*, September 1968, 6.

Sims, Judith. "ETC. ETC." *TeenSet*, October 1968, 3.
Sims, Judith. "ETC. ETC." *TeenSet*, January 1969, 4.
Sims, Judith. "ETC. ETC." *TeenSet*, March 1969, 3.
Sims, Judith. "ETC. ETC." *TeenSet*, February 1969, 6.
Sims, Judith. "In AUM." *AUM*, June 1969, 5.
Sims, Judith. "Janis Joplin and the Boys in the Band." *TeenSet*, September 1968, 32–35.
Sims, Judith. "Mail Scene." *TeenSet*, December 1966, 4–5.
Sims, Judith. "1967, The Summer of Love: There Was a Brief Moment When the Sun Really Shone." *Los Angeles Times*, 1987.
Sims, Judith. "Twang, Thump, and Plunk: The Guitar." *TeenSet*, December 1966, 18–19.
Skinner, Claire. "The Importance of Archives." Wiltshire and Swindon History Centre. Last modified April 22, 2014. Accessed December 21, 2020. https://wshc.org.uk/blog/item/the-importance-of-archives.html.
Slide, Anthony. *Inside the Hollywood Fan Magazine: A History of Star Makers, Fabricators, and Gossip Mongers*. Jackson: University of Mississippi Press, 2010.
Small, Sukey. "Mail Scene," *TeenSet*, July 1968, 6.
Spalding, Roger, and Christopher Parker. *Historiography: An Introduction*. Manchester, UK: Manchester University Press, 2009.
Spizer, Bruce. *The Beatles' Story on Capitol Records, Part Two: The Albums*. New Orleans: 498 Productions LLC, 2001.
Stableford, Dylan. "Minimalism Is In: When It Comes to Magazine Covers These Days, Less Is Definitely More." *Folio*, November 24, 2008. Accessed April 18, 2020. https://www.foliomag.com/minimalism/.
Stanford, Michael. *A Companion to the Study of History*. Hoboken: Wiley, 1994.
Stein, Jay W. "Magazine Covers on the Library Display Shelves." *Reference & User Services Quarterly* 37, no. 1 (1997): 29–30.
Stone, Emma. *The Graham Norton Show*, series 15, episode 218, BBC, April 11, 2014.
Stone, Oliver, dir. *The Doors*, 1991. USA: Lionsgate, 2006. DVD.
Strohm, John. "Women Guitarists: Gender Issues in Alternative Rock." In *The Electric Guitar: The History of an American Icon*, edited by Millard Andre, 181–200. Baltimore: John Hopkins University Press, 2005.
The Monkees Dress Up Game. Sunshine Factory. https://monkees.coolcherrycream.com/games/dress-up.
Swaney, Dave. "The Rogue's Gallery of Rock Writers." *TeenSet*. March 1969, 49–51, 58.
Swenson, John. *Stevie Wonder*. London: Plexus, 1986.
TeenSet. "Albums in Review." October 1965, 8.
TeenSet. "Albums in Review." February 1966, 6.
TeenSet. "Albums in Review." September 1966, 20.
TeenSet. "Albums in Review." October 1966, 56.
TeenSet. "All-Star Croquet Match." February 1967, 32–39.
TeenSet. "All-Star Scavenger Hunt." April 1967, 34–40.
TeenSet. "As Time Goes By . . . The Rolling Stones." March 1967, 32–40.
TeenSet. "Buffalo Springfield Pin-Up." April 1967, 63.
Teen Set. "Capitol Records Teen Set Membership." Advertisement. 1965, 37.
TeenSet (cover). October 1967.
TeenSet (cover). February 1968.
TeenSet (cover). March 1968.

TeenSet (cover). August 1968.
TeenSet (cover). January 1969.
TeenSet. "Features–A Go Go Teenage Magazine." November 1965, 2.
TeenSet. "For the Comfort of Teenagers over Twenty Or . . . How to Be an Overaged Teenybopper and Like It!" September 1967, 38–39.
TeenSet. "Go Fly a Kite." May 1968, 8–10.
TeenSet. "'In' Hollywood." June 1966, 26.
TeenSet. "'In' Hollywood." October 1966, 17.
TeenSet. "'In' Hollywood." December 1966, 26.
TeenSet. "'In' London." March 1967, 46.
TeenSet. "'In' San Francisco." January 1967, 28.
TeenSet. "'In' San Francisco." May 1967, 46.
TeenSet. "Kustom" advertisement. October 1968, 63.
TeenSet. "Kustom" advertisement. November/December 1968, 8.
TeenSet. "Kustom" advertisement. January 1969, 64.
TeenSet. "Kustom" advertisement. February 1969, 62.
TeenSet. "Let Us Know Questionnaire." May 1968, 40.
TeenSet. "Look Back." February 1968, 14–17.
TeenSet. "*Rolling Stone* Advertisement." February 1969, 3.
TeenSet. "Table of Contents." March 1969, 3.
TeenSet. "TeenSet Questionnaire: Some Surprising Results." September 1968, 48.
TeenSet. "*TeenSet*'s First Annual Christmas Party and Ice Skating Debacle." December 1967, 32–39.
TeenSet. "The Beatles at Monterey." October 1967, 52, 60.
TeenSet. "The Groove." June 1968, 48.
TeenSet. "The Unimportance of Being Earnest: A Letter from an Editor." January 1968, 8–9.
TeenSet. "Truth or Fiction?" June 1967, 26, 57–58.
Time, "The Press: Aiming at the Hip." June 2, 1967, 36
Toller, Brendan. *Danny Says*, 2018; New York: Magnolia Pictures, 2016. Film.
Torkelson Weber, Erin. *The Beatles and the Historians: An Analysis of Writings about the Fab Four*. Jefferson: McFarland & Company Inc., 2016.
Tosh, John. *The Pursuit of History*. Harlow: Pearson Education Limited, 1984, 1991, 2002, 2006.
Van Dyke Parks (@parksvandyke). "Do I Dare?" Instagram photo, May 17, 2020. Instagram.com.
Vechten, Carl Van. "Negro Blue Singers." *Vanity Fair*. March 1926, 67, 106–8.
Vechten, Carl Van. "The Folksongs of the American Negro. The Importance of the Negro Spirituals in the Music of America." *Vanity Fair*. July 1925, 52, 92.
Wall, Mick. *Two Riders Were Approaching: The Life & Death of Jimi Hendrix*. London: Orion Publishing, 2017.
Ward, Brian. "'The "C" is for Christ': Arthur Unger, *Datebook* Magazine and the Beatles." *Popular Music and Society* 35, no. 4 (2012): 541–60.
Warwick, Jacqueline. *Girl Groups, Girl Cultures: Popular Music and Identity in the 1960s*. New York: Routledge, 2007.
Wiener, Allen J. *The Beatles: The Ultimate Recording Guide*. Holbrook, MA: B. Adams, 1994.
Weinstein, Elizabeth M. "Married to Rock and Roll: Jane Scott, Grandmother of Rock Journalism." *Journalism History* 32, no. 3 (2006): 147–55.

Weinstein, Marc. "Marc Weinstein at Shea Stadium." *The Daily Beatle.* Last modified February 14, 2010. https://webgrafikk.com/blog/uncategorized/marc-weinstein-at-shea-stadium/.

Weissman, Richard. *Understanding the Music Business.* New York: Routledge, 2016.

Whiteley, Sheila. *Too Much Too Young: Popular Music, Age and Gender.* New York: Routledge, 2005.

Whiteley, Sheila. *Women in Popular Music: Sexuality, Identity and Subjectivity.* London: Routledge, 2000.

Williams, Paul. "How Rock Communicates." In *The Penguin Book of Rock & Roll Writing,* edited by Clinton Heylin, 75–80. London: Viking, 1992.

Williams, Paul. *Outlaw Blues.* 3rd ed. Encinitas, CA: Entwhistle Books, 2000.

Wilson, Sharry. *Young Neil: The Sugar Mountain Years.* Toronto: ECW Press, 2014.

Winn, John C. *That Magic Feeling: The Beatles' Recorded Legacy, Volume Two.* New York: Three Rivers Press, 2009.

INDEX

Page numbers in **bold** refer to figures.

Abrahamson, David, 26, 128, 130
album covers, **175**, 184, 207
Apple Scruffs, 238n83. *See* Furlong, Nancy
Armstrong, Don, 54, 58, 60, 97, 184
Aspinall, Neil, 49
Atlas, Jacoba, 45, 50, 51, 95–97, 183, 207
AUM, 20, 45, 50, 102, 136, 144, 169, 184, 188, 199, **200**, **201**, 204, **205**, 206, 213, 233n21

Bangs, Lester, 10, 19, 51, 54, 63, 65, 72, 75, 78–80, 87, 118, 149, 190
Beach Boys, 29, 38, 39, 42, 91, 128, 139, 188, 236n32
Beatles, 5, 7, 9, 10–12, 17, 19, 25, 26, 28, 29, 34, 36, 38, 42, 44, 48, 49, 54, 56, 57, 60, 63, **66**, **67**, 68, 71, 73, 82, 83, 95, 99, **116**, 118, 119, 122, 123, **124**, 127, 128, 131–34, 140, 141, **142**, 161, 164, 166, 174, 191, 197, 210, 213, 214, 224n66, 226n46, 233n18
Belscamper, Diana, 27, 28, 34
Benmont, Tench, 60
blues, the, 25, 33, 112, 151, 152, 154
Bonis, Bob, 19, 45, **45**, **66**, **67**, 99, 119, 122, 123, **123**, 124, **124**, 127, **142**
Brennan, Matt, 5, 8, 11, 13, 25, 64, 65, 86, 89, 90, 209, 229n23
Brooks, Daphne, 10, 212
Buffalo Springfield, 18, 35, 65, 68, 91, 94, 95, 112, 128, 139, 144, 158, 159, 166, 197, 218, 238n71

Capitol Records, 17, 18, 38, 39, 42, 43, 44, 48, 50, 54, 56–58, 99, 138, 150, 167, 169, 170, 188, 214, 226n51, 235n13, 237n68; Brown Meggs, 39, 42, 44; *Capitol News!*, 39; Fred Rice, 39
Captain Beefheart, 159
Cashbox, 26, 39, 42, 60
Cheetah, 50, 181, 193
Chester, Nancy, 45, 114, 139, 171, 176, 178, 180, 207
Cleave, Maureen, 11, 63, 132
Christgau, Robert, 70, 71, 72, 75, 87, 149, 229n23, 230n30
Coates, Norma, 7, 8, 147, 211
Cohn, Nik, 69
counterculture, 3, 28, 34, 48, 97, 102, 134–36, 147, 171, 175, 176, 179, 181, 183–85, 188, 194, 204, 206
Crawdaddy!, 11, 12, 34, 51, 57, 65, 68, 70, 73, 81, 82, 95, 97, 126, 169, 170, 190, 193, 211
Cream, 3, 49, 95, 96, 112, **157**, 162, **165**, **175**, 176, 182, 188
Creem, 16, 68, 72, 74, 75, 79, 81, 82, 86, 149, 211, 214
cultists, 54–56; Andrew Sarris, 55; Jon Landau, 54, 55

Datebook, 5, 29, 32, 34, 63–65, 132, 202, 235n75
Davis, Amelia, 18, 113, 114
DeRogatis, Jim, 63–65, 72–75
DIG, 22, 24, 27, 29, 43
Donovan, 34, **125**, 174, 175, 180, 197
DownBeat, 25, 26, 51, 113, 154
Dylan, Bob, **62**, 82, 102, 104, 106, **107**, 118, 179, 189

editorial persona, 128, 130, 131, 141, 150, 166
EMI Studios, 49, 140, 141, 162, 224n66

257

Epstein, Brian, 25, 99, 134, 226n46, 233n18, 236n32
Evans, Mal, 49

Featherly, Kevin, 83
Feldman-Barrett, Christine, 6, 7, 166, 204
field theory, 81, 86
Fields, Danny, 27, 28, 63, 65, 229n7
film: *Almost Famous*, 10, 19, 73, 75, 78, 79, 80, 81, 86; *The Doors*, 19, 99, 124, 126, **126**; *Get Back*, 60; *Ticket to Write*, 73–75, 80
Flip, 27, 29, 39, 97, 199
Flippo, Chester (Chet), 54, 55, 56, 58, 150, 204, 206
Fong-Torres, Ben, 18, 45, 50, 51, 72, 79, 80, 114, 150, 183, 211, 226n68, 227n72, 230n40
Frith, Simon, 6, 9, 13, 64, 71, 81, 82, 208
Furay, Richie, 18, 35, 65, 68, 139, 144, 229n19
Furlong, Nancy, 18, 22, 141, 144, 164, 169, 212, 224n66

Gambaccini, Paul, 71, 72, 230n33
Gendler, Debbie, 7, 17, 18, 36, 38, 141, 210, 212, 226n46
genre, 199, 202, 231n75; music, 13–15, 20, 25, 34, 44, 49, 69, 169, 191, 203, 209, 211, 224n12
Gleason, Ralph J., 25, 69, 87, 93, 114, 149, 230n30
Gold, Carol, 4, 20, 45, 57, 128, 130, 155, 162, 164, 165, 166, 196, 239n27
Goldstein, Richard, 54, 69, 89, 149
Grateful Dead, 69, 99, 104, 112, 135, 160, 169, 202
Green, Robin, 12
Grier, Miles Parks, 14, 211
GTOs, 50, **200**

hagiography, 19, 68, 80, 86
Harris, Dixie Dean, 24, 29, 224n6, 224n8
Hendrix, Jimi, 3, 19, 20, 32, 44, 49, 82, 91, 95–97, 99, 106–8, **108**, 109, 112–15, 118, 127, 151, 162, 165, **165**, 183, 184, **187**, 189, 202, 204
historiography, 4, 68, 69, 87, 90
Hoganson, Jeff, 18, 161, 213, 214

Hollywood fan magazines, 5, 17, 24, 25, 27, 28, 31, 221n4, 224n8
Hopkins, Jerry, 8, 9, 45, 51, 149, 183

Indiana, Robert, 184

Jack, Richard Morton, 54, 57, 58, 136, 162, 171, 183, 196
Jefferson Airplane, 3, 28, 35, 69, 103, 109, 112, 143, 160, 178, 183, 190
Johnson, Pete, 45, 93, 94, 149
Joplin, Janis, 3, 28, 44, 45, 49, 68, 99, 102, 103, 104, **105**, 109, 114, 118, 147, **163**, 171, 182, 204, 233n24

Keightley, Keir, 14, 15
Kern, Steve, 18, 142, 144, 167, 212–14
Kimzey, Lou, 43, 48
Khan, Sajid, 34, 185
KRLA BEAT, 45

Landau, Jon, 54, 55, 70, 83, 87, 143, 238n76
Lennon, John, 60, **62**, 63, 106, 107, **129**, 131–33, 178, 180, 184, **186**
Life, 27, 178, 180, **180**
literary sage, 19, 78, 79

magazine theory, 13, 83, 87, 144. *See also* Abrahamson, David
Mansfield, Ken, 17, 39, 44
Marsh, Dave, 65, 72, 83, 87
Marshall, Jim, 3, 18, 19, 45, 50, 51, 58, 99, 102, 103, **103**, 104, **105**, 106–9, **107**, **108**, 112–15, 118, 124, 127, 174, 182, 202, 219, 220, 233nn21–22
McCartney, Paul, 15, 64, **67**, 101, **120**, **138**, 141, 142, 145, 154, 198, 224n66, 238n90
McRobbie, Angela, 6, 9, 208, 221n2
Meltzer, Richard, 69, 75
Mendelsohn, John, 12, 50
Milstead, Janey, 13, 31, 45, 50, 57, 61, 134, 196, 227n72, 228n1
Moby Grape, 34
Monkees, 7, 25, 26, 29, 32, 34, 49, **84**, 85, 95, 181, 188, 189, 192, 194, 197, 202, 204, 238n71, 240n43

Monterey Pop Festival, 3, 15, 93, 102, **103**, 109, 112–15, 164, 171, 174, 196, 213, 236n32, 239n10

Morrison, Jim, 19, 44, 49, 99, 109, 124, 126, **138**, **146**, 181, 182, 198

Moses, Ann, 10, 13, 15, 17, 18, 29, 31–34, 37, 44, 45, 51, 236n39, 237n50

Moser, Margaret, 5, 27, 60, 61, 65

Mossman, Kate, 11, 12

Mouse Studio, 160

music scenes, 3, 20, 44, 49, 56, 128, 130, 155; Boston, 160–61; Hollywood, 155, 158, 159; London, 162, 164–66; San Francisco, 135, 155, 159, 160

Nolan, Tom, 45, 51, 149

Nyro, Laura, 19, 91, 93, 94, 99, 127, 232n2

O'Dill, Lee, 45, 151, **152**, 154, 155

Ono, Yoko, 60, 184

Parks, Van Dyke, 3, 18, 60, 129, **140**, 236n32

Paul Revere and the Raiders, 76, 92, 128, 134, 197

popular music journalism, 3–6, 9, 10–12, 15, 16, 18–20, 33, 36, 39, 54, 58, 63, 65, 70, 73, 74, 80, 81, 86, 90, 144, 150, 166, 207, 208, 211. *See also* rock criticism; rock journalism

Powers, Devon, 5, 10, 33, 63, 64, 81, 86, 89

Prior-Miller, Marcia, 13, 14, 199, 203

record reviews, 20, 22, 188–91

Regensteiner Publishing Enterprises, 43, 45, 48, 56, 130, 150, 169

Regev, Motti, 5, 72, 81, 82, 86

Right On!, 32, 225n37

rock aesthetics (aesthetics of rock), 5, 13, 15, 81, 82, 83, 108, 115, 169, 191, 203, 211, 223n54, 229n23, 231n76

rock criticism, 8, 16, 51, 69, 70, 71, 74, 75, 78, 80, 81, 83, 86, 87, 89, 90

rock journalism, 3, 4, 8, 10–12, 15, 19, 20, 21, 25, 54, 56, 58, 61, 63–65, 68, 70, 73–75, 79, 80, 81, 86, 87, 89, 90, 127, 149, 207, 208, 211, 212, 214, 230n40

rock photography, 19, 58, 99, 127, 181, 182. *See also* Bonis, Bob; Marshall, Jim

rockism (rockist), 68, 148, 211, 212, 229n23, 230n40

Rodriguez, Robert, 64

Rolling Stone, 3, 8, 11, 12, 14, 16, 18, 34–36, 51, 56, 57, 61, 65, 68–75, 78, 79, 81, 86, 93, 95, 97, 99, 119, 127, 143, 144, 147–49, 182, 188, 190, 193, 194, **195**, 202, 204, 206, 207, 211, 215, 223n60, 230n40, 238n76, 239n27

Roxon, Lillian, 10, 12, 68, 89, 207

Sarris, Andrew. *See* cultists

Selvin, Joel, 18, 102, 108, 112–15, 171, 174

Seventeen, 5, 14, 22, 24, 27, 28, 198, 203, 221n2, 221n3

Sims, Judith, 3, 4, 13, 15, 16, 18–20, 31, 43–45, 48, 49–51, 54–58, 60, 65, 89, 93–95, 102, 103, 113, 114, 119, 122, 124, 127, 128, 130–36, 139, 140–44, 147–51, 155, 160, 161, 162, 164, 165, 166, 167, 169, 170, 171, 174, 176, 178, 180, 181, 182, 183, 184, 185, 188, 191–94, 196, 197, 198, 199, 202, 204, 206, 207, 211–15, 226n68, 233n21, 235n6, 236n39, 237n50, 238n76, 242n90

16 Magazine, 5, 6, 8, 15–18, 24–29, 30–32, **31**, 34–36, 39, 44, 45, 51, 56, 58, 60, 61, 63, 65, 73, 74, 158, 170, 171, 176–78, 181, 182, 185, 193, 194, 198, **199**, 203, 204, 208, 210, 212, 215, 227n69, 235n5, 241n77, 242n90

Slick, Grace, 20, 49, 58, 103, 102, 104, **105**, 109, 114, **145**, **173**, 182–84

Slide, Anthony, 17

Smothers Brothers, 164, 183, 238n87

Soul Teen, 32, 225n37

Spizer, Bruce, 42, 54, 56, 57, 97

Starr, Ringo, 26, **124**, **156**

Stavers, Gloria, 5, 8, 10, 13, 26–29, 31, 40, 44, 56, 60, 61, 63, 65, 74, 89, 198, 227n69, 235n5, 237n50, 241n77

Taylor, Derek, 49, 131, 139, 159, 236n32

teen magazines: fan, 3, 4, 7, 9, 12–18, 20, 22, 24–27, 29, 30–39, 42–45, 48, 49, 50, 51, 54, 56, 58, 60, 61, 64, 65, 68, 73, 74, 81, 87, 91, 94, 97, 63, 123, 124, 131, 134, 141, 142, 144,

149, 151, 155, 167, 170, 174, 178, 180, 181, 182, 188, 193, 198, 199, 202, 203, 204, 208–12, 214, 215, 221n2, 229n10, 237n50, 242n90; lifestyle, 5, 14, 22, 24, 54, 198, 221n2; type, 14, 22, 24–26, 28, 43, 29, 221n2

teenagers, 20, 22, 29, 39, 42, 50, 133, 134, 192, 193, 196, 202–4, 212

TeenSet: covers, **41**, **46**, **47**, **52**, **53**, **59**, **62**, **66**, **67**, **76**, **77**, **84**, **85**, **88**, **92**, **100**, **101**, **110**, **111**, **116**, **117**, **125**, **129**, **137**, **138**, **145**, **146**, **156**, **157**, **163**, **168**, **172**, **173**, **186**, **187**; discussion of covers, 45, 171, 174, 175, 176, 178–85, 188, 190, 192, 193, 197, 198, 204; editor (*see* Sims, Judith); historical usage of, 91, 93–99, 102–9, 112–15, 118–24, 126, 127; in history, 51, 54–58, 60; race, 3, 20, 48, 49, 150, 151, 154, 155, 182–84; record reviews (*see* record reviews); scene coverage, 155–66; *The Teen Set*, 18, **23**, 29, 38, 39, **40**, 42, 43, 44. *See also* Armstrong, Don; Flippo, Chester (Chet); Jack, Richard Morton; Spizer, Bruce

Tiger Beat, 6, 10, 13, 15–18, 25–27, 29, 31–37, 44, 45, 49, 51, 58, 65, 93, 170, 171, **177**, 178, **179**, 185, 188, 193, 204, 208, 223n59, 236n39, 239n10

Tyler, Carol, 7, 133, 210

Unger, Art, 5, 63, 64, 132

Van Vechten, Carl, 25

Wall, Mick, 96, 97
Ward, Brian, 5, 63
Ward, Ed, 75
Webber, Erin, 25, 73
Weinstein, Elizabeth, 8, 10, 11, 89, 207
Weinstein, Mark, 99, 118–20
Wenner, Jann, 69, 79, 93, 144, 149
Who, 3, 109, 112, 113, 164, 197
Williams, Paul, 11, 50, 65, 70, 73, 95, 108
Wright, Clinton, 37, **38**

Young, Neil, 19, 49, 91, 94, 95, 99

Zappa, Frank, 3, 34, 49, 68, 99, 128, 139, **143**, 227n77

ABOUT THE AUTHOR

Photo courtesy of the editor

ALLISON BUMSTED teaches humanities at Austin Community College. Her work has been published in the *Journal of Beatles Studies* and the edited volume *Words, Music, and the Popular: Global Perspectives on Intermedial Relations*. She has also appeared on many Beatles podcasts such as *Something about the Beatles* and *Another Kind of Mind*.

www.ingramcontent.com/pod-product-compliance
Lightning Source LLC
Chambersburg PA
CBHW052047220426
43663CB00012B/2476